NATURE
UNPACKED

*The traveller's ultimate
bush guide to
Southern Africa*

NATURE UNPACKED

*The traveller's ultimate
bush guide to
Southern Africa*

Megan Emmett

Photographs by Shem Compion

BRIZA

Published by
BRIZA PUBLICATIONS
CK 1990/011690/23

BRIZA
www.briza.co.za
PO Box 11050
Queenswood 0121
Pretoria
South Africa

First edition, first impression 2018

ISBN 978-1-920217-40-2

All photographs by Shem Compion unless indicated otherwise.
Other photographers are identified as follows in the credit alongside their images:
ME – Megan Emmett; AL – Alouise Lynch; BEvW – Ben-Erik van Wyk; BvW – Braam van Wyk;
CE – Callum Evans; DH – Dai Herbert; GM – Geoff McIlleron; GN – Geoff Nichols; JC – Jakkie Coetzee;
JL – Jonathan Leeming; LdP – Louis du Preez; LO – Les Oates; LS – Lambert Smith; NJ – Niels Jacobsen;
NL – Norman Larsen; NS – Nico Smit; PJ – Pitta Joffe; PO – Pamela Oberem; PW – Peter Webb;
RB – Richard Boycott; RF – Reneé Ferreira; SS – Shutterstock;
FoZ – Flora of Zimbabwe / LL – Lene Lauritsen; DP – Daryl Plowes; BW – Bart Würsten;
WMC – Wikimedia Commons / CS – Charles J Sharp; BD – Bernie Dupont; BG – Brian Gratwicke;
DK – Derek Keats; F&KS – Forest and Kim Starr; HH – Hans Hillewaert; JR – Jon Richfield;
MS – Marco Schmidt; PV – Paul Venter; RC – Roger Culos; RvH – Ryan van Huysteen.

The publisher would like to thank the following people for their contribution
to the sound component of the book:
Michael Olivier for coding the pages and processing the sound files;
Philip Nel for the sound recordings of the scientific names;
as well as those individuals and organisations who contributed animal calls.

Project manager: Reneé Ferreira
Cover design: Michelle de Almeida, The Design Drawer
Inside design and layout: Michelle de Almeida, The Design Drawer
Reproduction: Resolution Colour, Cape Town
Printed in China by Forwards Group

Contents

Introduction

The southern African subregion is of the most beautiful in the world. Here savanna plains dissolve into semi-desert dry lands or erupt into watery wonderlands. Biomes and landscapes are diverse from the species-rich Cape Floral Kingdom to the arid Succulent Karoo, subtropical forest, thicket, desert, swamp, woodland and grassland, all manifesting unique charms and species variety in unique settings. No single book could ever contain the full richness of the entire region, which encompasses ten countries: Angola, Botswana, Lesotho, Malawi, Mozambique, Namibia, South Africa, Swaziland, Zambia and Zimbabwe.

Just focusing on South Africa, the author's home, it ranks as the third most biodiverse country in the world in spite of it occupying just 2 per cent of the global land surface. It is home to between 250 000 and one million species including 10 per cent of the planet's plant species (the fifth highest number of plant species in the world) and 7 per cent of the reptile, bird and mammal species. Many of these species are endemic, occurring nowhere else in the world. South Africa is also home to a wealth of terrestrial, aquatic and marine ecosystems and has three globally recognised biodiversity hotspots.

The vast expanses of bushveld or savanna in southern Africa, a zone of mixed woodland and grassland, a system structured by fire and mega-herbivores, has captivated travellers for time immemorial and it is these reaches that one typically associates with the popular pachyderms and iconic game in the form of striped equids, tall patterned giraffe, wart-faced swine or honking hippos. Of course, where there is diverse herbivore life, predators abound and the savanna regions boast the most powerful, beautiful and impressive of these in Africa. But there is also much more to every ecosystem than large mammals; the spectacle of African wildlife extends across bird, invertebrate, reptile and amphibian groups too, these communities shaped by the plant life found in a given area, which itself is determined by underlying geology and the soils this generates – everything interconnected and spectacular in shape, form and diversity.

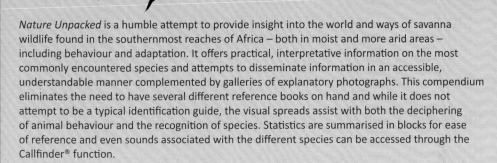

Nature Unpacked is a humble attempt to provide insight into the world and ways of savanna wildlife found in the southernmost reaches of Africa – both in moist and more arid areas – including behaviour and adaptation. It offers practical, interpretative information on the most commonly encountered species and attempts to disseminate information in an accessible, understandable manner complemented by galleries of explanatory photographs. This compendium eliminates the need to have several different reference books on hand and while it does not attempt to be a typical identification guide, the visual spreads assist with both the deciphering of animal behaviour and the recognition of species. Statistics are summarised in blocks for ease of reference and even sounds associated with the different species can be accessed through the Callfinder® function.

Nature Unpacked offers itself as a travelling companion to those visiting southern Africa for the first time or for the tenth. It is also the ideal companion for those who live and work within her extent. It is a must-have for any and all amateur naturalists and is based on the kind of information field guides are groomed to disseminate to their safari clientele. These guides need to be well-rounded naturalists to accommodate the varied interests of their clients and the starting point is always to address the commonest of subjects in all fields. With a foundational knowledge of the common topics, aspiring naturalists are then able to grow their body of knowledge over time by delving into the more authoritative reference works. But if all that is required is something to provide a little insight into the animal or bird in front of a traveller, then this book fulfils that purpose too, in a way more technical field guidebooks may not.

Whatever the context, whomsoever the reader, it is the author's experience that a little knowledge and understanding of nature engenders a perpetually growing desire to learn more. Time spent observing, reading and experiencing the wonders of the bushveld accumulates and amounts to a passion that burgeons and a soul well fed. May all your adventures in the outdoors, accompanied by *Nature Unpacked*, be amazing and fulfilling.

Acknowledgments

This book reaches the shelves with grateful thanks to many. To my friends and family for their constant support and encouragement for what I do. To mentors, teachers, colleagues and fellow nature-lovers along the way who have so willingly shared their knowledge with me and with whom I've shared countless enriching bush experiences. To June Cilliers ("Mrs Van As") who instilled a love of the written word in me from early on, I am indebted to you. To Shem Compion for his wonderful photographs and his shared passion for the ways of the wild, which always makes working on projects together so rewarding. To Michelle van der Westhuysen for the image work and reproduction. To the team at Briza, and Reneé Ferreira in particular, for the enormous effort necessary to produce a natural history book such as this. To every person who supplied additional photos, checked facts, proofread text (in particular Johan Marais and Duncan MacFadyen) or cast any kind of knowing glance over the spreads to make this book come together. To the love of my life, Andrew Parker, who exhorts me at every opportunity and who is my inspiration and joy. And finally, my deepest gratitude to the Lord God for creating the extraordinary landscapes and ecosystems that have always captured my imagination and for blessing me with my passion for the bush, an ability to learn about it and the priviledge of teaching others about it.

ME

How to use this book

The chapters have been colour-coded for ease of reference and every chapter is prefaced with a table of contents. Simply flip to the desired section and choose the species about which you'd like to learn more.

Blocked and icon information is available in the mammals and trees sections, providing technical details in a concise, easy-to-reference form.

The interpretative images direct the reader's eye to the different topics on the selected species so you can read whichever paragraph is of interest to you without having to wade through the entire body of text.

The sections on birds, reptiles, frogs and invertebrates focus more broadly on the biology of the group but also offers species-specific information that is interpretative rather than purely technical.

The Briza Callfinder® can be used to listen to animal and bird sounds, as well as to the pronunciation of scientific names. The Callfinder® unlocks sound from the printed page. Switch the Callfinder® on and, holding it in a vertical position, simply touch any image or text where you see this icon ⟪⟫. Where the icon appears on a photograph, the Callfinder® will play the animal's sound. Wherever the icon appears next to a name, you can listen to the pronunciation of the animal or plant's scientific name (see box below for more about scientific names).

MAMMALS

Impala
Aepyceros melampus

Height:	900 cm
Weight:	50 kg (♀ 40 kg)
Gestation:	6.5 months
Offspring:	1
Lifespan:	6–12 years
Diet:	Mixed feeder

Impala are attractive, medium-sized antelope with shiny, tawny, multi-toned coats. They are abundant because they are exceptionally well adapted to their lifestyles. They live in transitional woodland-grassland habitats (ecotones) and feed on both grass and leaves (as well as fruit and flowers) according to whatever is most abundant seasonally. They need to drink daily and are always found in close proximity to water. They are common prey for a variety of carnivores (including lion, leopard, cheetah, spotted hyena, jackal) and pythons, baboons or large birds of prey also take the lambs.

Impala have an arsenal of exceptional senses including large ears to hear the smallest noises and huge, side-positioned eyes with excellent peripheral vision. While feeding, impala take turns to lift their heads up to watch for danger. A loud, nasal alarm snort is used to signal threats and scatters the herd into eruptive flight. Impala are very agile, easily clearing obstacles in densely vegetated habitats with 3 m × 12 m leaps and they may flick their hind legs up almost vertically while they flee.

50

Scientific names

Every described species on earth has a unique, two-part scientific name ascribed using an international set of rules, which allows people all over the world to communicate unambiguously about a given species. Common names are not always exclusive to species, they vary from region to region and do not offer any information on the evolutionary history of the species. Scientific names comprise a generic name (genus) and a specific name (species). The former is always written with a capital letter and the latter with a small letter, and the entire name is *italicized*. Scientific names are rich in information and indicate a species relationship to another, i.e. animals sharing a genus (the first level of taxonomic organisation) are more closely related. These names are descriptive, suggesting clues to the species appearance; bearing the name of the person who first discovered or described the species; referencing the region where the species is found; or reflecting the common name given to it by native peoples. Because taxonomy is a constantly evolving field, scientific names may be changed when science's understanding of species and their relationships to one another change.

Being the largest and often easiest of the animals to spot, mammals are a favourite amongst safari goers. These warm-blooded, furry creatures capture our imaginations with their often-extravagant physiological designs and interesting behavioural repertoires. Their instinct for parental care is a trait we humans also find irresistible about them. While the Big 5 – lion, leopard, elephant, rhino and buffalo – have proved the most popular finds over the ages, many of the larger carnivores and other pachyderms hold similar appeal. Yet smaller, shyer creatures are no less interesting if we stop to notice and observe. Each species has a specific set of adaptations that equips it to its particular niche, or 'job description' if you will. These work in concert with the behaviour strategies it employs to avoid predators, find food, attract mates and raise families, the elements of each creature's ultimate goal, survival. This section decodes the designs, adaptations and behaviour of the most common mammals in both bushy and more arid habitats.

African elephant

))) *Loxodonta africana*

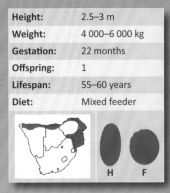

Height:	2.5–3 m
Weight:	4 000–6 000 kg
Gestation:	22 months
Offspring:	1
Lifespan:	55–60 years
Diet:	Mixed feeder

Elephants are the unmistakable, iconic, gentle, grey giants of southern Africa. The largest terrestrial mammal worldwide, they exhibit extreme intelligence and strength, modifying habitats to both the benefit and detriment of entire ecosystems. They occupy any habitat with adequate food, shade and water for them – from rainforests and savannas to deserts and mountains. They are adaptable altering their diet to accommodate availability or overcoming adversity by travelling long distances. They have a catholic diet and make use of grasses, herbs, sedges, aquatic plants, bulbs, tubers, roots, fruits, flowers, bark, wood, pods, seeds, leaves and entire branches.

While lions and hyena do prey on their young, elephants tend to suffer more losses through poaching, disease and starvation. They have acute senses except for eyesight, which is limited. The large ears ensure brilliant hearing, smell is well developed and the trunk is used to collect scent at different levels, and the chemoreceptive organ of Jacobsen on the palate is also well developed. Elephants are creatures of habit, feeding constantly but resting in the shade when it is hot after a drink or mud bath and then again during the night in between feeding. Large elephants lean against a supporting object to sleep standing up, smaller ones lie on their sides.

Elephants produce six sets of molars in a lifetime. These are large, oval, and flat on top with enamel ridges. Two sets occur on both sides and jaws, and as the leading molar becomes worn away, the next tooth pushes forward from the back. Each tooth is larger than the previous one to correlate with the growing body size. Once the last set of molars has worn away, the elephant starves to death, usually around the age of 60. The softer the food in an elephant's diet, the longer its teeth last.

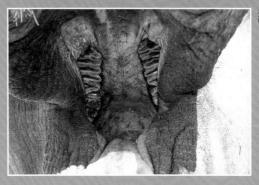

Tusks are modified upper incisor teeth that grow continuously. They are used for defence against predators, conflict with other elephants and as tools for foraging.

Individuals' tusks differ in size and shape, are broken, worn down, lost through injury or absent altogether, and animals are usually left or right tusk dominant, seen by the shorter length of one tusk. Older bulls may develop enormous tusks in older age when they no longer conflict with other bulls as much.

An elephant's ears can measure 1.2 metres and weigh 20 kg each. The large flap channels sound into the eardrum to effect excellent hearing. Ears also express mood and help with thermoregulation. They make up 20% of the elephant's surface area and the skin here is thin and well supplied with blood vessels. Blood pumps through the ears at about 12 litres per minute and by moistening the ears with water or mud and waving them, the blood is cooled before flowing to the rest of the body. Ears are held back against the body to conserve heat when it is cold.

ME

The trunk is unique and used to process the variety of foods elephants eat and functions as a limb, a nose and a straw. The trunk is a fusion of the nose and upper lip and contains thousands of muscles terminating in finger-like protrusions for grasping. It is sensitive, can stretch to reach things or shrink for travelling, suck up air, water, dust and even fruit to transport into the mouth or spray on the body, break and strip branches, scoop up several or grasp single items, or manipulate food in the mouth. Young elephants do not easily gain control of their trunks, which remain uncoordinated until they are 3 months old.

ME

Elephants communicate in various ways. Trumpeting and screaming are loud vocalisations inferring anger or excitement but more commonly they make rumbles and while some are audible, most are infrasonic and at low wavelengths. Elephants many kilometres away can perceive the infrasonic rumbles of their conspecifics. While spread out and feeding, this kind of communication helps the herd stay together and also alerts them to disturbances, enabling them to slip away quietly. If alarmed, the calves retreat to the middle of the herd and the largest elephants make a barrier with their bodies, charging predators if need be.

Elephants appear to be aggrieved by the death of one of their kind and they smell, pick up and carry around tusks or bones of dead elephants. Elephants have an advanced society and will rally to aid their sick or wounded. Very small babies always travel under their mothers' belly between her legs for safety, shade and assistance.

Elephants have unusual near-ungulate feet and are able to walk silently. They walk on their toe bones cushioned under the heel with a shock-absorbing cartilaginous pad. Forefeet are largest to support the heavy forequarters and the hind feet step into the tracks of the front ones. The hind track is more oval in shape. There are five toenails on the front feet and four on the back. Toenails are used to cut off tufts of grass while feeding or scrape fruit together to scoop up with the trunk.

Elephants rely on water and need to drink every day to aid digestion. Over 100 litres is drunk in a day, often at one sitting and clean water is preferred. They will travel long distances to access water, may dig for it underground and are known to be possessive during times of shortage, chasing off other species. Elephants take regular baths, spraying or immersing themselves, and they enjoy swimming, which cools them off, or bulls may engage in play fighting. They will also take a mud or dust bath to regulate temperature and protect their skin from the sun. They rub their bodies against rocks or trees to remove the mud once dry.

Elephants are herbivorous and eat a variety of materials. They eat about 5% of their body weight in food daily, equivalent to 300 kg for a large bull. They also feed constantly and digest their food rapidly to make space for more, ensuring enough nutrients are able to stream through their systems, especially during drier times. Only about 40% of what they eat is digested and bulls produce about 150 kg of dung per day through which many creatures sort to eat the undigested material. Seed coats are also scarified in the elephant's stomach, which enhances germination. Elephants are geophagic, chewing soil to supplement dietary mineral deficiencies.

Elephants alter habitats and drive ecosystems through their destructive habits and use of woody plants. They push over trees for access to foliage or in social displays, and debark them for water and nutrients, but the fallen trees are then browsed by shorter herbivores or resultant microhabitats occupied by small creatures like rodents or birds. Nutrients are recycled through decay, fires or by termites. Elephants also provide water to myriad animals by digging holes in dry riverbeds or creating depressions by wallowing that subsequently form pans that collect rainwater.

Elephants live in herds of related cows with their offspring, led by the oldest cow, or matriarch, who has the most experience. Bulls leave the herd at puberty (about 12 years old) and live alone or in small groups. Old bulls may be accompanied by a few younger ones that learn from him. Elephants are highly social animals with a complex society and a rigid discipline system to keep order and prevent injury to one another. Herd life centres around rearing the calves. Babies are seldom more than a metre or two from an adult and constantly reassured with touch. Elephants are long-lived and continued lifelong learning occurs and is passed between generations.

Elephants learn how to behave through mimicking the adults. Females practise motherhood by nannying the calves from a relatively early age, aiding them in feeding or navigation, and protecting them. Young bulls engage in head butting and play mounting to establish rank and develop their skills for winning dominance later on.

Large herds may segregate with smaller groups of closely related animals forming new herds. These kinship groups maintain contact with one another and all the herds in an area that are distantly related constitute a clan. Clans frequent particular home ranges typically allied to bulls' ranges.

Bull elephants develop local hierarchies that are established through ritualised play fighting and they recognise each other and know one another's strength. This process begins when bulls are young and continues until the age of about 40.

Elephant bulls experience a reproductive condition called *musth.* Elevated testosterone levels result in elevated aggression and they travel long distances emitting an infrasonic musth call as they go to attract cows on heat. Strong-smelling urine stains the inside of the bull's back legs, and temporal gland secretions mark his temples. Only musth bulls get to mate with cows and competition is eliminated when older bulls challenge and suppress musth in younger or less fit individuals. Young bulls only come into musth for short periods while it may last for months in older ones. Consequently, bulls only get a chance to mate between 25–35 years old despite the onset of puberty at 12. Equally matched bulls fight violently for access to an oestrus cow. Cows can conceive from eight years old and mating is stressful due to the large size difference between her and the mature bull that will mate with her.

Bulls and cows look similar due to bulls' internal testes except once animals get older and then bulls are significantly larger than cows. Cows have an angled forehead, a curved back and two large teats between their front legs. Bulls have rounded foreheads, straight backs and often a conspicuous penis when relaxed. They are also generally alone or in small herds while cows reside in breeding herds. Both sexes have temporal glands on the sides of their foreheads. Bulls secrete from these profusely during musth but cows and juveniles only have moisture here when under stress. Elephants may collect scent from these glands with the end of the trunk during greeting ceremonies.

Lion

 Panthera leo

Height:	1–1.2 m
Weight:	120–250 kg
Gestation:	3.5 months
Offspring:	1–6 cubs
Lifespan:	10–18 years
Diet:	Carnivore

Lions are the largest African carnivores. They have a wide habitat tolerance and even penetrate into deserts along dry river courses. They require the barest of cover to stalk medium- to large-sized prey animals – from mice to buffalo (even elephants), birds up to the size of ostrich, reptiles, insects, fish and carrion. Common prey species include giraffe, wildebeest, zebra, impala, waterbuck, warthog and kudu.

Lions are also the only social cats in the bushveld. By cooperating in prides, lions are able to kill bigger animals or improve the chance of a successful kill where there is little cover. They are also able to improve the survival of their young through cooperation. Lions are super-predators and dominate the bushveld predator hierarchy. They will steal food wherever they can from other predators and mutually kill each other's cubs. They may even kill smaller carnivores as food. The kills that lions make are attended by hyena, jackal and vultures who will attempt to scavenge the leftovers. Their only real competition are hyenas but only if these exist in significantly greater numbers and even a clan of hyenas do not stand too much chance against a pride if males are present. Elephants chase and even kill lions to protect their young as will herds of buffalo. Hyena, man, other carnivores and pythons take cubs.

All the lionesses in a pride are related and remain within the pride for life. They may split up into subgroups and operate in different parts of the territory but will join up from time to time. Young males are ousted from the pride in their third year and they must lead a nomadic lifestyle, keeping a low profile until they are able to contend for a territory from about the age of five. They are fully mature at seven years old, at which time their manes are at their fullest. After tenure of a territory, ousted older males also resort to a nomadic lifestyle and are often killed or die from lack of pride support by ten years old.

It is commonly thought that a pride of lion comprises a single dominant male and his females, but this is not the case. A territory is held by several males in partnership, known as a coalition. There can be between two and five males in a coalition and their territory overlaps with a number of different mutually exclusive female territories. Working as a team, it is easier to dispossess older lions of their domain and keep hyenas at bay, lions' chief competition. Collectively the males are a stronger force, can defend a larger territory

and protect more females. They will split up to do patrols but rejoin as necessity requires. The coalition may be (but not always) made up of brothers. In this instance the cooperative effort serves the perpetuity of the family genes.

Male lions seldom kill one another unless disputing a territory, but rather they take great care to avoid confrontation. Fighting creates an immediate risk of injury and any injury could imply disability in defending territory or catching food. Instead lions spend a great deal of time advertising their position through roaring and scent-marking. Lions mark their territories by urine-spraying bushes and other obvious objects. They defecate conspicuously and scrape with their feet on the ground where they have urinated, transferring the scent to their feet to pass on while they patrol their boundaries. Mature male lions have huge manes of hair over their necks and shoulders. This makes them look large and impressive to contenders and to females. When male lions fight they do so head-to-head, raking each other with their claws. A dense mane of hair serves to protect their necks from a fatal blow.

Females do most of the hunting although males do assist with larger kills like giraffe and buffalo. Males are adept hunters when they are on their own. Males will be the first to eat and sometimes take over the entire carcass to the exclusion of the females that killed it or even their own cubs. The females tolerate this behaviour both because the males are larger and stronger than them and because the males afford the females protection by defending the territory against hyenas and other male lions. Foreign males that move into the territory will kill all the cubs in a pride under one year old. This infanticide is executed to bring females into heat quickly so that they might mate with the pride females and then spend their tenure as the territorial coalition defending their own offspring. Interestingly, the females do not conceive immediately and the males need to establish themselves before they will. This mechanism prevents wasted reproductive energy, as should the new males be displaced soon after takeover, a similar process will occur and the females will again lose their cubs.

As it is the criterion to belong to the carnivore family, lions have a well-developed carnassial shear. The carnassials are made up of the forth upper premolar and first lower molar. These teeth are laterally flattened and articulate against each other acting with a scissor-like blade action to cut meat and sinew. The long, sharp canines are used to grasp and kill prey and are useless in feeding. The strong lower jaw is powered by well-developed muscles that attach to the massive skull. A lion's skull weighs over 3 kg. Lions have extremely rough tongues and can actually separate meat from bone by just licking it.

Lions roar to advertise their territory or to locate other members of the pride. They do this at night predominantly as this is when they are most active but also because the air is stiller and sound carries further. It is estimated that the roar of a lion carries over 7 km depending on the time of year and weather. Lions recognise individual roars and will respond to one another if it is relevant to do so. Lions are able to roar so loudly due to the suspensorium, which is a 'voice box' device at the top of the windpipe suspended with cartilage. The larynx of other species is ossified in place. The cartilage allows for movement of the suspensorium and as a result the vibrations caused during vocalisation are significantly enhanced and thus louder and they project further. Of the African cats, the lion is most closely related to the leopard (also *Panthera* genus) because of their similar voice box structure. Lions also moan, purr, growl and snarl, and the cubs meow.

Lions have protractile claws. The claws can be pushed out by muscle contractions when the lion has need to fight or hunt but they relax back into a protective sheath when not in use, which keeps them from becoming blunt while the cat moves around. There is a small claw on a lion's wrist which is higher than the rest and this is called a dewclaw. The dewclaw is used when pouncing on prey to secure it.

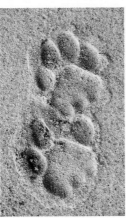

The cat family (Felids) usually have very rounded spoor. Lions are the largest of the cats with their tracks measuring 13–15 cm in length. The track has three lobes on the back pad (hyena have only two) and the toes are slightly oblong in shape and clearly separate (they do not fit together as the hyena's do). The protractile claws do not impress in the track (with cheetah being the exception). Lions have black tips to their tails and black behind their ears. These are 'follow me' signs. The black tail is at exactly the right height for a cub to follow a female through tall grass. Cats express their moods with their tails and ears and so having these areas highlighted is valuable for communication and coordination during hunts. While the black is obvious from behind, from the front they remain completely camouflaged.

Lions are expert stalkers. They can use the barest of cover to get close to prey by holding the head and body close to the ground. With their eyes firmly fixed on the victim, they move carefully, freezing immediately if the prey lifts its head. Lions will get as close as possible to their prey before the final dash and pounce. Sometimes a chase is necessary but this is always short. Lions can cover 100 metres in six seconds in final chase. The point of attack is usually the rump or shoulders of the animal and the sheer weight of the lion causes the prey to fall, at which time it is grabbed by the throat or muzzle for the final strangulation or suffocation.

Lions are opportunistic feeders eating mostly medium to large antelope but including anything from a mouse to an elephant. They will follow other predators or vultures to kill sites to steal food, including putrid meat, and they ambush animals by lying in wait at isolated waterholes. They may dig warthogs out of their burrows or pick off antelope lying up in the grass. They rid populations of their sick and weak members. They hunt predominantly under the cover of darkness but will hunt during the day if opportunity presents itself. Lions gorge themselves when they feed, leaving them almost immovable but food passes through their guts quickly to allow for a second meal soon after. Lions will drink water regularly if it is available. They fulfil the majority of their moisture requirements from the bloody meat they eat.

Lions are extremely lethargic for the majority of their lives, spending about 20 hours a day

resting. This is necessary to recuperate from the intense periods they spend patrolling and hunting. Although lions may seem comatose at times, they are often alert and can be spurred to action in seconds. After a day's resting and before they get active for the evening, a pride of lions will engage in contagious behaviour including yawning, grooming, defecating, urinating and communal roaring. This creates pride cohesion.

Mating in lions is a very intense affair. A pair will mate every 20 minutes for four days and nights with each bout lasting one minute. Lions have a low fertility rate and a very small percentage of mating results in conceptions. In fact, for every cub reaching one year old, the parents would have mated 3 000 times. The protracted copulations serve two functions. Firstly they stimulate the female to ovulate and secondly they provide the opportunity to confuse paternity. The male that begins mating with a female may become so exhausted by day three or four that another of the coalition members will take over. Since both believe the cubs to be his, both have a vested interest in protecting the offspring.

Although females often elicit mating by presenting their rumps (lordosis) to a male, by the end of a bout she appears irritable, turning to swat the male with her paw as he extracts. This is due to the fact that the male has a barbed penis and the extraction is extremely painful. The neck-biting and snarling that takes place during mating is ritualised.

Males determine that a female is in oestrus (ready to mate) by flehmen. They frequently smell the rump of the female or the area where she has recently urinated. By pulling back the top lip in a grimace (called flehmen grimace), muscles on the palate are contracted to force the steroid hormones into the organ of Jacobsen. This chemo-receptive gland is designed to detect hormones that indicate reproductive status.

Lion cubs are born blind and weak (altricial). The gestation period is very quick since lionesses need to hunt in order to survive and provide for the pride. They would be severely disadvantaged if they were weighed down by heavy pregnant bellies for protracted periods of time. As a result, the cubs are underdeveloped at birth and need to be kept in hiding while they grow strong enough to join the pride and hold their own. This is the converse to their prey. Antelope need only to eat grass to avoid starvation and a pregnant belly is no inhibitor to this. Once they are born, they must run to escape predators and so their young are born precocious

(able to move and see immediately) but this comes of having longer to develop in the womb. Lionesses often synchronise their breeding. This is useful as all the mothers will then mutually suckle each other's cubs. However, if there are very new cubs in a pride as well as cubs three months old or more, the mother of the younger cubs will keep her offspring away from the pride for longer than the usual six weeks. This is because the older cubs are stronger and have easier access to the milk on offer to the exclusion of the smaller cubs.

White rhino

Ceratotherium simum

Height:	1.8 m
Weight:	1 500–2 500 kg
Gestation:	16 months
Offspring:	1
Lifespan:	40–45 years
Diet:	Grazer

Rhino are part of the Big Five – the top five wild animals traditionally most dangerous to hunt. White rhino are the largest land mammals after elephants and with their broad, square lips adapted to grazing, these animals are found in relatively flat, grassy habitats where there is thick cover in which to hide while they rest, and adequate water to drink and in which to wallow. A group of rhino may be referred to as a 'crash' and while their bulky size and strength makes them relatively immune to predators, their calves are susceptible to lions and hyena and the species suffers greatly at the hands of poachers.

Horns are unique to rhino and used in fighting or to protect themselves and offspring. They are made of keratin and grow continuously from a blood- and nerve-supplied bed on the face. Horns can grow 2–6 cm in a year but are simultaneously worn away through usage and rubbing, especially in bulls. Cows generally have longer, thinner horns. The longest white rhino horn on record is 1.58 metres. The skin over a rhino's shoulders is 25 mm thick to reinforce this area against blows from opponents' horns.

White rhino are adapted for their life as grazers. The thick neck and large nuchal hump over the shoulders supports the low-slung head and is the force behind the horns, which are used in defence. Rhino have poor sight but excellent smell and having their heads close to the ground facilitates the use of the nostrils to pick up the scent of both food and other rhino. Hearing is also excellent and the ears are well positioned atop the head and move constantly and independently to detect noises. When a sound is detected, both ears focus in that direction.

They communicate with a variety of sounds, such as snorting, growling and squealing, as well as visual cues such as flattening the ears.

The muzzle is about 20 cm wide and the rhino uses its lips to graze, not its teeth. The more flexible upper lip guides grass into the mouth while the harder lower lip is used to press against to cut the grass with a neat upward swipe. The grass is chewed with big, grinding cheek molars. Rhino move their heads in a semi-circular pattern while they graze, stepping forward each time the arc is completed. They are selective grazers and keep neatly cropped lawns of palatable grasses amongst the taller grass, alternating the use of their favoured feeding areas. Sometimes rhino chew soil to supplement dietary mineral deficiencies.

Rhino are very water dependent and drink daily to assist with digestion. They can go no longer than four days without water during times of stress. Bulls ideally defend territories containing water but if not, they leave their turf to access it elsewhere. During these forays into foreign turf, the intruding rhino must behave submissively to ensure access to his neighbour's water source by urinating in a stream instead of spraying, and by flattening his ears and squealing if necessary.

White rhino are wallowers and will roll in the mud and cake themselves completely to cope with heat and prevent sunburn. Once dry, the mud is rubbed off against trees, rocks or stumps and removes external parasites in the process. Rhino use their rubbing posts repetitively and these become smooth and polished over time. A rubbing post is particularly used to reach difficult areas like the belly and inner legs. Terrapins often pick parasites directly off rhinos' skin while they wallow.

Rhino spend most of their time feeding or resting, which they do both diurnally and nocturnally in alternating bouts. They feed for long periods each day due to their size and consequently high energy demands. They typically rest up in the shade when it is hot but also hide in thickets on cold or windy days. A sleeping rhino breathes heavily while its ears do not cease their incessant flicking. A noise or disturbance may spur the rhino to alertness at a starling speed.

Rhino are often in the company of red-billed oxpeckers that glean ticks and other external parasites off their hides. The oxpeckers also help to warn the rhino of danger as they themselves flush up noisily when disturbed. Rhino are prone to skin lesions and oxpeckers may irritate these and other wounds to drink blood and in this way may also be a pest to the rhino, keeping sores open and susceptible to infections.

ME

Cows are usually accompanied by their latest calves and tend to live in groups with other cows. Newly independent adults also form groups of up to five even with mixed sexes. White rhino will aggregate in areas of good grazing or near water and finding ten individuals together is not unusual.

ME

Cows generally live in home ranges that overlap with one another and coincide with the territories of different bulls. Ranges vary from 6–20 km^2 depending on food and water availability and fluctuating slightly seasonally.

Bull rhinos are territorial and solitary, keeping the company of females only during courtship. Maturing at about four years old, bulls usually only become territorial when they are about twelve years old and somewhat more experienced. They are tolerated in other bulls' territories in the interim providing they remain submissive. A bull's territory is between 0.75 and 14 km^2 depending on resources and the borders of these often trace natural barriers like rivers and ridges, or roads.

Much of the social and territorial behaviour of a rhino centres on olfactory signs. A bull patrols his boundaries and well-used paths urine-spraying backwards onto bushes as he goes. Scraping his feet while he urinates impregnates them with smell, which is left behind as he walks. Territorial bulls also kick their dung when they defecate to get the smell on their feet.

Enormous middens are constructed along the territory boundaries and added to by myriad passers-by. Cows and subordinate bulls leave their dung intact as balls. These sites are centres for social information. Middens also form very visual territorial beacons and the scrape-markings left on the ground every 30 metres or so after urine-scraping are another form of beacon. Bulls only really fight when there is an oestrus cow or a territory at stake, otherwise actions are ritualised and posturing is adequate to resolve encounters.

Rhinos have drawn out mating and copulation lasts a full 30 minutes. Bulls detect oestrus cows from steroid-laden urine left behind in their territories using flehmen. Once he finds the cow on heat, the bull will try to prevent her from leaving his territory and will chase away other contenders, which can be a noisy business. The cow may reject the bull, sometimes aggressively so but the bull is generally very persistent and herds her, chasing, squealing and even clashing horns with her. Courtship can last 14–20 days and the pair will remain together for up to six days after mating.

A stressed rhino may curl its tail up, bounce with a nervous gait around the same spot, turn one side to the disturbance or rub its horn on the ground. If necessary, rhino can charge at 40 km/h. Cows are extremely protective of their young and when running away, the calf always runs ahead where the mother can keep her eye on it.

Black rhino

)) *Diceros bicornis*

Height:	1.6 m
Weight:	400–1 000 kg
Gestation:	15 months
Offspring:	1
Lifespan:	30–40 years
Diet:	Browser

While they look very similar, the lifestyles of the black and white rhino differ significantly. Black rhino are browsers and live in wooded areas where they find their food and can hide away. They tend to be secretive animals. They have shorter heads than white rhino that they carry high on the shoulders to facilitate browsing. They consequently lack the nuchal hump so prominent in white rhino. The black rhino's prehensile lips are adapted to picking leaves and manipulating twigs that are cropped at distinct angles because of the slope of the cutting edge of its molars. Black rhino are smaller than white rhino and have smaller, rounder ears. When they flee danger, the calf trails behind the mother that clears a path through the wooded habitat for them. The animal is not black in colour as the name suggests and is one of Africa's top 10 most endangered animals.

Rhino have large feet with three toes, one large one in front and one on either side of the foot. The heel has a distinct, rounded 'W' shape and the cracks in the skin on the soles of the feet mark in the tracks. Two parallel lines are often evident amongst the tracks of bulls where they have marked by scraping their feet. The white rhino's track measures about 30 cm long. Black rhino have smaller tracks (24 cm) than white rhino, with a larger space between the toes and a less pronounced constriction on the heel of the foot.

The black rhino makes a snorting sound, which is repeated. Other sounds used for communication include screams, squeals and growls.

))

Leopard

 *Panthera pardus*

Height:	60–80 cm
Weight:	30–90 kg
Gestation:	100 days
Offspring:	2–3
Lifespan:	10–15 years
Diet:	Carnivore

Leopards epitomise secrecy and adaptability, living in many different habitat types and eating whatever prey is most common – from rodents, reptiles and fish to large antelope and small carnivores, but mainly medium-sized antelope like impala and duiker. Leopards scavenge and may raid stock. They prefer areas with good cover for hunting, hiding and denning, and they make use of drainage lines, rocky outcrops and thick bush. They spend the majority of the day resting in thick cover before getting active under the cover of night. When it is cold, they will sun themselves on rocks. Male leopards are also called 'toms'.

Leopards rise up on their hind legs to claw hard surfaces like tree trunks. They do this to flex their spines and stretch, and for claw maintenance, fraying pieces of the claw sheaths being removed via the friction. The resultant scratch marks on the trunk may serve as a territorial marker.

Leopards primarily use their brilliant sense of sight to locate prey. Their eyes are adapted to seeing in the dark, having a high number of light-sensitive rods and a reflective *tapetum lucidum* behind the retina, which increases the stimulation of the retinal light-sensitive cells and improves vision in low-light conditions. Binocular vision is imperative for gauging depth and distance in hunting and is provided for by the forward-facing eyes. Leopards have long tactile whiskers to help them move around in darkness and to detect minute changes in air currents critical for exploring and hunting.

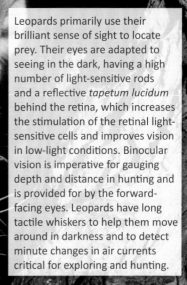

Leopards hoist their kills into trees to avoid competition from lion and hyena that are unskilled climbers. Hyena wait below to grab dropped scraps and fortuitously, larger parts or occasionally the whole kill that may fall down. Where the threat of these competing predators does not exist, leopards feed on the ground. Leopards hoist kills as heavy as they are, using the dewclaws to good effect while climbing and hoisting. They are powerful animals with large skulls and strong necks (particularly older toms). Leopards straddle their kills when moving them, accommodated by the high shoulders and concave chest, traits critical for climbing and hoisting too.

Leopards are expert stalkers, approaching to within 5–10 metres of their prey before attacking. Prey is grabbed with the fore claws and bitten on the throat or behind the head. They are opportunistic hunters and use almost 100 different food types including termite alates, stranded fish, ground birds, rodents, reptiles, porcupine, aardvark, rock hyrax and other small mammals, and even baby buffalo. They steal kills from cheetah and may hunt diurnally too. Before eating, leopards pluck the hair or feathers of their food and discard the entrails of larger prey, covering them to mask the smell. Kill remains are also covered with vegetation or soil if it is cached.

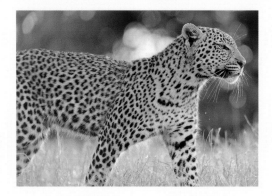

Leopard cubs are left alone for many hours while females hunt and patrol. These periods provide opportunities for the developing cubs to explore their immediate surrounds and to play with one another, exercising the muscles and refining the skills they will need to survive as adults. From early on in life, leopards experience the feast or famine condition their lifestyles dictate.

The golden pelt is patterned with rings of black spots that form rosettes and these are unique to each animal. The spots camouflage the leopard by breaking up the shape of its body and this allows the leopard to blend into its habitat while resting, hiding or hunting. The underside of the animal is almost pure white. A melanistic, genetic variant of the normal spotted leopard is occasionally found and black leopards are known as panthers. A very rare strawberry form also occurs.

Leopards have long, white-tipped tails, which provide 'follow me' signs for young cubs to follow in tall vegetation. They also offer conveniently positioned targets to cubs practising their pouncing skills. The primary function of the long tail is for balance when climbing or running in hot pursuit. The small, round ears also have markings that act as a 'follow me' sign. From behind, the black markings are evident to cubs but the ears are cleverly sized to keep protrusions to a minimum for stalking.

Leopards call with a rasping sound resembling the sound of a wood saw. A vibrating, non-ossified suspensorium similar to that in lions, projects the sound of their calls over long distances, which in turn is detected by their acute sense of hearing. Leopards vocalise to advertise territory, to make contact with offspring or to locate mates. A female's call is longer than a male's, with a higher rasp frequency.

Leopards advertise their territories overtly to avoid confrontations and possible injury. Leopards use urine to mark their territories, which is loaded with olfactory messages. They also rub their faces on plants and objects along boundaries imbuing these with cheek gland secretions. Toms scrape the ground while urinating to get the smell on their feet. The scrape marks are visual markers while the scent on the feet leaves an olfactory trail where he walks. Toms also defecate conspicuously and take deliberate patrols to emphasise their territory limits.

Leopards mate for two to five days copulating every five to ten minutes. Females may seek out a male, calling and marking incessantly and even leaving their territories to seek out a tom. After each bout, the female turns and swats the male violently as he extracts his barbed penis. Gestation is quick and cubs are born helpless and blind but spend the first weeks of their lives hidden away in heavy cover, caves or holes while they gain strength. Despite this, 50% of cubs die, many being killed by other predators. The female suckles her babies for three months after which she hunts food to which she leads them. At about nine and a half months, cubs join their mother on hunts and usually start killing for themselves around 11 months old. Females allow their cubs to remain in their territories for 18 months or more and may even permit hunting trips by newly independent sub-adults.

Leopards are solitary except females and growing cubs. Both sexes have territories defended against members of the same sex. Females select territories dependent on available prey and den sites while males select for the availability of females. Territories vary from 5–100 km² depending on resources and toms defend areas encompassing numerous female territories so that locating females in oestrus is possible. This is done via the chemicals left behind in their urine and females seeking a mate will call constantly. Male and female remain together only during courtship and mating but the male has no further parental role.

African buffalo

))) *Syncerus caffer*

Height:	140 cm
Weight:	650–800 kg
Gestation:	11 months
Offspring:	1
Lifespan:	20+ years
Diet:	Bulk grazer

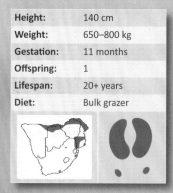

African buffalo are massive and impressive bovines with a reputation for being temperamental. Their size, strength and fearsome charge resulted in their inclusion amongst the Big Five, the most dangerous animals to hunt historically. They live wherever they have adequate tall grass to graze, water to drink and shade in which to rest. They may take small quantities of browse when under stress and are generally only hunted by lions although leopards and hyena may make an attempt on a vulnerable calf. Buffalo are heat sensitive and graze during cooler times of the day and night (during hot summers). During the hottest times of the day, buffalo seek out shade and ruminate. They may also wallow in mud. Bulls also wallow to show status rolling in mud or tossing it with their horns. Sometimes access to a wallow depends entirely on an individual's status. Buffalo rest during the night and during this time will lie touching one another.

Buffalo have an excellent sense of smell. They approach unfamiliar objects or situations with noses raised to sniff the air. They also use smell to communicate and to organise within the herd. They are very vocal animals and contact call continuously while feeding. Sight and hearing are good and also used to find food or to detect predators but these are less acute than smell. When threatened, buffalo give a distressed bellow and the herd responds collectively, the calves sheltering beside the cows in the centre while the bulls defend the flanks and rear. Buffalo flee together as a unit or stand their ground and mob predators. A buffalo can charge at 60 km/h.

Buffalo eat long grass, which they graze noisily while on the hoof. They eat vast amounts to meet the needs of their large bodies and are unselective. A wide row of incisors is used together with a flexible tongue to chop the grass but they lack the pliable lips of selective feeders. Buffalo trample areas where they feed, making stands of grass more suitable for grazers like zebra, wildebeest and grazing antelope.

Buffalo sexes differ with the bulls being bigger, black and often strewn with drying mud or soil. Female buffalo are reddish-brown, which as are juvenile animals are also quite hairy. Bull buffalo have huge horns with large bosses forming a 'combat helmet'. Cows and younger animals have narrower horns and bosses and young bulls have hair on their bosses. Buffalo have large, droopy, hairy ears that hang down below the horns.

ME

Cattle egrets are often found following herds of buffalo, mingling bravely in between their enormous hooves as they graze. The egrets harvest the insects they kick up. Occasionally egrets also perch on top of buffalo and remove parasites directly from the skin. Fork-tailed drongos also hawk insects flushed up by buffalo, darting in speedily before returning to a perch. Sometimes to improve their options, they give a false alarm call to startle the herd into running a few paces. Oxpeckers attend to buffalo herds en masse and the rarer yellow-billed oxpecker can usually be seen with them.

Buffalo drink water daily, twice daily during dry seasons, to assist with the digestion of grass. They typically make their way to water in the late afternoon in a determined fashion with much belching and an accompanying cloud of dust. On arrival, the herd moves right into the water until ankle or belly deep and begin drinking, sucking up sometimes 35 litres in a short sitting.

Buffalo live in mixed herds possibly numbering hundreds and fluctuating in size seasonally. Large herds may split up in summer and amass in the dry season. A herd comprises clans of closely related cows and calves that tend to remain in close proximity to one another. The herd is further ordered by rank and this improves when a cow has a calf at foot. Adult bulls are affiliated with and dominate the female clans. Young bulls do not become dominant or mate until about 8 years old because a bull's status depends on his size and strength which increases with age. Younger bulls may form age-related bachelor groups.

Buffalo have home ranges where they feed usually to the exclusion of other herds, but because they need to go where the water and food is, they are not territorial. The herd is led by specific individuals known as pathfinders, which are not dominant but simply direct the herd. Even sub-herds have pathfinders for when the herd segregates. Home ranges fluctuate depending on resource availability.

Highly ranked buffalo enjoy privileged positions within the herd, moving and feeding in fresh pastures ahead of the rest or in the centre of the group where they are safest. Dominant bulls gain access to oestrus cows earned via a display of combat ability. Older bulls are larger and stronger and therefore more powerful when clashing heads with opponents, the impact of which is absorbed

by the huge bosses. Such contests are only necessary when a suite of postures has failed.

Old buffalo bulls past their reproductive peak usually live alone or in small groups. Nicknamed '*dagha-boys*' after the Zulu word for mud, these individuals spend the majority of their time near water and wallowing. They are often inflicted with skin diseases, old battle wounds and a bad temperament because of their aged condition. Food around waterholes is often softer and easier to digest but without the protection of a herd, dagha-boys become vulnerable to lion attacks further adding to their aggressive demeanour.

Buffalo mate and calve during the rainy season when there is much green grass for the lactating cows to eat. Bulls test cows with flehmen and then guard oestrus cows. Cows are evasive and uncooperative, which attracts other bulls. Dominant bulls displace subordinates and by the peak of oestrus, a dominant bull is likely to be in attendance of and will mate with the cow. Cows will give birth in the herd but can get left behind if the calf cannot keep up when the herd moves off. Although a calf may stand in just 10 minutes, it takes a few weeks for it to overcome its feeble sense of coordination and clumsy running ability.

Hippo

)) *Hippopotamus amphibius*

Height:	140 cm
Weight:	1 400–3 000 kg (♀ 1 400 kg)
Gestation:	8 months
Offspring:	1
Lifespan:	35–40 years
Diet:	Grazer

Unmistakable with their grey, barrel-shaped bodies, enormous heads and large, four-toed feet, hippos are the largest land animals after elephants and rhinos. While a hippo's skin is generally thick, the epidermis is thin and dries out easily so hippos spend daytime hours submerged in water. They live in permanent water bodies in the vicinity of the grass pastures where they feed at night. Males and females are difficult to tell apart since the bulls' testicles are internal but bulls are generally larger, more active and scarred. Hippos are fairly immune to predation but lions, hyenas and humans do kill adults. Calves are more susceptible to predation, especially by crocodiles.

Hippos are well adapted for life in the water with all their vital senses well developed and perched high on the top of the head, including the eyes, nostrils and ears. When hippos submerge, they can stay underwater for 5 or 6 minutes. The nostrils and ears close off to stop any water from getting inside them. Baby hippos only submerge for short periods. Hippos can sleep underwater but surface involuntarily every few minutes to breathe.

To protect themselves from desiccation, hippos have a natural sunscreen, which they can secrete from their mucous glands if their bodies are exposed for long periods. This blood-red fluid helps for a while but after an extended time, the skin dehydrates and cracks. When water is scarce, hippo pods pack together in muddy pools to keep moist and move long distances at night to find deeper water. Cows will attempt to hydrate calves with dribbled saliva.

Hippos have a thick layer of fat to insulate them against the cold and they also come out of the water to bask in the sun to warm up. They tend to do this at cooler times of the year or day. Often an entire pod will haul onto a sand bank at once to bask. Hippo calves tend to lose heat more rapidly than adults and may pull themselves onto their mothers' back while in the water to warm up.

Hippos save on the amount of food they need to eat because they reserve much energy by being buoyed-up by the water. An adult hippo usually eats 15–40 kg of grass in a night, which equates to about 1.5% percent of its body weight. Other large mammals eat about 5% of their body weight as a rule. Hippos mostly graze on grass and only occasionally eat the water plants growing in the rivers where they live.

Hippos feed on grass at night when it is cool enough to leave the water. They feed alone except cows and calves. Leaving the water at dusk, they head to favoured short-grass feeding grounds 1–2 km away along well-used pathways. They return to the water before the sun gets hot. They feed noisily and pluck grass unselectively with their wide lips. During drought times, hippos may walk 15 km in a night.

Hippos have 3-chambered stomachs yet they practise foregut fermentation which exposes their food to micro-bacterial action and the breakdown of cellulose early on in the digestive process. They do not chew the cud like ruminants but are bulk grazers like hindgut digesters. Hippos defecate in and near the water bodies where they live and contribute to the ecology of these systems by adding nutrients for fish and invertebrates.

Hippos sometimes lick carcasses but since they do not have mouths or dentition suited to eating flesh, the reason is unclear. It could be the stomach contents of the dead herbivore that they are after, or the salts on the dried skin during droughts, or it could be they are using the chemo-sensitive organ of Jacobsen on the roof of their mouths for exploration of the environment. Hippos are also known to assist particularly juvenile antelope across crocodile-infested waterways.

Hippos are not adapted to swimming, lacking webbed limbs or flippers but they do porpoise with some success. To move in the water, they simply walk along the bottom pushing off with their feet. This action dredges water channels, keeping them open and flowing. To stay under, hippos breathe out before submerging and create negative buoyancy. They need to resurface to breathe, which they do with a puff of air and water spray from their nostrils.

Hippos do not navigate obstacles well and they cannot jump. They are able to charge at almost 40 km/h if necessary and when threatened, they head straight back to the safety of water along

the same well-used pathways by which they left. Because hippo paths are convenient footpaths for human use, many humans have come face to face with hippos in this way, to their detriment.

Hippos live in pods presided over by a territorial bull. Bull hippos defend territories, which may contain more than one nursery herd of females and their young. An average herd of hippos is about 10–15 animals strong but anything from two to 2 000 can be found. Bulls are very aggressive and much conflict occurs. When fighting, they attempt to wound the upper body of their opponent with their sharp canine teeth.

Territorial bulls show off their dominance by yawning. Hippos have incredible muzzles that can stretch very wide open. This puts their lower canines, which are modified into huge tusks, on display for all to see. These grow continuously, may reach 30–50 cm long and are continually sharpened through articulation against the pair on the upper jaw. A hippo uses its tusks to defend itself and its young, or to fight.

Territories are asserted by displays like charging or porpoising and only the most serious challengers fight. The ritualised process involves vigorous paddling of the tail that showers dung in all directions, while at the other end the mouth opens to show off the sharp canines. Much roaring accompanies this. Territories are marked on land with tail paddling of dung against trees and the iconic hippo-honk advertises territory vocally. Hippos also growl, grunt or squeal for other social applications.

When it comes to mating, bulls are not very tactful and a female in heat is simply accessed by the dominant bull pushing through the pod and smelling rumps. An oestrus female is chased into the water and forced into position even if this means she has to dodge grumpy snaps from the bull in order to steal breaths. The water buoys up their massive bodies during mating, alleviating the cow's discomfort of having a bull twice her weight upon her.

Hippo calves are born in shallow water and babies are able to swim and walk within minutes. Calves suckle underwater by pinching the cow's teat between its tongue and palate and while it drinks, its ears and nostrils are folded closed to avoid drowning. Cows protect their calves fiercely, not even tolerating unwelcome attention from the bull hippo.

Giraffe

)) *Giraffa camelopardalus*

Height:	4–6 m
Weight:	700–1 400 kg
Gestation:	15 months
Offspring:	1
Lifespan:	25 years
Diet:	Browser

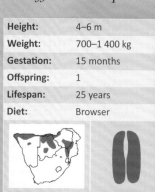

The giraffe is the tallest land mammal, living in the savanna and feeding on the most nutritious leaves. It can eat 34 kg in a day and is in turn eaten by lions and hyena (especially younger animals). Their long necks allow them to browse foliage otherwise out of reach for all other herbivores except elephants. They bend down to drink and to chew bones or soil for the minerals. The species name camelopardalis means 'camel-like leopard'. It has a leopard-like pelage and walks like a camel, moving the two legs on the same side at a time to prevent them tangling. Giraffe gallop like hares and reach up to 50–60 km/h. The giraffe's large size means it has few enemies but can defend itself with a powerful kick. Giraffe are especially vulnerable when they lie down at night. They only sleep curled up for 5 minutes at a time.

Bulls and cows have bony, skin-covered horns called ossicones. Males' are thicker and bald on top while females' are thinner and tufted. Males also have a median horn on the forehead, which enlarges with calcification from necking impacts. Other calcified knobs also form. Giraffe are born with cartilage horns unattached to the skull. As the calf grows, the horns ossify from the top down until solid bone and fuse with the skull at 4 years old in males and 7 years in females.

Giraffe are ruminants and browse selectively on nutritious foliage. The biggest bulls can browse almost 6 metres up and because females are shorter, they do not compete with them for food. Bulls also tend to stretch up to browse while cows will bend down. Giraffe's constant browsing of particular trees can cause waistlines around the tree or may stunt their growth.

Giraffe get moisture from the leaves they eat but drink if water is available. Bending down potentially subjects the brain to high blood pressure considering the heart circulates 60 litres of blood every minute and the brain may be as high as 5 metres above the ground and 2 metres from the heart. However, giraffe have a network of small capillaries in the neck that dilate and constrict to control the flow of blood when the giraffe bends down and stands up. Valves in the neck also assist this process.

Giraffe have many adaptations that enable browsing, especially of thorny trees. The tongue is 45 cm long, prehensile and extends beyond the mouth. This gives giraffe extra height and helps them grip leaves or strip branches. The tongue is also very rubbery, has papillae and is coated in copious saliva so thorns do not easily penetrate it. The muzzle is narrow and the upper lip supple to pick leaves between thorns. Long eyelashes and whiskers protect the eyes while they do so. A modified atlas-axis joint at the skull's base allows the head to tilt vertically.

The giraffe's patches break up its outline; it needs only to stand still to disappear amongst trees. The patches are caused by a variation in fur colour and every animal has a unique coat. The giraffe's patches may also scatter heat, helping animals to thermoregulate. The patch arrangement varies between isolated populations and at least six different races are recognised in southern and east Africa. Males are typically darker than females and sometimes a metre taller.

Giraffe have brilliant sight, both in the light and dark. Their height gives them further advantage when it comes to spotting danger and other animals tend to associate with giraffe to benefit from this, and respond to their reactions. Giraffe are inquisitive and stare at predators lying in the grass or at unfamiliar intruders, sometimes even moving closer.

Giraffe are gregarious but live in temporary associations so the individuals in a group may change within a matter of hours. There are no lasting bonds except between mothers and young calves and any combination of sex and age occurs. Bachelors may remain together and young animals form crèches overseen by one of the mothers. The skin behind a giraffe's ears is white and useful as a 'follow me' sign or to remain in visual contact in a landscape.

Bull giraffe are solitary and move between groups searching for cows in oestrus. They are not territorial and a hierarchy develops depending on age and size (that infers heavier skulls), established through ritual necking amongst young males. Necking becomes serious if there is an oestrus cow at stake. Giraffe engaged in necking appear to be swaying in the wind or dancing in slow motion. The goal, however, is for a bull to arc and thrust his neck sideways and hit the other with his bony horns and knobbly skull. They stand head to rump and side on. Rivals do their best to avoid blows but injuries do occur in serious matches.

Giraffe weigh 100 kg at birth and are on their feet within 15 minutes. During birth, the cow squats to prevent the calf from falling the full 2 metres as it exits the birth canal front feet first, then head. Calves initially lie-up and lower the neck if they need to hide. The mother stays close to protect and feed her calf but may go off for hours to feed. Once a little bigger, calves form crèches for safety and mothers take turns to stay with the group and they defend their young bravely. Calves basically grow out of harm's way, adding 1 metre to their height in the first six months and double that in the year.

Plains (Burchell's) zebra

🔊 *Equus burchelli*

Height:	135 cm
Weight:	320 kg
Gestation:	12 months
Offspring:	1
Lifespan:	20 years
Diet:	Bulk grazer

The plains zebra is iconic with its black and white stripes. They graze in herds in open woodland or grassland where brilliant senses of sight, smell and hearing alert them to threats. They prefer short green grass, particularly spring or post-fire flushes but also eat taller grass, which they crop short enabling more selective blue wildebeest and antelope to then feed on it. These species benefit from shared vigilance by associating together. Lions and hyena prey on adult zebra, and leopard and cheetah also prey on foals. A zebra's tufted tail flicks continuously, acting as a fly-swatter and animals often stand head-to-toe to mutually keep flies off one another's faces.

Each zebra has a unique pattern of stripes. Plains zebra have brown 'shadow stripes' on the rump between the other stripes, a trait exclusive to the subspecies. When a foal is born, the mother screens it from other zebra to allow her pattern to imprint on the foal. Stripes make it tricky to tell the sexes apart. Females have a broader black wedge under the tail and between the hind legs. Males have a narrow black stripe.

Different theories exist as to why zebras have stripes. Camouflage is one option and stripes supposedly break up the shape of the animal but zebra are often found in open areas and are active and noisy so this may have limited application. Another theory suggests that the blur of stripes in a group of fleeing zebra makes it difficult for predators to identify an individual target. Weaker or older animals tend to lag behind and are easy pickings although zebra do attempt to rally around their weak when threatened. Stripes may also have a thermoregulatory role.

Zebra are generally found in close proximity to permanent water. Because they consume much roughage in their diets, they must drink daily. They prefer clean water and will carefully skim this off the surface of a waterhole or dig a hole beside it, allowing clean water to filter into the depression before drinking. In some areas zebra migrate in order to maintain access to water as well as good grazing and are therefore not territorial. Many harems aggregate together in productive areas.

Zebra use their strong movable upper lips to push grass between their sharp incisors and snip it off. They are primarily bulk grazers but in dry conditions, may sometimes browse or dig up rhizomes. They are hindgut fermenters and digest large amounts of food, producing large quantities of gas. This bloats their bellies contributing to a

well-rounded appearance and flatulence when they run away. Even sickly zebra appear fat from their bloated stomachs and the condition of the mane (whether erect or floppy) is a better indication of health.

Zebra are not territorial but rather a stallion protects a harem of four to six mares and their foals. Colts leave the natal herd at about two years old and then between five and 12 years old will begin abducting fillies from other herds to create their own harems. Each harem is, however, fearlessly defended by the resident stallion that fights violently to protect his herd. Contenders may also fight amongst themselves for access to fillies. Once a young male mounts and impregnates a filly, she becomes his. This may take as long as a year to accomplish. He then pursues another.

A stallion defends himself and his harem with powerful kicks and biting. Zebra have two rows of well-developed incisor teeth and males have sharp canine teeth, which deliver painful bites. Mares and foals typically flee danger as a group and the stallion may run behind. Usually alarm is accompanied by a high-pitched and repeated 'kwa-ha-ha' contact call. Stripes may help to keep the group together when they flee since black and white are especially visible colours in the low light conditions during which predators typically hunt or as a result of the dust churned up by frantic hooves.

There is a rank hierarchy amongst the mares in a harem according to age and also to the order of abduction. The first filly that is abducted becomes the dominant mare. Zebra may queue up in rank order to perform certain tasks such as rubbing against rocks or termite mounds. The herd mutually groom one another as a bonding exercise.

Zebra enjoy dust-baths rolling over on their backs in loose earth. This helps to smother ectoparasites and plays a thermoregulatory role. They also enjoy rubbing head and shoulders against objects. Zebra like to sleep, resting during the heat of the day or for longer periods after dark. They may remain standing or lie on their sides (especially younger animals) but one animal generally remains vigilant for danger during these times.

A zebra foal can stand on its own just ten minutes after birth, walking within half an hour and running within the hour. A zebra's gestation is a year long and as a result, foals are born well developed sand ready to run for their lives from birth. Baby plains zebra are browner and hairier than adults.

Impala

)) *Aepyceros melampus*

Height:	900 cm
Weight:	50 kg (♀ 40 kg)
Gestation:	6.5 months
Offspring:	1
Lifespan:	6–12 years
Diet:	Mixed feeder

Impala are attractive, medium-sized antelope with shiny, tawny, multi-toned coats. They are abundant because they are exceptionally well adapted to their lifestyles. They live in transitional woodland-grassland habitats (ecotones) and feed on both grass and leaves (as well as fruit and flowers) according to whatever is most abundant seasonally. They need to drink daily and are always found in close proximity to water. They are common prey for a variety of carnivores (including lion, leopard, cheetah, spotted hyena, jackal) and pythons, baboons or large birds of prey also take the lambs.

Impala have an arsenal of exceptional senses including large ears to hear the smallest noises and huge, side-positioned eyes with excellent peripheral vision. While feeding, impala take turns to lift their heads up to watch for danger. A loud, nasal alarm snort is used to signal threats and scatters the herd into eruptive flight. Impala are very agile, easily clearing obstacles in densely vegetated habitats with 3 m × 12 m leaps and they may flick their hind legs up almost vertically while they flee.

Being relatively small antelope, impala necessarily reduce blood-loss to ticks by being fastidious about personal hygiene. They spend long periods grooming themselves and other herd-members (reciprocating in the hard-to-reach head and neck areas). Modified lower incisors are slightly loose and behave as a comb to get rid of dirt and ectoparasites. Impala are also generally in the company of red-billed oxpeckers that assist with grooming.

The multi-toned colour of the impala's coat (dark above and paler on the belly) produces a camouflaging technique called counter-shading. The darker colour on the back and flanks absorbs graduated light falling on them from above, reversing the effect of the illumination to make the animal appear two-dimensional and thus less obvious to prey.

Many animals perform pilo-erection, lifting the hair on their bodies to achieve various objectives, for example to appear larger or frighten predators. Impala do pilo-erection on cold mornings to trap a layer of air close to their bodies. The body warms the layer of air to better insulate the animal against the cold. Their coats become duller when they do this.

Impala are gregarious, living together in herds. Ewes and lambs associate in breeding herds year-long while rams form bachelor groups. Herds provide safety in numbers against the many predators that feed on impala. The three black stripes on the impala's rump offer a 'follow me' sign to herd members inducing individuals to fall behind one another and thereby offering safety from pursuit or ambush to the individual hemmed in the middle.

The impala rut is a sight to behold. Shortening day-lengths from the end of January trigger elevated testosterone in rams that separate from their bachelor herds and set up territories. Rams rush about frenetically herding females and chasing opponents away with tails stiffened and deep roars. Serious encounters between rams involve intense horn clashes. The peak of the rut falls around May by which time the rams' antics have stimulated oestrus in the ewes and intensive mating ensues. At this time rams abandon feeding and grooming and as a result, territory tenure is shortened (to about eight days) accommodating for a degree of gene variation.

ME

Impala employ an ingenious breeding strategy during which all the ewes are impregnated during a three-week window in May–June with the result that during late November and early December, all the impala lambs in an area are born within a three-week period. This flood of newborns offers a feast for predators but they cannot eat all of them. A large proportion grows to a safe size before the breeding effort can be fully devastated and the overall population is subsequently bolstered.

Impala often associate with other species while they forage, whether to utilise common food resources or to benefit from shared vigilance. Impala regularly glean scraps of fruit or flowers left behind by the foraging actions of baboons who also offer an early predator-warning system to the impala from their vantage up in the trees.

Rams create large middens throughout their territories and in the no-man's-land between their territories. Ewes add their pellets to middens when they pass by, leaving behind olfactory information in the process.

The black metatarsal glands on the heels of an impala's hind legs are unique to the species but their actual function is uncertain. They are supposedly activated when an impala kicks up its hind legs in flight and could play a role in regrouping after a herd has scattered.

Blue wildebeest

 Connochaetes taurinus

Height:	1.3–1.5 m
Weight:	180–250 kg
Gestation:	8 months
Offspring:	1
Lifespan:	15 years
Diet:	Selective grazer

The blue wildebeest is silvery-blue, lined with dark stripes over the shoulders and flanks. These bands and the 'gnu' sound they make led to their alternate name, brindled gnu. They also snort and bellow. They live in open, grassy habitats since they are pure grazers, selecting sites with fresh forage of 15 cm or less, which are cropped with the broad muzzle. Wildebeest tend to trample their own pastures to maintain them. They avoid regions with very cold temperatures as well as predators such as lion, hyena, leopard, wild dog, cheetah and crocodiles.

Both sexes have horns. A bull's horns tend to be heavier and extend past the ears before curving up. His penis sheath also breaks the smooth curve of his belly. Females are browner with russet on the forehead and horns that curve before the end of the ears. Juveniles also have brown on the face.

The wildebeest has an unusual shape with high shoulders, long front legs and a strongly slanted back. These adaptations enable energy-efficient cantering, as they must often travel long distances following distant storms. Blue wildebeest constantly seek fresh forage and water and traditionally migrate to new areas to access these once depleted where they are. Herds combine into massive aggregations (most notably in the Serengeti and Masai Mara of East Africa) and will breed while on the move.

Where resources are more constantly available or where fences have cut off migratory routes, blue wildebeest are more sedentary. They form harems and a bull protects a demarcated territory. Cows enter a territory in search of resources at which time the bull will herd them and attempt to retain them. This is especially true in early winter during the rutting season. Breeding is synchronised so that calves arrive simultaneously at the start of summer when there's much green grass. Females remain in a herd lifelong, moving in home ranges that expand or contract seasonally, while young males form bachelor groups from two years old, using the fringes of bulls' territories until they stake their own.

Blue wildebeest feed when it is cool and at night, seeking shade during the day when it is hot. In the absence of cover, they face the prevailing breeze to allow wind to cool the blood flowing through their horn bosses. They are very water dependent and drink daily even taking muddy water, and usually remain in close proximity to water. Wildebeest can be quite influential on ecosystems around permanent water sources, trampling pastures to short grass at the expense of specialist species like sable and roan antelope.

Bulls make their territories near water and include a sandy patch for a stomping ground. They rake the ground with their hooves to release scent from pedal glands and horn-rub bushes or the ground to transfer secretions from the preorbital gland. They often get covered in mud in the process. They also make large dung middens on their stomping patches. Territorial animals spend much time alone and are vulnerable to predators, a risk worth taking to ultimately win females. Intruders are chased away and bulls wrestle on their knees if confrontation is necessary.

A blue wildebeest calf is tan and looks quite different to the adults. It is exceptionally precocial, standing up and running within minutes and can keep up with the herd within a day. This adaptation suits their migratory habits. The horns get their upward curve at eight months.

ME

Warthog

🔊 *Phacochoerus aethiopicus*

Height:	65–85 cm
Weight:	80 kg (♀ 65 kg)
Gestation:	5–6 months
Offspring:	2 to 3
Lifespan:	18 years
Diet:	Grazer

Warthogs are the only 'pigs' adapted to grazing in savannas, feeding on lawn-like swathes of grass in summer but changing to underground rhizomes and bulbs in winter. They pick up fallen fruits too. They prefer open habitats like grasslands or areas near waterholes and avoid forests or desert. The warthog gets its name from its obvious facial warts comprised of thick skin and cartilage. Females have a single pair below the eyes while boars have two pairs. Boars' warts are much larger and the extra pair on the cheeks helps to protect their faces during combat. Warthogs are the smallest ungulates to be attended by red-billed oxpeckers and being short-sighted and short-legged, warthogs rely on these parasite-removing birds (and other animals' alarm calls) to warn them of danger in the form of lions, leopards, hyenas or wild dogs. Piglets are hunted by pythons, cheetah, jackals and raptors.

A warthog's tusks, called tushes, grow sideways and are modified canine teeth. The lower tusks are shorter (up to 13 cm) and sharper, being employed with slashing motions in defence against predators. The upper tusks grow to about 60 cm and it is against the inner groove of these tusks that the lower ones articulate, sharpening with each movement of the mouth which renders them are as vicious as daggers and able to inflict mortal wounds. Older females may have tusks that curl right over the snout.

Warthogs are grazers using above- and below-ground parts. They feed selectively on more nutritious species. To effect feeding, the shovel-shaped face with hardened upper snout, large flat molars and modified jaw-articulation are well suited. The short neck provides leverage while grovelling and warthogs often kneel on their front legs, which are calloused, while feeding. They can dig several centimetres even in hard ground. Warthogs are hindgut fermenters and they defecate coarse textured dung fortuitously. They are also water dependent and drink daily.

Warthogs are day-active, returning to their burrows before dark. Warthogs have little subcutaneous fat and are susceptible in cold or wet conditions. The stable microclimate inside burrows provides vital shelter from weather conditions, including access to shade on hot days. They typically use a network of old aardvark holes, modifying them with their forefeet and shovel-like snouts. They prefer large burrows with numerous exits and sows construct shelves for their piglets to lift them up in case of flooding. Warthogs may share burrows on a first-come-first-serve basis.

Warthogs raise their tails when running away. The action is an involuntary muscle reaction and the tail acts as a 'follow me' sign to piglets and other warthogs, especially in longer grass. Warthogs make for bolt holes when threatened, reversing into them so that their tusks face out towards the danger. Piglets enter first and the adult will about-turn at the last second in a swoosh of confusing dust. Generally warthogs are cautiously hesitant when exiting burrows.

Warthogs mate at the start of the dry season with boars staking out the entrances to sows' burrows. On finding an oestrus sow, they trail them while strutting. If interrupted by other boars, males rush at one another aggressively with manes up and paw the ground or head-butt on their knees. The victor then continues with a bouncy, hip-swaying gait, chomping his jaws and salivating.

parasite infested. The normal litter size is 2–3 but abandoned piglets may join other sounders. Up to 50% of piglets die in these early weeks due to sudden temperature fluctuations and predation. Piglets may sleep on the sow's back to keep warm.

One or a few sows live together in sounders with their offspring. The boars live in bachelor groups or alone and only join the sounders during the rut. Sounders can have between five and 16 members (during more productive times) and are not

Piglets are born in October but remain hidden in burrows for six weeks where sows suckle them 12–17 times a day or every 40 minutes. Piglets usually emerge during November to begin grazing or change burrows. Sows carry tiny piglets in their mouths between dens should burrows become

territorial but share home ranges. Animals tend to reside in areas where they were born and sounders may remain bonded through successive seasons. Warthogs interact socially via allogrooming, pulling one another's mane hair through their front teeth or mouths.

Warthogs practise osteophagia (the chewing of bones), geophagia (the chewing of soil) and coprophagia (the consumption of faeces). They do this to supplement deficient nutrients, to colonise their guts with digestive microbacteria or to reprocess poorly digested plant material. Warthogs also visit carcasses to consume the exposed stomach contents of other herbivores.

ME

Warthogs are usually quiet but they can grunt and snort. Piglets squeak if stressed. The jaw-chomps of a boar courting a sow can be heard 50 metres away.

Warthogs put what little hair they have to good use. The coarse mane can be raised to make the warthog look more intimidating to enemies. Distinct white cheek whiskers in younger animals probably serve to emulate the adults' formidable tusks and dissuade predators from attacking them. Warthogs thoroughly enjoy mud wallowing which helps to keep their naked bodies cool and also to remove ectoparasites. Once the mud has dried, they rub it off on any suitably positioned object concurrently removing the mud-caked ticks.

Vervet monkey

🔊 *Cercopithecus aethiops*

Length:	1 m (tail 60 cm)
Weight:	4–5 kg
Gestation:	5.5 months
Offspring:	1
Lifespan:	12 years
Diet:	Omnivore

H   F

Vervet monkeys are attractive with grey pelage and black faces, fringed with white fur. They are arboreal, preferring riverine areas where their food is abundant. Their diet is diverse, including fruit, flowers, leaves, buds, seeds, gum, insects, bird's eggs and nestlings. Vervet monkeys have about 36 calls including six different alarm signals, indicating different predators, for example a prowling leopard or an aerial threat such as a bird of prey. Other carnivores also prey on vervets, as do pythons. When anxious, vervets alarm constantly. Aside from baboons, the only other monkey found in southern Africa is the samango monkey, which lives in forests.

The white fringe around the face highlights facial expressions during interactions. Vervets may also reveal their white eyelids to intimidate another and these contrast with the black face. Long whiskers assist with navigation and the hands have agile fingers and opposable thumbs – features critical for climbing, grooming and manipulating food. The long tail is used for balance when leaping or running along branches. It is prehensile and acts as an additional limb during foraging. They have very sharp canines which they see to protect themselves, fight and forage.

ME

ME

Forward-facing eyes provide vervets with binocular vision necessary to judge depth for jumping. They have colour vision to find ripe fruit, their primary dietary ingredient. Green fruits contain bitter or toxic tannins and alkaloids. Colour vision is also used to communicate and dominant males sit with their legs splayed to show off their blue testicles and red penis which denote status. They, in fact, flash their genitals at any given opportunity and in a number of ways. Subordinate males respond by retracting their penis. Night vision is poor so vervets are hidden in dense foliage by nightfall, huddling together for assurance and warmth.

ME

Vervet monkeys have territories, the trees of which they scent-mark from cheek and chest glands. A large, common resource like a fruiting tree will draw many vervets to one area and while they may feed together for a time, there is often some tension between troops. Troops comprise about 20 individuals ranked according to status with males outranking females and offspring inheriting the mother's status. There is usually one dominant male overall. Rank allows an animal access to the best feeding or sleeping sites and in the case of males, access to females. The hierarchy also absorbs aggression in a troop, so dominant animals fight with subordinates but instead of retaliation, subordinates in turn pick on lower-ranked individuals. The lowliest member has many bite marks on its tail.

Vervet monkeys have advanced social systems in which members interact. Most of the social

SS

activities take place while resting during the heat of the day. Closely related monkeys tend to interact more and rally together during disputes. However, allogrooming forges partnerships that may subsequently result in a favour from a higher-ranking animal to a lower-ranked one. Visual communication conveys messages between individuals, for example barring of teeth could indicate aggression.

Vervet monkeys post sentinels to keep watch for danger while the troop forages. Dominant males are most reliable, raising the alarm most often. The white belly of the sentinel perched up high is easy for the troop to see and the alarm may be passive or active. If the sentinel suddenly abandons his post without any vocalisation, the troop quietly slips into cover to remain undetected. If an alarm call is given, vervets watch the sentinel to see where the threat is and react accordingly. A bird of prey will send the troop deep into the canopy while a snake may cause them to chatter agitatedly while standing up. Vervets also respond to avian alarm calls.

Infants cling to the front of the mother where her teats are easily accessed. All the females in a troop care for the young and will rush to a baby's defence. Play is an important learning mechanism for young monkeys during which they discover skills and exercise muscles they need to survive as adults. Young animals also mimic older animals to learn what to eat, how to integrate socially and what different alarms calls mean.

SS

Chacma baboon

)) *Papio cynocephalus ursinus*

Height:	1–1.5 m
Weight:	15–40 kg
Gestation:	6 months
Offspring:	1
Lifespan:	20–30 years
Diet:	Omnivore

Chacma baboons are large, terrestrial primates with dog-shaped heads and a kink in the tail. They live in big troops, which the dominant males defend through cooperation. For this they have massive canine teeth and can injure even large predators. They spend the day on the ground in a variety of habitats, searching for food. Their omnivorous diet includes fruit, seeds, bulbs, rhizomes, grass stems, invertebrates, small mammals and birds, and any other edible morsel they find opportunistically.

Baboons have forward-facing eyes with binocular vision to gauge depth and distance necessary for climbing trees and cliffs. They also see in colour to identify ripe fruit and to recognise sexual readiness. The female has scarlet sexual skin around her rump that turns a variety of shades of pink throughout her cycle, being brightest when she is on heat. Because they see in colour, baboons do not see well at night and therefore sleep in tall trees along rivers or up against cliffs at night.

Dominant males eat meat, occasionally hunting small antelope. They have three priorities in a day: to find food and water, make time to socialise and avoid predators in the form of leopards, eagles and crocodiles. The alarm is raised with noisy barks. Baboons only take to trees to sleep, escape danger or access fruit.

Baboons are habitual, waking early and climbing down the trees to sun themselves and perform the social activities of grooming, playing, mating or fighting. The troop then begins to forage, moving as they do, up to 15 km in a day. They usually rest at the hottest time of the day and then forage back towards their sleeping site. They arrive in time to engage in more social activities and by the time it is dark they have taken to the safety of the boughs.

Baboons have dexterous hands, nailed digits and opposable thumbs that are used to forage and manipulate food. They overturn rocks, dig up grass clumps, pull out water lilies and peel tough skin off fruit. Cheek pouches in their mouths hold as much food as the stomach and they stuff their pouches and then process the food later in safety. In this way baboons never have to abandon a meal if threatened. They have cushions to pad their buttocks, called ischial callosities, as they spend much time sitting.

There is always competition within a group. More dominant animals have access to prime resources so subordinates forge alliances and curry favours from them through grooming. Smaller subgroups form and these groom, feed and sleep together, and males in the clique, called godfathers, come to the rescue of females. Disputing baboons often grab an infant as bargaining leverage and the godfathers protect them. They have also been known to care for weaned, orphaned babies.

A band of dominant males rule the roost in a social system known as an oligarchy. All animals in the troop are ranked with males dominating over females and females with infants having elevated statuses for that period. Females stay in the same troop for life and inherit their mother's status. Males emigrate at 6 or 7 years old as they achieve better status as immigrants and can potentially breed in new troops. Males advertise their dominance by displaying their impressive canines.

Baboons are not territorial because they roam to find food and water, and different troops' home ranges overlap. However, they have

favourite sleeping sites, which smell strongly from regular use. If roosting places are in short supply, these are defended with barking, chasing and branch shaking. Furthermore, if disturbed at night, baboons urinate and defecate upon the disturbance below.

Baboons dig for water opening up pits in dry riverbeds that are subsequently used by other animals especially during dry times. Baboons are water dependent and must drink daily. They associate with many different herbivores and respond to one another's alarm calls. Animals like impala, kudu and civet eat fruit and scraps that baboons drop out of trees. Baboons are undeterred by buffalo and elephants using the same area.

Female baboons are promiscuous and solicit mating from males by flashing white eyebrows or presenting the rump but at the peak of her oestrus, she will only mate with a dominant male. Baby baboons are black with pink faces and ears at birth, and helpless. For the first five weeks, they cling to the mother's belly where they can access her teats and suckle on demand. From then they can walk and ride jockey on the mother's back.

Baboons are long-lived and grow slowly with stages including infant, juvenile, adolescent and adult. Like other long-lived animals, behaviour is learned through experience and observation. For example, young baboons learn what to eat as well as the subtleties of community life by watching older baboons.

Baboons have a large vocabulary and they scream, squeal, bark and chatter. Dominant males make the iconic, echoing 'ba-hoo' which carries over long distances, especially when uttered from a vantage point. Vocal communication maintains contact while foraging, raises the alarm and demonstrates mood. Baboons have very expressive faces and use their lips and brows for non-verbal communication. For example, smacking lips and soft grunting is friendly while displaying teeth is a threat or show of dominance. Baboons present their rumps to one another to make peace.

Tree squirrel

Paraxerus cepapi

Length:	35 cm (incl. tail)
Weight:	200 g
Gestation:	8 weeks
Offspring:	1 to 3
Lifespan:	8 years
Diet:	Omnivore

Tree squirrels are small, agile, golden-coloured woodland dwellers residing in natural cavities in trees and are sometimes called mopane squirrels for their association with that tree. They are diurnal, foraging by day only but are most active in the mornings and afternoons, resting when it is hot. They are essentially vegetarian, eating flowers, seeds, berries, bark and grass but supplement their diet with insects. Tree squirrels cache food in pantries but on a much smaller scale than European squirrels. Food items are secretly buried in small holes, covered and patted down with the chin.

The tree squirrel's alarm call is bird-like but loud and persistent. Their predators may include birds of prey, snakes or larger carnivores like wild cats or mongooses. Other species may respond to their alarms that get more urgent with time, reaching a high-pitched whistle. Other squirrels also begin alarm calling or may rally together to mob predators like snakes.

Tree squirrels live in family groups. They nest and sleep in trees but are equally terrestrial and arboreal when they forage. They use natural cavities in trees as their dreys, which they line with vegetation and clean regularly while nesting. They also retreat to holes when threatened. Family groups acquire a common odour through grooming one another, sleeping together or dragging anal glands over family members. Any squirrel not bearing the common scent is chased off.

Being small animals, tree squirrels lose heat quickly and therefore spend much time sunbathing when it is cooler. Basking may last a few hours before a squirrel moves off to forage in the mornings and typically coincides with mutual grooming. They may repeat the process before retiring for the night.

Tree squirrels are adept at their lifestyles, deftly manipulating objects or hanging acrobat-style from their hind legs to get at hard-to-reach morsels. They climb effortlessly on flimsy branches or jump and grab repeatedly to access desirable foodstuffs and then sit at a vantage point to simultaneously eat and watch out for trouble.

Feeding on a diet of seeds and grass, tree squirrels take to the ground readily but do so cautiously, walking jerkily with tails flicking. They forage on their own using their acute hearing and sight to detect danger, bounding into the nearest tree for cover. In the absence of cavities in which to retreat, they may lie flat against a branch or circle a tree trunk keeping the tree between it and the threat. Tree squirrels can also easily clear 2 metre gaps between trees if necessary.

Family groups are territorial and are very vocal in advertising these. They scent-mark with urine, or lip and anal gland secretions. The male is the territory's chief defender. A female in oestrus promotes her status with insistent, high-pitched chatters attracting different males, which the territory owner spends much effort chasing around. Other females may come into heat concurrently keeping the territorial male very busy.

Tree squirrels make attentive parents and the female remains with her helpless, blind newborns in the drey for the first few days to look after them. She may need to move them to new dreys, which she does by grasping one of their back-legs, the baby clinging to her shoulder. The male also contributes to rearing his family. Babies wean quickly and are then not fed to encourage them to begin learning how to fend for themselves by watching the adults. Before leaving to forage in the mornings, youngsters are held down and groomed obligatorily by their mothers. They reach sexual maturity at ten months old and may then leave the family group.

Ground squirrel

)) *Xerus inauris*

Length:	41–49 cm (tail 21 cm)
Weight:	500–1 000 g
Gestation:	6–7 weeks
Offspring:	1 to 3
Lifespan:	15 years
Diet:	Vegetarian / termites

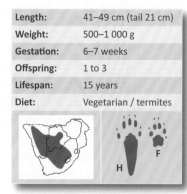

A larger, more robust squirrel than its tree-dwelling cousin with some striping and a big bushy tail. Unlike tree squirrels that frequent ground and arboreal habitats and forage alone, the ground squirrel is strictly ground dwelling and more communal. It is diurnal and uses open habitats, particularly in arid areas. While foraging they are susceptible to attack by predators like raptors and quickly dive for the cover of their burrows at the first sign of trouble. Generally, they attack and mob snakes rather than the other way around. When alarmed, they utter a high-pitched whistle or scream.

Female ground squirrels and their young live in colonies visited by males only when a female comes on heat. The dominant female is particularly defensive of her colony, chasing off other groups of squirrels as well as the males that stop over sometimes. Colony members groom one another meticulously and recognise each other by smell. Babies remain in the safety of the warren for a month and initially forage within 10 metres of it. Females remain with the colony while males disperse at a year old.

The squirrel family is known as the Sciuridae after *skiouros,* the Latin word for shady tail referring to the bushy tail that is used as an umbrella by some species.

Ground squirrels live in intricate warrens in the ground that are constantly under construction. Excavations result in a mound at the warren entrance. Warrens are scent-marked with urine and lip or anal area secretions. They may share their living quarters with yellow mongoose or meerkats for enhanced vigilance and mutually respond to one another's alarms. The ground squirrel jerks its tail and whistles its alarm with growing urgency to which colony members respond by dashing straight-tailed back to the warren.

Ground squirrels eat every part of the plants they can find as well as termites when necessary for protein. They seldom roam far from their warrens so vegetation in the immediate vicinity of their homes becomes degraded.

Ground squirrels are weather-sensitive and their activity patterns depend on the ambient conditions. They avoid rain, wind and extreme heat by sheltering in their warrens and sunbathe to warm up on cool days. They use their bushy tails as umbrellas to shade themselves while feeding and may flick sand onto their bodies too. Activity above ground is usually in the region of six or seven hours a day.

Rock hyrax (Dassie)

)) Procavia capensis

Height:	50 cm
Weight:	3–4.5 kg
Gestation:	7.5 weeks
Offspring:	1 to 6
Lifespan:	12 years
Diet:	Mixed feeder

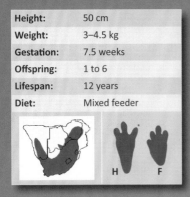

H   F

Rock hyraxes are small, guinea pig-like herbivores that live in rocky habitats and are adapted to the inhospitable conditions in such places. They look and behave much like rocks so that they camouflage easily into their environment. They have stone-coloured, rounded bodies and they sit motionless for long periods as much to sun themselves as to remain concealed. To compensate for temperature extremes, they are strictly diurnal, coming out of their night refuges after the sun is up and returning before sunset. They take to crevices to avoid predators, including caracal, leopard and Verreaux's eagle.

Verreaux's eagles are the hyrax's primary predator. Hyraxes have eyes that are modified to look into the sun in order to detect the eagles. An umbraculum shields the eye and the kidney-shaped pupil may also play a role. To escape attack, hyraxes shelter in rock crevices and are seldom more than 15 metres from one. Hiding places can be in short supply, which is one reason hyraxes live in groups. An older female acts as a sentinel, sending the group under cover immediately at her barked alarm. Hyraxes make 21 different sounds including growls, grunts, wails, squeals, snorts, whistles and twitters.

In spite of short limbs, hyraxes are good jumpers and climbers, and can efficiently traverse steep or slippery surfaces. They also manipulate plants with the front feet. Hyraxes' feet are comparable to elephants' in that they are hoof-less and the feet also do not fit neatly into the carnivore or primate groups. There are four stumpy nailed digits on the front feet and three on the back. Naked, padded soles provide much-needed traction enhanced by moisture produced by glandular tissue in the feet.

Because of their reliance on rock crevices for safety, hyrax colonies are often isolated and the food in the immediate vicinity of their homes is heavily used. They are mixed feeders and much of the diet comprises poor-quality forage as well as aromatic and poisonous plants. Hyraxes feed by cropping foliage with the cheek teeth sharpened on the outer edge through use. Their digestive system is modified with a large sac behind the stomach where bacteria process the cellulose in their food. This sac then joins onto the caecum with a short bit of intestine. The caecum has two horn-shaped processes, like in birds, and manufactures fatty acids to supplement their energy supply. Under extreme circumstances, hyraxes may travel up to 20 km to find food. Water is obtained from their food, succulents and dew, or from rain puddles.

Rocky habitats are prone to very low minimum temperatures and hyraxes are adapted to keeping warm. They have a double layer of insulating fur, a woolly inner layer and a thicker, rougher overlying guard coat. Hyraxes also perform 'heaping' to share warmth whereby they huddle up in layers upon each other with rumps facing inward and heads out. There may be as many as four layers in the heap with the younger animals on the top. They spend hours sunning themselves to warm up and remain indoors on colder days.

A hyrax's fur protects and streamlines it, and amongst the pelage long, tactile hairs help it to orientate in dark crevices. They also have long whiskers. The fur in the centre of a hyrax's back is longest and covers the dorsal gland. The hair on the dorsal spot can be erected during aggressive social interactions to displace others from a sunny spot, for example. It may also play a role in individual recognition or developing a group scent during heaping. Submissive hyraxes hold their dorsal hair flat and such posturing prevents actual fighting. Hyraxes groom their fur with grooming claws on the hind feet, usually after a stint of basking. Dust baths also help to get rid of parasites.

Male hyraxes are extremely territorial, defending their harems and turf from other males. Repetitive barking is used to advertise territory. A harem comprises as many females as space and food allows but usually less than 20. Members are often in close contact with one another and develop a common smell, newborns even climbing onto adults to obtain the scent. Any individual lacking the common odour is chased off, along with young males when they reach a year old. Territorial males use their sharp teeth to attack intruders or drive off stubborn youngsters. Ousted males are extremely vulnerable while they travel around to find new homes.

ANTELOPE ARE A DIVERSE GROUP of hooved herbivores and occur in a variety of sizes, from the tiny blue duiker, no bigger than a small dog, to the enormous eland, comparable with the largest cattle. Although each kind has its preferred niche or habitat, the antelope described in this section all prefer more vegetated areas such as savanna, valley bushveld or forest. There is some overlap with the arid-zone antelope and eland or steenbok, for example, also occur in semi-desert areas. Because of size difference between male and female nyala, this species provides the cut-off for antelope gender terms. Nyala females are ewes but males are bulls. So antelope smaller than the nyala female are referred to as 'ram' and 'ewe' while antelope larger than a nyala bull are referred to as 'bull' and 'cow'. The antelope described in this section prefer bushy areas.

Waterbuck

Kobus ellipsiprymnus

Waterbuck occur wherever there is good grazing within 2–5 km of water since they drink regularly to avoid dehydration. They consume large quantities of roughage, choosing protein-rich grasses where possible, and produce soggy droppings. They are easily recognised from their grey, shaggy coats and the white 'follow me' ring around the rump. When startled, herds may take to water.

Height:	1.2 m
Weight:	180–270 kg
Gestation:	9 months
Offspring:	1 or 2
Lifespan:	11 years
Diet:	Grazer

A musky gland secretion may help to waterproof their coats but does not immunise the animals against predators, which include lions, leopard, wild dog, hyena and crocodiles. Territorial bulls are particularly smelly, the scent detectable from 500 metres away. Bulls are very territorial, advertising their status by standing in the open with head held high and thick neck visible to contenders. White marks on his face emphasise his demeanour and waterbuck are not shy to put their impressive horns to use, fighting frequently. Herds move between territories in search of good grazing and water, and the resident bull will attempt to retain and mate with the females. Young, satellite bulls sometimes use territorial bulls' territories if they behave submissively. They even help defend the territory, probably in the hope of inheriting it. Most young males form bachelor groups until they are six years or older. They also show submissiveness to territorial bulls in order to access food and water. Status amongst bachelors is determined through pushing contests with older, larger animals being dominant. Calves are mobile from early on and while lying up will find their own hiding places and choose to flee from threats rather than lay still.

Eland

Tragelaphus oryx

Eland are the largest antelope in southern Africa and consequently almost immune to predation except the calves that suffer attacks from large predators. Adults run quickly or may band together to defend themselves or give their calves chance to escape. Eland are athletic jumpers and can easily clear a fence 2 metres high. Eland are nomadic and do not defend territories, rather they move to locate the best resources. They can walk extremely fast, adults producing a 'click' noise as they move, and at a trot cover ground rapidly.

Height:	1.5–1.7 m
Weight:	450–700 kg
Gestation:	9 months
Offspring:	1
Lifespan:	20 years
Diet:	Mixed feeder

Breeding is governed by a system of seasonal temporary associations where females, sub-adults and bulls occur together in herds. Sometimes they form aggregations up to 1 000 animals. After breeding, males form bachelor herds or go off alone and females separate from young animals that seem closely bonded to one another. Animals allogroom and a rank system keeps the order amongst groups maintained by subtle ritualised threats.

Males dominate over females and older animals dominate over younger ones. A jab of the horns quickly corrects an out-of-place animal.Males give way to stronger males but equally matched bulls fight for oestrus cows, horn-locking, pushing and twisting. Older, dominant bulls are impressive with blue-grey colouring, thick necks and large dewlaps.

A mop of hair between their horns covers glands and is regularly coated in mud from head-rubbing the earth or where cows have urinated. They horn-thrash bushes and bellow to advertise their status.

Eland are mixed feeders eating grass in summer and browsing in winter to maximise on available nutrients and moisture in food. They use their horns to twist and snap branches out of reach. They do not have to drink regularly and are adapted to dry areas, getting moisture from their food or using water conservation techniques such as feeding at night when foliage moisture content is higher, producing concentrated urine and dry dung pellets, standing in the shade on hot days, breathing slowly and allowing their body temperature to rise slightly, dissipating the heat when it cools after dark.

Kudu

)) *Tragelaphus strepsiceros*

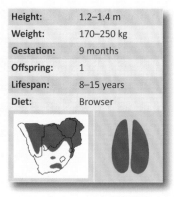

Height:	1.2–1.4 m
Weight:	170–250 kg
Gestation:	9 months
Offspring:	1
Lifespan:	8–15 years
Diet:	Browser

Kudu are the second tallest antelope in southern Africa and have remarkable jumping abilities, easily clearing 2 metres. They live in thickets especially along rivers, are crepuscular and very secretive. Small hooves help them to walk silently, hind feet registering directly onto the front track. Huge ears help them hear even soft noises in their dense habitats and they use a loud, deep bark to alarm call, the loudest of any antelope.

Kudu tend to freeze if startled, allowing the disruptive markings on their bodies to camouflage them. They lift their tails in flight showing the fluffy, white underside, a beacon to followers of their own kind, or predators such as lion, leopard, hyena or caracal. The tail drops as soon it stops and predators battle to relocate the target they were following. Bulls have huge, spiralled horns, the most impressive of all African antelope, which they flatten against their backs to keep them from snagging while running.

Males are larger than females with pale yellowish legs and strong, thick necks with a beard of hair. This enhances their lateral displays, a passive system in which males size one another up by walking in a circle with neck swollen, mane raised and a stiff-legged gait. Contenders will fight if equally matched and many a kudu bull has died interlocked in the horns of another. Cows live in small herds with their offspring and may aggregate in larger groups near good forage. Males are solitary, in bachelor groups or join up with the herds. Kudu breed in the wintertime so calves arrive in summer when the grass is long for eating and hiding in.

Bulls only have a short window of opportunity to breed as they mature at 5 years old but are initially displaced by older bulls so only really get to mate at 7 or 8 years old.

Competition is stiff and the large energy investment, combined with lack of nutrition, cold winter temperatures and

possible injury means that kudu bulls often die at the end of the season. Kudu are browsers including leaves, herbs, forbs, fruit, flowers, seedpods, succulents and tubers and are not especially water dependent as they get moisture from their food. They do drink regularly, usually as it starts getting hot.

Nyala

Tragelaphus angasii

Nyala are striking antelope living in thickets in dry savanna woodlands and eating leaves, small quantities of grass and bark or following primates to pick up dropped fruit and flowers. They drink at times when their food is particularly dry.

Height:	1 m
Weight:	60–110 kg
Gestation:	7.5 months
Offspring:	1
Lifespan:	15 years
Diet:	Browser

Ewes are red-brown and striped along the spine with many white lines, while bulls are significantly larger, grey with white stripes on the back, spots on the flanks, and spiralled horns. The lower leg in bulls is yellow and a shaggy, white fringe runs down the animal's back, under the neck and along the belly. Young animals resemble females. The nyala's tail is white when raised as a 'follow me' sign to others as they flee from any medium or large carnivore. They also have small hooves that register as they walk to reduce noise.

They bark deeply in alarm and also react to impala, kudu or baboon alarm calls. These traits suit them for their lives in dense habitats, also ideal for hiding newborn animals for 2–3 weeks. If threatened, the odourless calf instinctively flattens itself onto the ground to avoid detection.

Nyala live in temporary associations joining or splitting up freely although there are persisting bonds between ewes and calves. Sometimes big aggregations up to 100 individuals may form at a waterhole or good foraging site.

Mature bulls are solitary, interacting with females when encountered and tolerating other bulls. Local dominance hierarchies are established between males through passive displays. They do not defend territories but demonstrate dominance by scraping soil with their horns and rubbing their heads on bushes or thrashing them while pawing the ground.

A bull remains with a female group if an oestrus ewe is present. Ewes emit a strange clicked vocalisation to advertise their oestrus and bulls perform flehmen. However, ewes will not actually mate with a bull until the final hour, giving dominant bulls in the area ample time to supplant less favourable ones. They do this through lateral presentation during which males parade around one another in a high-stepped gait, mane raised, tail lifted and head lowered. The bulls' coats exaggerate the whole process and the first to be intimidated drops out and stops posturing. Lateral presentation can occur at different intensities but only equal matches will actually engage, pushing heads and clashing horns.

Klipspringer

🔊 *Oreotragus oreotragus*

Height:	50–60 cm
Weight:	10–15 kg
Gestation:	6–7 months
Offspring:	1
Lifespan:	15 years
Diet:	Browser

Klipspringers are small, slightly hunched, golden-coated antelope. The pelage has a rough appearance from multi-coloured hairs. Klipspringers (or 'rock-jumpers' directly translated) live in rocky habitats and are superbly adapted to do so. They camouflage well amongst rocks and are incredibly sure-footed.

Modified cylindrical hooves have blunt tips, rimmed on the inside with a cartilaginous pad for leaping between boulders or up cliffs. They give traction, absorb shock and help the antelope make sudden direction changes. The fur is hollow, flat and springy. This combination insulates the klipspringer from the temperature extremes in rocky areas, helps to conserve moisture and also provides shock-absorption should it fall.

Klipspringers form lasting pairs, seldom ever moving far from one another, because they live in isolated habitats where mates are hard to come by. They defend a territory together, protecting their piece of turf and resources from others but not showing much aggression in encounters.

They stand statue-like in prominent places to repel intruders, make dung piles, horn bushes and deposit tarry preorbital gland secretions on the ends of twigs. They may descend from their rocks to exploit resources and several family groups may do so simultaneously but they retreat to their own turf if threatened.

Leopard, hyena, caracal, baboons, Verreaux's and martial eagles, and jackal all pose a threat to klipspringers that have the advantage of seeing danger approach. They freeze to blend with the rocks or whistle-snort an alarm, sometimes in duet. They easily outrun most predators in their own habitat.

Klipspringers browse in nibbles skilfully plucking fruit or flowers or standing on their hind legs to access desirable items. They chew soil and bones to supplement deficient minerals and drink water from rock pools if it is available.

Sable

Hippotragus niger

An impressive and attractive large antelope with long, ridged arcing horns. They have thick necks with a small dewlap in front, a dark haired mane and striking black and white facial markings. Females are chestnut in colour while males blacken with maturity. They inhabit areas with abutting woodland and grassland as they rely on grasses during wet seasons but make use of forbs and some browse to supplement their diets during drier times. They have a partiality for the spring flush in miombo woodland. They are water dependent and drink daily if not more often.

Height:	1.2–1.4 m
Weight:	220–235 kg
Gestation:	8 months
Offspring:	1
Lifespan:	17 years
Diet:	Grazer

Typically sable remain in a particular area for a protracted time and then suddenly depart, moving long distances between suitable foraging areas. Herds comprise about 20 cows and young but these are often segregates of larger herds that join up during drier times close to water and the best possible food sources. Females remain in the herds in which they were born and inherit the home ranges of their predecessors. Herds are governed by a rank hierarchy maintained through a series of posturing and dominance activities between cows, like aiming the horns at another or prodding the rump with them. The most senior cow plays the role of leader and lookout.

Bulls are loners and engage in intensive territorial activities, patrolling, sniffing, leaving dung beacons at regular intervals and pawing the ground, horning bushes and breaking branches. They practise combat techniques as young bulls, learning to master the use of their horns while they are not yet full length. Combat usually takes place with animals on their knees. A territorial bull will herd females when they enter his turf and try to prevent them from leaving, especially during the mating season. A two-month birth peak occurs towards the end of the rainy season and calves lie-up in long grass or other concealment for about 3 weeks before joining the herd.

Blue duiker

Cephalophus monticola

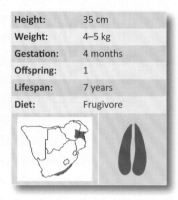

Height:	35 cm
Weight:	4–5 kg
Gestation:	4 months
Offspring:	1
Lifespan:	7 years
Diet:	Frugivore

The blue duiker is a tiny, forest-dwelling antelope with a blue-grey coat, dark face and the smallest of horns at just 5 cm. Like other duiker, it holds its head low and has large hindquarters. In southern Africa, blue duiker can be found in forests along the coastal plains and take to areas where the undergrowth is not too dense. They tend to lie out in more open sections and only dart to really thick cover to hide. Like other duiker, blue duikers freeze when threatened, or dive and freeze. Blue duikers are chiefly preyed on by crowned eagles.

They are primarily frugivorous but consume a few leaves, flowers, fungi and ants. They have relatively large mouths with a wide gape and low-crowned cheek teeth so they can manipulate and crush large, hard fruits. They may dig with their feet while foraging, stand up on their hind legs and drink rain off leaves for moisture.

Because they are small and diurnal, blue duikers are vulnerable to predation and as such they live in pairs or small family groups with up to two of their successive offspring. Pairs are very strongly bonded, probably staying together for life, and seldom move far from one another, engaging in regular playing, social licking and grooming, and scent-marking together. They defend a 2–4 ha territory with males chasing male intruders away, and females chasing female intruders.

They spend much time scent-marking their territory and each other (and offspring) with colourless, odourless secretions from the prominent curved preorbital glands on the face, often pressing their faces together to combine scent.

The male does the marking of trees with preorbital secretions, and this he does at a rate of about 6 times per hour, but both sexes have hoof glands and leave urine and dung as scent markers.

Tree-horning is another form of territorial marking and blue duikers leave obvious scratches on saplings from this exercise, especially near boundaries, usually scraping their feet at the conclusion thereof. They advertise and alarm signal with snorts, whistles and stamping. The tail has a white underside and is flicked up and down as a visual 'follow me' sign to keep in contact with family members. Sexual activity is intense but there is little fighting amongst all but captive duikers.

When the lambs arrive, they are hidden in thick vegetation and during this time, presumably not to draw attention to the mother and her suckling baby, the male goes away for a month. Other males may enter his territory then but remove themselves once he returns.

SS

Common duiker

Sylvicapra grimmia

The common duiker, also known as grey or Grimm's duiker, is slate grey sometimes with red or yellowish hues. A dark tuft of hair sits on the head, between the horns in the case of the male, and a dark stripe runs from forehead to nose.

Height:	50 cm
Weight:	15–21 kg
Gestation:	7 months
Offspring:	1
Lifespan:	11 years
Diet:	Browser

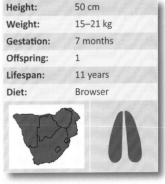

The obvious preorbital glands secrete a tarry substance probably for scent-marking. They are solitary except courting pairs and lambs are very precocial, growing quickly and attaining adult size by 6 or 7 months old. They like bushy cover and dive for it directly when disturbed. 'Duiker' comes from the Afrikaans word meaning 'to dive'. Their predators include an array of medium to large predators, especially leopard, as well as birds of prey. They have good ears to hear trouble coming. Common duiker are browsers, typically eating leaves, twigs, fruit, flowers, seeds and forbs, digging for tubers or nibbling bark but they have also been recorded eating nestling ground birds, reptiles, mopane worms and mice, unusual ingredients for an antelope's diet and probably consumed to supplement protein.

Bushbuck

Tragelaphus scriptus

Height:	70–80 cm
Weight:	30–45 kg
Gestation:	6 months
Offspring:	1
Lifespan:	12 years
Diet:	Browser

SS

A loud, deep, resonating alarm bark is ventriloquistic and a bushbuck in danger will freeze to blend with its surrounds. They are prone to secrecy but also common in some areas and can become noticeable where densities are high because food and water are abundant. They feed at night or early on in the day often amassing in open areas with rich food sources. More usually, they are solitary or in small same-sex groups. Bushbuck rams use lateral display in the same manner as nyala or kudu, and do not have territories. The lambs lie-up for an extended period of 4 months.

Bushbuck are browsers that live in riverine forests and thickets near to permanent water and they are strong swimmers. Medium to large carnivores prey on them, especially leopard. They are the smallest of the spiral-horned antelope but can defend themselves effectively and aggressively with their stout, sharp horns.

Steenbok

🔊 *Raphicerus compestris*

Height:	50 cm
Weight:	11 kg
Gestation:	7 months
Offspring:	1
Lifespan:	10 years
Diet:	Mixed feeder

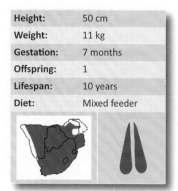

The steenbok is a small, stone-red antelope with white underparts. 'Steen' means brick in Afrikaans. The ram has two pencil-like horns. Steenbok live in open habitats with scattered cover and eat mostly forbs but also consume grass, seeds, flowers and fruit. Bulbs and rhizomes may be dug up, as they are capable diggers. They also find scraps amongst porcupine excavations.

They do not need to drink regularly, getting moisture from their foodstuffs and conserving moisture and energy by lying in the shade when it is hot.

Steenbok live alone but males and females use abutting or overlapping territories, which they scent-mark with preorbital, pedal and throat glands. They make use of latrines and even though these are covered, they are still believed to demarcate territory. Pairs are found during courtship or an adult with offspring, which are usually similar sized as they grow quickly. Martial eagles and medium to large mammalian carnivores catch steenbok so they spend much time lying in long grass out of sight or even in old aardvark holes.

Their white underparts offer a form of predator deception, the white rump being obvious as steenbok bound away but not so, once they stop. Flash colouration encourages pursuers to focus on the obvious target, which they lose once the antelope stops.

Reedbuck

)) *Redunca arundinum*

A small and shy nocturnal antelope that lives in pairs
or family units in territories defended by the male.
They utilise dense habitats and feed predominantly
on grass, switching to browse if necessary in the
dry season when they may also be seen feeding in
daylight. They drink water regularly and bed down
during bouts of resting on trampled grass.

Height:	90 cm
Weight:	80 kg
Gestation:	7–8 months
Offspring:	1
Lifespan:	9 years
Diet:	Grazer

A characteristic rocking-horse gait or posturing with neck up to reveal the white colour, and legs held rigid advertises the male's status as dominant and he horns bushes and defecates or urinates to reinforce his territorial ownership. Stiff-legged stotting is used by reedbuck to advertise their presence too.

Reedbuck communicate with whistles. They do not run especially quickly and in flight, flick their tails to reveal white patches on the thighs and pronk while snorting with each bound. Hind legs are kicked up and the opening of the inguinal glands results in a popping sound. They take to cover to escape predators such as leopard.

81

T**HE ANTELOPE** described in this section all prefer more arid and open areas such as desert and grassland.

Oryx (Gemsbok)

Oryx gazella

Height:	1.2 m
Weight:	200–240 kg
Gestation:	9 months
Offspring:	1
Lifespan:	19 years
Diet:	Grazer

A large, handsome grey, white and black antelope with long, sword-like horns and a long black tail that inhabits arid habitats in the western half of southern Africa. It thrives in a diversity of dry places and is a water-independent species. Gemsbok graze and can digest large quantities of fibre and roughage. The mouth, teeth and jaw are adapted to close-cropping coarse desert grasses of which they will select the most nutritious species and parts. They also take browse, melons and flowers and dig for tubers, roots, rhizomes and bulbs. Gemsbok wander huge distances to find food, often congregating in hundreds where thunderstorms have yielded green growth.

Gemsbok are nomadic, moving in small herds to utilise scattered resources. Large bulls characterised by thick necks and fully developed scrotums are usually solitary and territorial but tolerant of subordinate males that travel with the female groups. Territories are huge and advertised with low-crouch posturing, dung piles at strategic points, horn thrashing of bushes and pedal gland ground-scraping. Bulls may abandon territories during very dry times or to follow females. Within the herd, there is a stable rank hierarchy headed by the alpha bull when in attendance and a high-ranking cow leads the herd. The hierarchy is maintained with head and horn movements, tail-swishing and ear-flicking. Calves are a pale rufous colour to blend with their dry habitat while they lie up for a month or two. A calf may lie right in the open but remains remarkably motionless even when approached or covered by flies. Calves may also form crèches.

The gemsbok's deadly horns are its defensive weapons against lions or hyena, and they have been known to reverse into thorn bushes to protect the rear end while dealing with a predator. Lions ambush gemsbok and hyena run them to exhaustion. Their flight is swift and they have great stamina. Horns are used as part of aggressive displays and for competition within the species

too. Males' horns are thicker and slightly shorter for this reason. Typically gemsbok in a herd will keep a social distance between them greater than the length of their horns and lie facing in opposite directions to avoid accidents. Horns are present from birth as hair-covered bumps but grow rapidly during concealment.

This is an extremely desert-adapted species with a low metabolism and water requirements, and behaviour that accommodates energy and water conservation. This includes lying in the shade when it is hot or orientating the body to expose as little surface area as possible. They dig for water in dry riverbeds and use cooler times of the day and night for activities, as grazing then renders vegetation highest in moisture. Gemsbok only pant if their body temperature exceeds 41 °C and breathing is moderated to reduce moisture loss from the respiratory tract. Urine is concentrated. They allow their body temperature to rise a few degrees above normal (35.7 to 40 °C) and then dissipate the heat by standing on a dune at night to collect a breeze. There is an intricate network of superficial blood vessels in the moist nasal area where blood is cooled by evaporation. Arterial blood en route to the brain is cooled to protect the brain from fatally high temperatures. To increase airflow over these capillaries, animals may pant.

Springbok

🔊 *Antidorcas marsupialis*

Height:	75 cm
Weight:	35–50 kg
Gestation:	6 months
Offspring:	1
Lifespan:	10 years
Diet:	Mixed feeder

An attractive, medium-sized gazelle, the only one in southern Africa, with contrasting light and dark body colouration and hindquarters higher than shoulders. Both sexes have ridged horns that are lyre-shaped and tails flick incessantly. Springbok are generally smaller in the southern parts of their range and both black and white forms occur. Springbok inhabit short grass savannas, often in dry, harsh environments. They opportunistically select the best vegetation they can find, preferring new grass after the rain and congregating in such areas after showers, but changing to leaves, buds and acacia flowers as required and often driven to migrate to more productive areas as the dry season progresses. They drink when they can or alternatively get moisture from roots and tubers, producing extremely concentrated urine and dry faecal pellets to conserve moisture. Springbok are sensitive to cold.

They are gregarious, forming mixed-sex herds except for solitary, territorial males. Bachelors may live apart from 6 months old, only qualifying for territories after 2 years of age. Rams defend areas with resources likely to attract ewes and mark these with dung middens, posturing during urination and horn-sweeping of bushes. Females are herded with the head stretched forward and tail held out stiffly as they pass through. Territory owners are regularly challenged and much horn-stabbing and wrestling ensues. Territorial animals are vulnerable to predators and cannot forage optimally. The rut may occur at any time of the year, at which time rams grunt, chase intruders and round up the ewes to induce simultaneous oestrus. Consequently, lambs are born close together, a predator avoidance technique. Lambs are hidden for a few days but are mobile enough to run with the herd within 3 weeks. Females with young form nursery groups. Springbok may breed twice a year if resources permit.

A pouch along the spine houses a crest of long, white, erectable hair. At rest the browner fur conceals this but with the contraction of special muscles the hair bunches up and stands erect. The crest can be raised to effectively conduct heat, springbok aligning their bodies so incident solar rays fall on the reflective white surface. It is also raised during pronking to enlarge the animal's profile. Pronking is a demonstration of vigour whereby animals jump up repeatedly, legs held stiff, back arched and head down as if on a trampoline. Individual bounds may be 3 metres high. It is used in several contexts, one of which being around predators to dissuade pursuit, and less fit individuals are consequently targeted. Cheetahs are the springbok's chief predator but lions and leopards also hunt them, and jackal take the young. The alarm is a loud nasal whistle and results in explosive leaps in all directions, the initial sprint fading into a trot.

Blesbok

Damaliscus dorcas phillipsi

Blesbok and bontebok, (Damaliscus dorcas dorcas), are subspecies. Bontebok are believed to be the result of a group of blesbok that were isolated historically by a climate change event and had to adapt to living in the unique vegetation of the Western Cape. Blesbok live in open grassy areas and do not frequent wooded habitats. They are pure, selective grazers. The two closely-related antelope look different as a result of their separation.

Height:	90 cm
Weight:	55–85 kg
Gestation:	8 months
Offspring:	1
Lifespan:	11 years
Diet:	Grazer

Blesbok

Bontebok

Blesbok have lighter brown coats with less white (in bontebok, the white goes right over the rump). Bontebok have dark almost black horns and no band separating the white blaze on their faces. Blesbok and bontebok hybridise to form *bontebles*, fertile but genetically compromised offspring.

The striking colours emphasise the various postures used by blesbok to communicate social messages of dominance. Rams hold territories and herd small female groups when they come into range. Rams hold their heads low and ears out, curling the tail up while they chase up females. They use preorbital gland secretions to scent-mark territory, transferring odour rubbed onto grass stalks onto

the horns which are also imbedded with earth and plant material from horning. They also use dung middens. Outside of the breeding season, territorial males are tolerant of bachelors but fight violently when mating is at stake. Females give birth in the herd and precocial young can run within 20 minutes.

Herds rest during the heat of the day standing head down during these times. Stamping, snorting, head shaking or short, circular gallops may break the peace intermittently. Blesbok live in mostly isolated, fenced-in populations and are subject to predation by leopard or jackal which may take the young.

85

Black wildebeest (White-tailed gnu)

Connochaetes gnou

Height:	105–120 cm
Weight:	110–160 kg
Gestation:	8 months
Offspring:	1
Lifespan:	20 years
Diet:	Mixed feeder

A rare, endangered and endemic animal, the black wildebeest is relatively small with forward-facing, upward turned horns and a white, flowing tail. The body is dark to black and fringed with a mane and beard. The thick, dark coat provides insulation against the extreme temperatures experienced in its open, predominantly grassland habitats. Biology is, however, similar to its savanna cousin, the blue wildebeest (see page 54).

Because black wildebeest numbers are relatively low in South Africa, the genetic integrity of populations is at risk from hybridisation with blue wildebeest. Although separate species, they break the rule by producing fertile offspring.

Originally it was understood that hybridisation only occurred when animals were forced together but it has subsequently been discovered that wildebeest hybridise readily. The similar behaviour and synchronised breeding seasons of the two species is responsible for this and typically the larger blue wildebeest bulls displace the smaller black males and crossbreed with black wildebeest females.

Hybrid offspring look different from one case to the next with the horn shape being the most obvious feature. It is surmised that blue and black wildebeest shared a kind of co-evolution, with differences resulting when a historical environmental opportunity presented in the form of the abundant, permanently open-structured habitat of the Highveld grasslands.

Ancestral black wildebeest made a behavioural shift to greater territoriality that relied on visually unobstructed habitats and that then drove the evolution of the animal to develop different physical characteristics to the common wildebeest ancestor which continued living in more closed habitats.

Red hartebeest

Alcelaphus buselaphus

A high-shouldered, tawny coloured, glossy antelope with contorted horns. It lives on open plains often near the edges of more wooded country. Herds comprise territorial bulls that herd and protect a group of ranked females, subordinate males and youngsters. These may be sedentary units, or herds may move between different bulls' territories.

Height:	115 cm
Weight:	120–140 kg
Gestation:	8 months
Offspring:	1
Lifespan:	13 years
Diet:	Mixed feeder

Bulls advertise their status visually by standing prominently on raised areas such as termite mounds, useful vantages for watching for predators too. The alarm is raised by stomping or snorting, which sends the herd into single file flight, calves running beside their mothers or dropping and freezing.

Territories are won through impressive fights, combatants wrestling with their rigid horns and attempting to throw each other off balance. The clashing of the horns can be heard from some distance away. Dung middens demarcate turf. Outside of the rut, aggression is much reduced and bulls even abandon their territories to seek out desirable forage.

Hartebeest eat both grass and browse. In areas where rain or fire stimulates fresh green growth, herds may aggregate in their thousands. Red hartebeest drink water where its available but in drier parts of its range will dig up tubers or consume melons for moisture.

Calves are born and hidden in seclusion and the mothers consume their dung and urine to keep them scent-free until they join the herd at about 2 weeks old. Hartebeest are very alert animals and even approach predators like lions when spotted. They may stot – an exaggerated, bouncy run – to demonstrate their fitness and alert predators that they have been spotted.

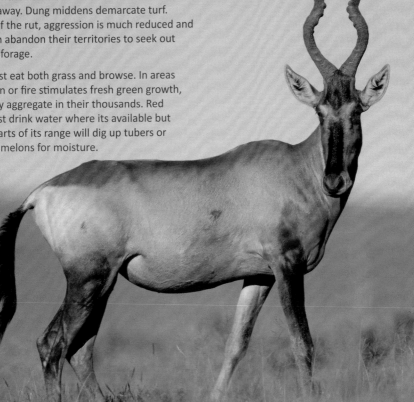

SS

Cheetah

Acinonyx jubatus

Height:	80 cm
Weight:	40–60 kg
Gestation:	3 months
Offspring:	1 to 6
Lifespan:	16 years
Diet:	Carnivore

Cheetahs are super-specialised for speed clocking speeds of between 75 and 110 km/h. The fastest land mammal can, however, only maintain a sprint for a few hundred metres before it is spent. Cheetahs live in open areas or wooded savanna with little undergrowth to enable them to hunt. They usually catch small to medium-sized antelope but also eat ground birds and smaller mammals such as hares. Two diagnostic black 'tear marks' line the sides of a cheetah's nose, running from the corner of the eyes to the corners of the mouth. They have a golden coat dotted with solid black spots, a slender body with a small head and a long tail.

Leopard vs cheetah

These two cats are often confused but are in fact quite different. The leopard has a powerful build with a large head and neck, and its body is covered in rosettes. Cheetahs are slight of build with small heads and their spots are solid. Cheetahs also have dark tear marks which leopards lack. As far as lifestyles go, the leopard is a solitary, ambush predator that hoists its prey into trees. Cheetahs may form coalitions of males, chasing their prey in fast sprints and then feeding in situ on the ground once they have caught their breath. They frequently lose kills to larger predators. Leopards are habitat generalists while cheetahs have more specific habitat requirements.

Even though they run extremely fast, cheetah need to get as close as possible to their prey before launching an attack. They making use of available cover to stalk, freezing if the quarry raises its head. They usually select an animal on the outskirts of its herd, and once in pursuit, must gain on the target quickly or will abandon the chase. Prey is tripped with a paw and then suffocated around the throat. Cheetahs catch their breath before feeding, dragging kills into the shade where possible.

The cheetah's anatomy is designed for speed. Long legs, flexible spine and thin waist facilitate long strides and semi-retractable, unsheathed claws give traction during chases. The long tail acts as a rudder, counter-balancing the animal on direction changes and the small, streamlined head has small ears to reduce drag. A deep-set chest houses large lungs and heart. Teeth are small, reducing skull weight and making room for enlarged nasal cavities for oxygen intake. Nostrils are aerodynamic

to maximise airflow during sprints. Pads under the feet are hard and ridged for both traction and braking ability.

Too exhausted after sprinting, cheetahs cannot feed immediately like other predators. Being a lightweight, it is mostly defenceless against larger carnivores like lion, leopard, hyena and even vultures, and regularly loses kills to them. To avoid unwanted attention, cheetahs hunt during the day when other predators are usually resting but even this is not always an adequate deterrent for these opportunists.

Cheetah risk injury by hunting prey that is too large. A great deal of strength is needed to pull down large ungulates such as wildebeest or zebra. While their bodies are large, they lack the power of a leopard or lioness behind their attack. Males tend to overcome this limitation by teaming up in coalitions to pull down larger prey. Generally, however, cheetahs target immature members of large herbivore species. They are finicky feeders, slicing meat from the surface of a kill and discarding the innards, barring the heart and liver. Bones and skin are typically too tough for them to attempt. Generally, they do not scavenge.

Cheetahs are not as social as lions but do prefer to live in small family units, usually made up of a mother and her growing cubs. Males, often brothers, form coalitions of about three for hunting and to compete with other males. Ritualised threat displays are typically employed to chase off intruders but when an oestrus female is at stake, males will use front paw slaps. Females have larger territories than males but these overlap with the males' turf. They do not, however, join up unless it is to mate. Territories are scent-marked with urine and scat.

Cheetahs do not climb well but do use elevated places such as sloped tree trunks or termite mounds to gain vantage while resting or to find prey. They are most active while it is cool in early morning and late afternoon and take to shade during the heat of the day. If it is cold, cheetahs may delay their activities temporarily in favour of warming up in the sun.

Cheetahs make various high-pitched, bird-like sounds unusual for a large cat. They do this to communicate with cubs or in greeting. Contented cheetah purr loudly but when distressed may growl, snarl, hiss, bleat, cough or moan.

Adult cheetahs use the crest of hair down their backs when in confrontation or if threatened, pilo-erecting the longer hair to accentuate their size and appear more formidable. Up until three months old, cubs have a mantle of grey fur along the saddle of their backs resembling the formidable honey badger and believed to deter larger predators from attacking them.

Cubs are born in discreet hiding places and frequently moved. A mother carries her litter one at a time by the scruff of the neck. She brings them meat at just five weeks old and cubs wean in three months. They begin hunting at eight months and

become independent at 18 months, becoming nomadic until they are old enough to vie for territories. They may wander great distances during this time and are vulnerable to large predators as well as competition with others of their own kind for food.

Wild dog

Lycaon pictus

Height:	75 cm
Weight:	20–30 kg
Gestation:	2.5 months
Offspring:	7 to 21
Lifespan:	6–12 years
Diet:	Carnivore

Also known as painted wolves, every wild dog is dressed in a unique dappled coat. The huge satellite dish-like ears are quintessential and often all that can be seen twitching over the top of the grass while dogs rest in the shade. This is the second most endangered carnivore in Africa, having historically suffered terrible population blows at the hands of farmers or game wardens that considered them vermin.Now habitat unavailability and diseases like rabies and canine distemper challenge the survival of the species. Lions are also a nuisance to wild dogs, killing both adults and pups and stealing their kills.

Wild dogs live in super-organised, cooperative societies and together a pack of dogs, relatively small in size, are more efficient at catching prey or raising large litters of pups. Wild dogs are by no means diminutive predators and stand up to other large predators, outnumbering them. A pack of wild dogs will tree a leopard or drive off a lone hyena, ganging up to bite at its vulnerable flanks. Wild dogs live in savanna woodlands or broken hilly country with open plains and hunt small to medium-sized antelope, especially impala but also kudu, duiker and steenbok and occasionally wildebeest, zebra and even smaller buffalo.

Wild dogs live in packs of between a few individuals up to 30 dogs in which the alpha pair are the only breeding members. All the other dogs assist with hunting and helping the alpha pair raise the litter of numerous pups. Litters are incorporated into the pack until it becomes too large and same-sex groups break away to join up with an opposite-sexed breakaway group. All individuals have a shared genetic interest in raising the litter. A beta male and female are next in rank to the alpha pair and should anything happen to the alpha animals, they will take over.

Wild dogs are nomadic with home ranges exceeding 450 km^2. They move to follow game or to avoid predators. However, between May and July, the pack becomes sedentary in order to breed. At the end of the dry season, many prey animals are in poor condition and easy prey to feed a growing family. The pack dens in a disused aardvark burrow because puppies are blind and helpless at birth. If the den becomes compromised in any way, the female moves her pups to a new site, picking them up by any convenient body part. By two and a half months old, the pups are ready to leave the den and straggle behind the adults during hunts. They track the adults by scent or are retrieved by the adults after the kill.

Members of the pack perform different functions, guarding the den and pups, or hunting to provide for the family. All the adults groom the pups and keep them from wandering off. Meat is taken back to the den in the dogs' stomachs and regurgitated as chunks for the puppies and baby-sitter. Much excitement is associated with feeding time, the adults yipping to alert the pups of their return and the pups begging, which induces the adults to regurgitate. Hungry adults also beg food from the hunters with much whining, licking and nudging of the provider's face.

Wild dogs hunt by coursing, chasing prey to exhaustion and then disembowelling it. They can run at 50–60 km/h for several kilometres. The kill is very quick and the pack can consume an adult impala carcass in just 15 minutes. Eating rapidly helps them to avoid attention from other predators like lion, leopard and hyena that will steal kills.

Adaptations that suit wild dogs to their habitats include large, round ears for acute hearing, well-developed nasal passages to facilitate breathing during long chases, heavy skulls with powerful muscles actuating the massive lower jaw bone and strong bite and modified dentition. Upper incisors wear into sharp canine-like teeth to grip and the carnassial shear is reinforced with a sectorial (lower first molar) to increase its cutting ability.

There are no territorial boundaries to speak of but wild dogs defend their den and the alpha pair use anal-dragging to mark the home range. The rest of the pack mark with urine and body-rubbing. Excited bird-like twittering announces the beginning of a hunt or the success of a kill while members remain in contact or reunite with a melodic 'hoo' call. The alarm is raised with a growl-bark.

As a following mechanism, wild dogs have white-tipped tails – especially useful to these smaller carnivores in tall grass. The tail also communicates a dog's mood with a relaxed dog hanging it down; stiffened it indicates aggression and curled between the legs it shows submission.

Wild dogs have a ritualised greeting ceremony and the begging demonstrated by puppies is integrated into adult communication and appeasement, which helps to suppress aggression within a pack. During the ritual, dogs lick one another's faces, nuzzle the corners of the mouth and whine. All dogs show submission to the alpha pair. The infantile behaviour probably originates from the fact that puppies are the most privileged members in a wild dog pack.

Spotted hyena

🔊 *Crocuta crocuta*

Height:	85 cm
Weight:	60–80 kg
Gestation:	4 months
Offspring:	2
Lifespan:	20 years
Diet:	Carnivore

The spotted hyena is one of the most successful carnivores in southern Africa, proficient at both hunting and scavenging. It is large with immense forequarters for carrying heavy loads, has incredible stamina, powerful crushing jaws and exhibits great resourcefulness. These are the only mammals able to digest bone, benefiting from the calcium and protein extracted. Hyenas are extremely mobile, covering up to 70 km in a night. They usually hunt the young of large antelope like wildebeest but will opportunistically take almost any mammal, bird, fish, reptile, vegetable matter, carrion or garbage they can find.

The spotted hyena's name derives from the dark spots on its pelage, more pronounced in younger animals. Young hyenas are usually darker too. Hyenas are social animals and ritualised greeting ceremonies reinforce cohesion amongst clan members so they can attack prey or lions, their main enemies, or defend territory as a team. The hyena is more closely related to cats than dogs and belongs to its own family amongst the carnivores, Hyaenidae. There are four species in the family: the spotted hyena, the brown hyena and aardwolf (which are found in Africa; see page 104 and 116) and the striped hyena (found in Asia).

Hyenas produce 14 calls, including whoops, grunts, groans, lowing, giggles, snarls, yells and whines. The 'whoop' travels far and is often heard at night. It advertises territory or rallies clan members.

Individuals recognise one another's calls. The notorious giggled vocalisation is made while feeding together on a kill as a sign of deference or during hysterical encounters with lions.

Spotted hyenas are precisely designed for their hardcore lifestyles. The large head and massive skull provide broad attachment for muscles that actuate the incredible jaw, also powered by the muscular neck. Heavy canines provide lethal grip, molars crush dense bones and the sharp carnassial shear slices through cartilage and tough skin. Enlarged forequarters and bigger front feet give the hyena its slanty posture but also enable it to use an energy-efficient gait for coursing. Hyenas have exceptional senses and follow three-day-old scent trails easily. An erectile crest over the neck and shoulders may be employed to intimidate rivals or predators.

The genitals of both male and female look similar and they are difficult to sex. Females are larger and their pseudo-penises lack the triangular glans (tip) of the males'. The unusual female genital develops due to exposure to high androgen levels in the womb and females have high testosterone levels. The genitals are central to the hyena greeting ceremony, a form of social bonding. Two hyenas from the same clan stand head to tail and lift their legs to expose the erect genitals to the other's nose (and jaw) to display trust.

Clans are the social groupings in which hyena live, dominated by females. Within the clan, females are ranked amongst themselves, and cubs inherit their mother's status. Coalitions of females and their young work together to hunt or may break off to form new clans. A clan communally defends a territory of about 130 km^2. Young males emigrate at about two years old and gain slightly better status elsewhere. Males work hard to earn social favour and mate with females. Members of a clan may separate and reunite randomly.

Hyenas chase prey to exhaustion, alone or cooperatively, choosing quarry by walking right into a herd of animals. They quickly establish the weakest members and play an important ecological role in eliminating these. Hyenas are very successful hunters thanks to their extraordinary endurance and have been known to chase prey at 60 km/h for over 2 km or follow herds almost 30 km before making a move.

As scavengers disposing of carcasses, hyenas help to control diseases like anthrax. Hyenas will deprive lions of their kills if they have the advantage of four hyenas to one lioness but in spite of this advantage, hyenas tend to hunt more when lion numbers are

ME

low. Where lions are numerous, hyenas scavenge more regularly. They regurgitate indigestible hair and hooves as pellets.

Hyena scat is white when dry due to the high calcium in their diet. Leopard tortoises may even consume hyena scat to supplement their calcium requirements. Scat plays a role in both the visual and olfactory marking of hyenas' territories. They make and regularly visit latrines. They also scent-mark with anal glands that are inverted and wiped onto a blade of grass. The secretion is pungent and the action is known as pasting. Cubs practise pasting from four weeks old.

Hyenas den communally, usually in the disused burrow of an aardvark. Cubs dig small tunnels inside the den to crawl into if threatened. Adults tend to remain outside near the den entrances on hand to suckle their cubs, which they do not do mutually. Hyenas produce very rich milk which cubs feed on exclusively until weaned at 14–18 months old. In this way, the cubs are kept safe at the den and unwanted attention from other predators is kept to a minimum and no food is taken back to the den.

Hyenas typically give birth to twins and the cubs are born with eyes open and canines fully erupted. Dominance is so well developed from birth that two female cubs will immediately compete for dominance, especially the litter of a high-ranking female. Often one sibling kills the other. Since females naturally dominate males, different-sexed siblings do not generally fight. Hyena cubs are inquisitive and playful, chasing one another, climbing over the adults or picking up sticks or other objects. These activities contribute to developing lifestyle skills.

The birth canal runs through the hyena's pseudo-penis and consequently is twice as long as other mammals'. The opening is much narrower than the cub's head and while still pushing through the birth canal, cubs lose their source of oxygen as the umbilical cord disconnects from the placenta. Many first-time mothers have stillborn cubs from oxygen deprivation but are more successful second time around once the uro-genital opening has been split.

Black-backed jackal

Canis mesomelas

Height:	40 cm
Weight:	7–10 kg
Gestation:	2 months
Offspring:	1 to 6
Lifespan:	10 years
Diet:	Carnivore

Black-backed jackals are highly adaptable, resourceful animals that live in a broad spectrum of habitats, preferring to rest and forage in the open where they have a good field of vision. They are able to thrive in even harsh environments and have a reputation for being wily and for sharing learning amongst their population, especially predator avoidance. Black-backed jackals have a saddle of long, dark hair on their backs, a black-tipped tail and large, pointy ears. Excellent hearing facilitates their lifestyles, helping them detect small prey such as rodents or insects, or become aware of large kills some distance away. The other southern African jackal is the side-striped jackal which lacks the dark saddle, has a stripe on its side and a white-tipped tail. This jackal is more common in woodland areas and shares a similar biology to the black-backed jackal.

Jackals are omnivorous, monopolising whatever is seasonally available. Insects and rodents form their mainstay but they also hunt larger prey and scavenge. They also eat much fruit. Jackals hunt small prey by leaping up, back arched, then trapping their quarry with front paws and snapping the spine with a bite to the back. Larger prey is run down. Jackals are essential in controlling rodent numbers and removing weak animals from the ecosystem. They also clean up carcasses left behind by larger carnivores.

A jackal's teeth cater to its catholic diet with long, curved, sharp canines and canine-like outer incisors effecting a deadly grip on prey. The scissor-like carnassial shear cuts meat and shears bits off bones while broad molars are used for crushing insects or chewing fruit.

Jackals den in late winter with pups arriving in August to October. They only use the den until the pups are weaned at about 3 months of age and can join the adults to forage. Jackals modify aardvark burrows for their dens, ensuring the main underground space is 1–2 metres wide and that several escape options are present. They also change burrows frequently to avoid predators and parasite infestations.

Black-backed jackals live in extended family groups comprising the monogamous pair and their pups, including the previous litter that assist with raising the new pups. The older pups help to guard the den, find and regurgitate food for the youngsters and mother, and play with or groom the young pups. In the process, they gain valuable life experience for raising their own offspring and finding territories of their own is delayed until they are a little older and shrewder.

Black-backed jackals are territorial and share the duties between the pair. Mates see off same-sexed intruders. They deposit scat as territorial markers upon elevated objects like rocks or vegetation, or even on top of larger predators' droppings.

They advertise vocally with a wailing call, particularly late in the evening or when the breeding season begins. Neighbouring pairs answer one another. The mated pair's bond is so established that if one animal dies, the other inevitably loses its territory. Jackals tolerate visits from neighbours when there is a large kill.

ME

Jackals patrol and forage using an energy-efficient bouncy trot. They move more cautiously when stalking rodents or insects, stopping to listen while they do. They rest while it is hot, lying in thick vegetation or in holes. When it is cold, they may sleep on impala middens or flattened elephant dung for insulation.

Competition between predators sees them mutually killing one another's offspring. This helps to keep populations in check but seems to be particularly true of jackal and caracal (see page 113). It seems in areas with high jackal densities, lower populations of caracal exist and vice versa. Predators that have similar diets may also outcompete others in an area by reducing the prey base. Many large predators, including lion, hyena and leopard, kill adult jackals and then may or may not eat them. Pythons and large raptors hunt jackal too.

Bat-eared fox

Otocyon megalotis

One of two foxes found in semi-arid habitats (the other being the Cape fox) this little carnivore is adorned with a bushy black tail at the end of its curved spine and enormous, dish-like ears. The ears are used to locate harvester termites and beetle larvae, the fox's primary dietary ingredients. The ears are moveable and adjusted towards the slightest subterranean sounds, able to amplify the noises so the fox can pinpoint its quarry precisely. Other menu items include scorpions, locusts, small mammals and wild fruits.

Height:	30 cm
Weight:	4 kg
Gestation:	2 months
Offspring:	4 to 6
Lifespan:	11 years
Diet:	Insectivore /Omnivore

Bat-eared foxes pair for life and live in small family groups. Pairs rest lying close to one another. When they are denning, the male remains with the cubs while the female forages. They sleep in burrows in ground that usually comprise several entrances and vegetative screening. These they take over from other burrowing species. Bat-eared foxes are artful dodgers and can change direction rapidly without losing momentum if being pursued and in this manner evade their predators, including raptors and larger carnivores. The bushy tail is used as a rudder and as a decoy during pursuit. They are non-territorial and playful animals.

Few vocalisations are used for communication: the contact call is a 'who-who' sound while the young utter a shrill chattering sound when alarmed.

Brown hyena

 *Hyaena brunnea*

Height:	80 cm
Weight:	40 kg
Gestation:	3–4 months
Offspring:	1 to 4
Lifespan:	24 years
Diet:	Omnivore

Brown hyenas are brown, shaggy, dog-like animals that are clan-orientated, living together in loose groups but foraging alone. Sloped backs, strong jaws and excellent smell are just a few of the adaptations suiting them to their lifestyle. They are predominantly scavengers and consume a vast variety of foodstuffs, accommodating for scarce availability in their arid habitats. It is no challenge to open an ostrich egg and they even raid seal colonies along the Namibian coast. They will also cache surplus food.

Brown hyenas, like their spotted cousins, paste with anal glands to scent-mark their territories but perform an even more elaborate process. It first applies a white paste and then a black one above it on a grass stalk from inverted anal glands. They paste every 300 metres, which can equate to 600 pastings in a single evening as they traverse wide areas. The smell is pungent and lasts for a month to warn off intruders. Every hyena's scent is unique and carries a resume of information for other hyenas. Chemical communication is essential for these animals as they spend much time apart even from clan mates due to the large size of their territories (up to 300 km²).

Adult males can be nomadic and are preferred by females in distant clans over resident males as mates since they are less likely to be relatives. They are excellent parents, hauling heavy carcasses over long distances to provision cubs at the den. The denning period is the most socially intense part of the brown hyena's life. Females may mutually suckle cubs. Brown hyenas are formidable carnivores and can hold their own against other large carnivores.

They do not communicate vocally over long distances, but group members do utter a variety of yelps, squeals snorts and growls.

Cape clawless otter

Aonyx capensis

The Cape clawless otter is a robust aquatic mammal with dense brown fur complemented with white on the belly, neck and cheeks. Each foot has five clawless digits and its hind feet are partially webbed. The skull is massive with powerful crustacean-crushing teeth and jaws, and well-developed whiskers assist with navigating underwater and detecting prey. Cape clawless otters inhabit a diversity of both fresh and marine water environments.

Length:	1.8 m (tail 40 cm)
Weight:	16 kg
Gestation:	2 months
Offspring:	1 to 3
Lifespan:	15 years
Diet:	Carnivore

Hunting by sight and feel, they catch crabs, rock lobster, fish, frogs, birds, insects, molluscs, reptiles and small mammals. The webless but rough front paws with opposable thumbs are specifically modified to feel for and grip prey on river bottoms and digits are poked under rocks or into holes in order to find prey, which is then pursued in a direct chase if necessary. They feed in the water, manipulating their food with primate-like dexterity, lying on their backs and holding it against their bodies in the process. They may drag large quarry to land and feed with much noise. Cape clawless otters are intelligent and playful yet tenacious if threatened and the flexible body, loose skin and vice-like grip help it to evade enemies, crocodiles and large raptors being among them.

Otters keep to themselves mostly and are graceful and adept swimmers, moving quietly in the water and then disappearing if disturbed. While they may waddle awkwardly on land, they are capable of a rapid, bounding gallop and slide down banks on their bellies. Females transport young in their front legs effectively staggering on their hind ones. The tail acts as powerful rudder in the water, a defensive weapon and the third leg of a tripod on land if the otter wishes to sit up. They are mainly solitary but females and young may associate in small groups and interact energetically. They chase each other, play fight, drop and retrieve pebbles or play cat-and-mouse with their fish-food.

They recline in holes or thick vegetation known as holts and mark sleeping and rolling sites with sweet-smelling spraints deposited in latrines. They seem to be dancing while they defecate, performing ritualised foot lifts as they circle around. A strict hygiene regime is maintained and otters wash their face and feet regularly, dry their coats by rolling and rubbing on grass, earth or rocks, then sunning and grooming. They are especially active in the late afternoon.

SS

Dwarf mongoose

))) *Helogale parvula*

Length:	40 cm (tail 16 cm)
Weight:	300 g
Gestation:	2 months
Offspring:	2 to 4
Lifespan:	6 years
Diet:	Carnivore

Dwarf mongooses are gregarious, social animals living together in cooperative groups of about 12 individuals, sometimes up to 30 and demonstrate a well-developed organisation of roles within their society. They are the smallest mammalian carnivores and are often numerous in their dry, open woodland habitats. They are very agile, athletic and are accomplished hunters.

Excellent sight and smell assist in the location of prey, which comprises mostly insects but also snails, scorpions, centipedes, reptiles, eggs and even some small mammals. They forage during the day by sorting through piles of leaf litter or digging in the ground. Their predators include raptors, small carnivores and snakes and to avoid these, dwarf mongooses have horizontally elongated pupils for an enlarged field of vision, they are adept climbers, have small bodies that fit into small spaces and they are able to change direction rapidly at full tilt. They usually run with a springing gait, lifting up off the ground as they move.

Dwarf mongooses feed spread out and contact call incessantly. Members are very vocal and sounds vary, including peeps, churrs, twitters and rolling chatters depending on the prevailing circumstances. Subtle fluctuations indicate different kinds of threats and possibly even their proximity to it. Such an advanced vocabulary is required because dwarf mongooses suffer predation from multiple sources and different reactions are needed for aerial vs. terrestrial threats and may involve darting for cover or group mobbing attacks.

Dwarf mongooses bed down at night in deserted termite mounds punctured with holes. Throughout their small home range of about 1 km^2, the group will have several refuges and within a day, they forage from one site to the next to ensure they have overnight accommodation. In the interim, they use any available shelter or bolt hole if threatened. It takes about three weeks to cover their entire home range and by the time they reach their starting point, food resources are replenished.

Dwarf mongooses typically forage by digging with their sharp claws, heads immersed into the pit while they dig. They pounce on insects or leap to catch them from the air. Rodents are pinned with the forepaws and bitten on the head but it takes several bites and much shaking to dispatch larger prey. Snakes are bitten and dropped repeatedly, with larger serpents being tackled collectively from opposite ends. A mongoose holds its lips back to avoid insect stings while chewing.

A well-developed hierarchy exists and the alpha pair is most senior, remaining paired for life. The alpha female leads the group and the alpha male defends it. The rest of the community is made up of offspring and immigrants that assist the breeding pair through babysitting and caring for the young, as well as sick or wounded members, grooming, guard duty and defending the troupe.

Females dominate males and rank is then determined by progressive age except that tiny infants outrank adults. Subordinates always submit to superiors by crouching or rolling onto their backs twittering gently. Performing duties like babysitting regularly can enhance status. Immigrants outrank residents once they are able to earn acceptance into the group. If one of the dominant pair dies, the next in rank succeeds them, often decided through a grooming contest that lasts for days and results in opponents becoming saliva-drenched.

As cooperative breeders, an alpha pair dominates the troupe. It is only this pair that breeds. Mating is an epic affair with the alpha male mounting his female in the region of 2 400 times. Young arrive in summer when insects are abundant. The helpless infants are transported by the females between night-time refuges. They join the troupe to forage from about four weeks, an older member escorting each youngster, demonstrating what and how to eat.

Slender mongoose

🔊 *Galerella sanguinea*

Length:	60 cm (tail 28 cm)
Weight:	500 g
Gestation:	2 months
Offspring:	2 to 4
Lifespan:	8 years
Diet:	Carnivore

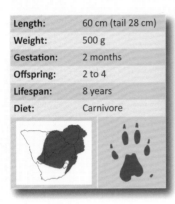

The slender mongoose is weasel-like with a red tipped nose and identified from its black paintbrush-tipped tail. It hunts alone for small vertebrates like rodents, and scavenges fruit and carrion. It is a capable hunter and dispatches even large, venomous snakes effectively. Slender mongooses escape predators with the tail held out straight.

Yellow mongoose

🔊 *Cynictis penicillata*

Length:	50 cm (tail 20 cm)
Weight:	550 g
Gestation:	2 months
Offspring:	1 to 4
Lifespan:	12 years
Diet:	Carnivore

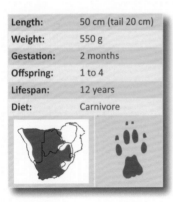

A smallish yellow mongoose identified by its white-tipped tail, it is probably the commonest mongoose in semi-arid areas. They live in small groups of 8–20 with a rank hierarchy but forage alone for insect prey predominantly. Small vertebrates and fruit are taken as necessary, as well as succulent plants for moisture. They sleep in underground warrens although some individuals remain active on warm nights. Yellow mongooses flee with their tails curved up.

Banded mongoose

🔊 *Mungos mungo*

Length:	59 cm (tail 22 cm)
Weight:	1–2 kg
Gestation:	2 months
Offspring:	1 to 4
Lifespan:	8 years
Diet:	Carnivore

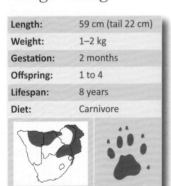

A social species that lives in troupes up to 30 but unlike many communal species, all the females in the

troupe breed and mothers may mutually suckle one another's young. Larger than the dwarf mongoose, it is brown with obvious banding and chatters incessantly while foraging. They excavate in the earth and leaf litter in woodland for insects and sometimes fruit.

Meerkat (Suricate)

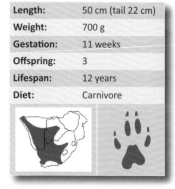

Suricata suricatta

Meerkats are diurnal carnivores that belong to the same family as mongooses. Active, inquisitive and prone to rising up on their hind legs, these animals that live in communal bands of about 6–30, are an entertaining species to observe. They live in a system of underground warrens that they dig themselves or share with ground squirrels. Meerkats forage in open terrain and work cooperatively to spot and warn of danger. They employ a sentinel system to do this.

Length:	50 cm (tail 22 cm)
Weight:	700 g
Gestation:	11 weeks
Offspring:	3
Lifespan:	12 years
Diet:	Carnivore

Meerkats are both predator and prey. They dig for insects, grubs, geckos, scorpions and millipedes, often lowering their heads right into their excavations. Every few seconds, a subadult or immigrant member of the troupe raises its head to look around, sitting up on its hind legs for the best vantage. The alarm is given if danger is detected. The more members in the troupe, the less time is wasted per individual on guard duty. Over and above this more passive warning system, sentries will be posted on a termite mound or tree stump to keep a determined watch on proceedings. The sentinel vocalises continually and if it ceases, the troupe immediately knows there is a problem. They have exceptional eyesight and can discern between different predatory species, for example a raptor or a snake from distances of about 2 km. Meerkats will gang up and mob predators intimidatingly to get them to move off.

Babies are born in summer and the colony works cooperatively for the common good. A dominant female gives birth and then a subordinate female will babysit the youngsters while the others, including the mother, forage for food. The mother does not perform sentry duties during this time as her primary role is to bolster her milk supplies. Subadults that do perform guard duty do so as a kin selection action as most individuals are related. Meerkats are territorial and scent-mark and defecate to identify their turf. They are hostile to other groups.

Civet

Civetictis civetta

Length:	130 cm (tail 47 cm)
Weight:	11 kg
Gestation:	2 months
Offspring:	1 to 4
Lifespan:	14 years
Diet:	Omnivore

Civets are striking black and white carnivores that resemble cats but are not from the felid family. White patches on their faces highlight facial expressions during occasional social interactions between typically solitary and shy individuals.

Civets live in dense woodland and have a diverse diet consuming whatever small animals they can find and overcome (birds, reptiles, frogs, rodents, fish) as well as plant material, especially fruit. They are renowned for their ability to ingest poisonous prey, including cyanide-rich millipedes and venomous snakes like puff adders. They also scavenge and may eat the stomach contents of dead antelope.

Teeth modified for both tearing and crushing aid their catholic eating habits. Civets make large middens called civetries, which are characteristically littered with signs of the diverse materials they eat, for example millipede rings and seeds. Civetries demarcate territory, as do dark-coloured, pungent secretions from their well-developed anal glands that are inverted and wiped onto objects in the process. This substance has a long-lasting smell and is called civetone. Anal gland secretions may also be used as a chemical defence against predators although civets generally slip silently away when threatened. Under duress they may raise the longer-haired crest of fur along their backs and stand sideways to intimidate attackers, which may include lion, leopard and hyena.

Genet

)) *Genetta* species

Genets belong to the same family of carnivores as civets do, namely the Viverridae, and are lanky, long-tailed, short-legged woodland creatures with black, white and copper markings. The large-spotted genet (Genetta tigrina) has larger spots on the body and a black tip to its banded tail while the tail of the small-spotted genet (Genetta genetta) has a white tip. White patches on the face play a role in the occasional social interaction between these solitary animals by enhancing their facial expressions. Genets use vocal communication to this effect too.

Length:	95 cm (tail 45 cm)
Weight:	2 kg
Gestation:	10 weeks
Offspring:	1 to 4
Lifespan:	13 years
Diet:	Omnivore

Genets hunt cat-like on the ground for invertebrates, small mammals and reptiles but are extremely agile climbers, searching in trees for birds, eggs or fruit, or climbing up to escape predators. They are able to retract their claws like cats, which facilitates their arboreal habits. To appear intimidating to the larger carnivores that hunt them, genets arch their backs and pilo-erect the hair on their tails, or escape using well- executed leaps. Genets use their anal glands to scent-mark territory, the musky smell lasting up to nine weeks. They also make middens near their dens full of insect-rich dung. During the day genets shelter in holes or in thick bush. They generally prefer more densely vegetated habitats and only venture into the open when hunting and under the cover of darkness. Cubs are hidden at dens from which they emerge after about 45 days. Individuals are sexually mature at 2 years old.

▲ *Large-spotted genet*

▼ *Small-spotted genet*

African wild cat

Felis lybica

Length:	90 cm (tail 32 cm)
Weight:	4–5 kg
Gestation:	8.5 weeks
Offspring:	2 to 5
Lifespan:	15 years
Diet:	Carnivore

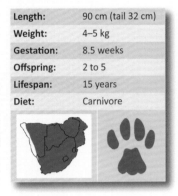

While similar, the African wild cat has longer, stripy legs, redder ears and sits more upright than the domestic cat, which originated in Egypt thousands of years ago and with which it easily hybridises today. African wild cats, except a female with her kittens, live alone in open habitats sheltering in holes, crevices or hollow trees. They communicate through a variety of sounds such as hissing, yowling and purring.

A male's territory may overlap with that of several females and while wild cats are apparently particularly intolerant of one another, they do seem to share hunting grounds outside their core territory areas. Both sexes mark their territories by spraying urine, and cheek- or chin-rubbing. Scat is buried. Kittens are born in summer when there is much prey available, develop quickly and are independent by about 5 months old. African wild cats have well-developed senses used to pursue prey such as rodents, birds, lizards and invertebrates. This is done in the characteristic feline manner of stalk, pounce and kill with a bite to the neck. In turn, the wild cat is preyed upon by most mammalian carnivores larger than itself, raptors and pythons.

Caracal

Caracal caracal

Height:	50 cm
Weight:	8–19 kg
Gestation:	11 weeks
Offspring:	2 to 3
Lifespan:	10 years
Diet:	Carnivore

The brick-coloured caracal has a reputation for its speed and dexterity in killing birds in the air, expertly killing two doves in one leap using both paws. Jumping ability is actuated by the strong hindquarters, propelling the cat 4–5 metres into the air from sitting, and the short tail helps with balance. Caracals do not only kill birds but are powerful predators and can kill prey as large as a leopard, including female kudu and adult springbok.

They kill with a bite to the neck or throat and eat from the rump after plucking fur there but without removing the intestines. Caracals have excellent climbing abilities too, pursuing dassies on rocks or sleeping eagles up trees. They may also cache food in trees. The large, padded paws are quiet as the caracal moves and equipped with tough, protractible claws useful for killing and climbing. The caracal tucks back its characteristic black ears when it stalks to remain concealed.

The ears are used for social interactions in combination with the striking facial markings and help to emphasise the expressions of the individuals in confrontation. The dark ear tufts highlight the position of the ears and caracals may indicate hostility by flicking their ears at each other while moving the head side to side. They are solitary animals but when a female has kittens, the black ears provide useful 'follow me' signs.

Youngsters disperse by about 10 months of age and move long distances from their natal range. They use open habitats such as plains, wetlands, rocky or mountainous areas and mixed woodland. Trees are needed to provide cover for hunting or escaping danger. Caracals usually dash into hiding without looking back when threatened by carnivores larger than themselves. Birds of prey, pythons and other predators eat kittens.

SS

Serval

)) *Felis serval*

Length:	1 m (tail 30 cm)
Weight:	12 kg
Gestation:	10 weeks
Offspring:	1 to 3
Lifespan:	12 years
Diet:	Carnivore

The serval is a golden cat attractively marked with spots and bars. Although small, the cat is tall with a long neck and legs and big ears that suit it to its speciality of hunting rodents and birds in tall-grass habitats. The long limbs allow the serval to see and hear above tall grass and the big ears isolate the smallest tell-tale sounds. Once a rodent is found, the serval stalks and pounces with an athletic leap, then pins its quarry on the ground with both forefeet after which it may play with its prey before eating it.

A serval's long-legged leaps are impressive and they can jump both high and far, changing direction at will. Long legs also allow servals to dig in holes for prey and to run quickly if need be. Their usual escape tactic is to take cover and crouch down but when required they bound away with sudden direction deviations. Predators include larger carnivores like hyena and wild dogs. Animals are solitary and maintain territories through urine-marking and by rubbing their faces on grass stalks while salivating. Although they do share ranges to an extent, they will avoid meeting up and when they do the reaction is intense – backs arch and coats bristle as opponents toss their heads up and down baring teeth and yowling. Paws are lifted up and may be used to prod the intruder.

Servals are actually fairly active during daylight hours too but do rest up in the middle of the day in a shaded clump of grass. Kittens are also hidden in dense grass or reeds and the mother spends inordinate amounts of time catering rodents for her growing brood. Males are chased off soon after weaning but female offspring may stay with the mother for some time. Animals are known to purr in each other's company. Servals usually live near water and readily paddle in the shallows in pursuit of vlei rats. They can also climb trees.

Honey badger (Ratel)

Mellivora capensis

The honey badger is a small yet ferocious predator if provoked, with a propensity for honey and bee larvae aside from its more typical prey of snakes, rodents and invertebrates. The honey badger is suited to bee-hunting by having ears that can close and a very tough, sting-impenetrable skin, especially over its shoulders. The looseness of the badger's skin makes it a hazard to its own predators since it can turn around when gripped. Sharp canines and a powerful jaw deliver a fearsome bite to predators and prey alike.

Length:	95 cm (tail 22 cm)
Weight:	12 kg
Gestation:	6 months
Offspring:	2
Lifespan:	20 years
Diet:	Carnivore

Honey badgers have short but very powerful legs and long, sharp claws, which they use to dig up prey or excavate dens in the ground. They often demolish rotten logs in the process of foraging and can easily break open hardened dung beetle balls to eat the larvae inside. Honey badgers have an excellent sense of smell, which they use to locate food. They forage alone but live in mated pairs, are very habitat tolerant, and generally quite nomadic. Although they do mark their home ranges with anal gland secretions, this is believed to be for the purpose of communication. Anal gland secretions are foul smelling and ejected in defence against predators too, mostly lions and leopards.

Honey badgers put up impressive threat displays but also resort to playing dead if their chemical defences, black and white warning colouration and downright ferocity are not enough to deter a hungry pursuer.

Honeyguide birds follow honey badgers to beehives to access them once opened by the badger. Pale-chanting goshawks also benefit from the badger's foraging techniques, dashing in to scoop up rodents that escape the badger's determined digging by exiting a burrow through a back entrance. It communicates through growls, grunts, a high-pitched bark and a nasal 'harr-harrr' sound.

Aardwolf

))) *Proteles cristatus*

Height:	45 cm
Weight:	10 kg
Gestation:	3 months
Offspring:	1 to 5
Lifespan:	15 years
Diet:	Insectivore

Long legs and a sloping spine give the aardwolf a typical hyena posture but its diet differs from other hyenas. It is an insectivore specialising on Trinervitermes *harvester termites that forage above ground at night. This source of food provides them with protein equivalent to similar quantities of lean meat while reducing competition with other carnivores and the effort required to hunt. The aardwolf helps to control termite numbers, consuming a kilogram or 200 000 termites in a night.*

They are adapted to their lifestyles by having tapering, almost hairless muzzles, reduced peg-like teeth and sticky saliva to lick up their quarry. They have modified ears that can rotate independently and provide very acute hearing, detecting even subterranean noises made by their prey. Because they are small and defenceless against larger predators, they use an impressive threat display whereby the fur, including mane and tail, is pilo-erected, increasing the side-view of the animal by 70%. To seem more intimidating, they roar deeply.

Animals are thought to form monogamous pairs sharing territories but they spend much time apart and feed alone. Territory boundaries are scent-marked with a smelly anal pouch excretion, which the aardwolf swipes on stalks of grass while waggling its rear and tail. The aardwolf pastes in lesser quantities throughout its territory while it forages, leaving a scent-trail probably to remind it and others where it has already fed. Dens and latrines are marked especially copiously. Scat, which is particularly large and smells of ammonia, is deposited in large quantities in latrines but is buried.

Dens are burrowed into softer ground but being weak diggers aardwolf typically make use of other ground dwellers' holes as homes or bolt holes. Males help to guard cubs and animals sunbathe at colder times of the year. Their arid savanna, short grass habitats are prone to freezing temperatures.

SS

)))

Aardvark

Orycteropus afer

Length:	150 cm (tail 50 cm)
Weight:	40–60 kg
Gestation:	7 months
Offspring:	1
Lifespan:	20 years
Diet:	Insectivore

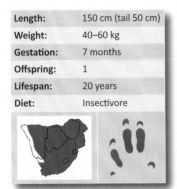

Aardvarks are solitary animals that feed at night. They are earthmovers, excavating holes and digging through even rock-hard soils very rapidly. Aardvarks dig to find food, a diet of ants and termites, or to make deep burrows in which to live, or to escape predators including lions, hyenas and leopards, which they have been known to out-dig when pursued.

They use a broad variety of habitats but do prefer sandy soils where digging is easier. They have powerful claws on their front feet for digging and large, rotating ears for hearing their tiny prey or predators. The ears fold away to keep sand out during digging. The elongated muscular muzzle is movable and used for sniffing out prey in holes. The hairy, slit nostrils can close to keep out sand and facial bristles protect the eyes. Termites are lapped up with the long, saliva-drenched tongue but mastication does not take place in the mouth where there are only a few reduced peg-like teeth, but rather in the gizzard-like stomach adapted for grinding. The short, strong tail is used to sweep away the earth excavated by the feet and leaves behind drag marks where the aardvark walks.

Almost 20 different mammal species, two reptiles and several birds subsequently use disused aardvark burrows and the aardwolf (see page 116) may feed in the wake of the aardvark. Distinctive oval pellet-droppings comprising termite heads and compacted soil ingested during foraging are deposited in a shallow scrape then covered.

SS

ME

Bushpig

))) *Potamochoerus porcus*

Length:	155 cm (tail 40 cm)
Weight:	70 kg
Gestation:	5 months
Offspring:	2 to 6
Lifespan:	20 years
Diet:	Omnivore

The bushpig could be considered the nocturnal version of the warthog (see page 56). However, some of their life history traits differ. Bushpigs are more omnivorous and forest dwelling than warthogs, which mostly graze grass in savannas, but like warthogs, use their muscular snouts to grovel in loose soil for food. The bushpig's menu includes vegetable material, reptiles, eggs, ground bird nestlings, buried insect larvae or pupae, frogs (especially rain frogs), dead meat and even young antelope. They are strong swimmers and take to water to forage for aquatic plants. They also enjoy mud wallowing.

Bushpigs live in sounders governed by a dominant boar. The boar protects his females and piglets from predators, using his barely visible but very sharp tusks in defence, and also from other boars that will be confronted with shoulder hairs bristled and jaws chomping. He may also roll on the ground churning up dust and clods of mud in an attempt to out-impress a rival. Snout-boxing ensues in more serious encounters. The tusks are also used to scratch marks on tree bark and ranges are scent-marked with tusk and pedal gland secretions as well as latrines. Although bushpigs are not strictly territorial, they sometimes form aggregations of about 30 animals (as opposed to the usual 12–15). Sows build nests out of long grass in which to give birth.

Bushpigs are colourful swine dressed in dark browns, reddish hues, light spots, and they have a white eye-ring. The back is rounded and crested with white hair. They grunt softly while foraging; the alarm call is a long, deep growl.

Cape porcupine

Hystrix africaeaustralis

Length:	84 cm (tail 13 cm)
Weight:	12–20 kg
Gestation:	3 months
Offspring:	1 to 3
Lifespan:	30 years
Diet:	Herbivore

The Cape porcupine is the largest rodent in southern Africa with a coat of long, sharp, loosely-attached, defensive quills. Porcupines raise their quills in confrontation with an enemy and rush backwards at it often, leaving quills firmly embedded in the offender's skin as a result of contact. In large predators such as lion or leopard, these may result in septic wounds. To complete the threatening ensemble they rattle their tails ominously, raise the crest of hair on their necks menacingly, stamp their feet and roar.

Porcupines are family animals and while they may forage alone, they live in pairs with their successive litters of offspring. Only the main pair mate and this they do daily for a few minutes, which stimulates ovulation and reinforces their social bond. To achieve a mounting, the male stands on his back legs and the female moves her tail aside and backs into him. He is well endowed and need not get very close to the female to mate successfully.

Babies are born well developed with incisors and some soft quills erupted and eyes open. To avoid rolling onto her quills, the female suckles the babies from flank-positioned teats. Young begin foraging alone from about five months old but until then are accompanied and defended by the adults. Porcupines have robust digestive systems and eat bark, roots, tubers and fallen fruit, including material from poisonous plants. They are noisy feeders and damage plants while foraging, often completely ring-barking and thus killing trees. They chew bones to supplement their calcium intake, a necessity to maintain both their quills and large, continuously growing incisors.

Scrub hare

)) *Lepus saxatilis*

Length:	50 cm
Weight:	2–3 kg
Gestation:	5–6 weeks
Offspring:	1 to 3
Lifespan:	8 years
Diet:	Herbivore

Scrub hares are characterised by their large ears and hind legs, traits necessary for an aboveground lifestyle and staying clear of predators such as jackals, caracals, leopards, pythons and Verreaux's eagle-owls. Scrub hares flee from threats at speeds of up to 70 km/h and may run in an irregular zigzag to outsmart pursuers, sometimes coaxing them to approach closely and subsequently to overshoot when a sudden change in direction is manoeuvred.

ME

They flatten themselves in thick undergrowth by day and produce well-developed, fully furred young, or leverets, that can move around from birth and become independent within a month. Scrub hares breed at a high rate and apparently under all conditions to ensure that population numbers remain high even though predation of scrub hares is high. Scrub hares eat grass, roots and tubers, and practise refection of their food, re-consuming vitamin-rich, soft, green caecotropic faeces directly from the anus at night to maximise nutrient uptake, producing harder, dry pellets by day.

Springhare

Pedetes capensis

Length:	90 cm
Weight:	3 kg
Gestation:	10–11 weeks
Offspring:	1
Lifespan:	7 years
Diet:	Grazer

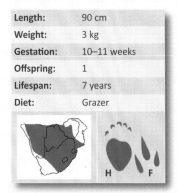

H   F

The springhare is a rodent that hops like a kangaroo propelled by large hind legs. A long, black-tipped tail balances the animal during hops while forelimbs are held close to the body. These are used to support the springhare while it feeds rabbit-like on grass and are modified to allow manipulation of their food. Springhares are selective grazers, nipping off choice bits of grass with their incisors or digging for rhizomes.

They are accomplished diggers as they live in burrow systems and require well-drained, sandy soils in flat open areas to build these. Sharp, curved claws facilitate digging and long eyelashes and bristles protect the eyes from flying sand. The long ears can fold away. Inside the burrow, long whiskers and sensory hairs help with navigation. Springhares do not forage far from their holes and bolt back into their own burrows when threatened, bounding with 2-metre leaps if necessary. The black-tipped tail flags from side to side as a distraction to all manner of predatory animals that eat them, including humans who relish the meat. If captured, the powerful hind legs and sharp claws can inflict painful wounds.

Burrows are usually clustered together. They can become extensive and include escape holes and side burrows. Springhares usually plug holes during the day and when they emerge after dark, they do so tentatively. Springhare burrow systems are also used by mongooses, mice, reptiles and pangolins. Springhares congregate on short-grassed, often-overgrazed areas to feed, but small springhares are seldom seen as they remain in burrows for several weeks until almost fully sized.

Lesser galago (Lesser bushbaby)

Galago moholi

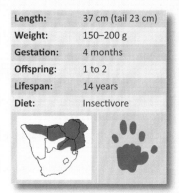

Length:	37 cm (tail 23 cm)
Weight:	150–200 g
Gestation:	4 months
Offspring:	1 to 2
Lifespan:	14 years
Diet:	Insectivore

Lesser galagos are small insectivorous primates super-specialised for an arboreal lifestyle. They have enormous eyes for seeing in poor light. These are immovable in their sockets but galagos bulge their eyeballs to focus and have flexible necks to look over their shoulders. Long whiskers protect their eyes while they forage in the dark. Their membranous ears are so sensitive they can hear insects; swivelling independently to pick up noises, or folding away completely.

Powerful hind legs and a long tail effect leaping while dexterous thumbs and toes assist with grip, as do the soft friction pads on the hands and feet. These features allow galagos to land on their feet with hands free for catching prey. Jumps can be 4 metres wide, 6 metres down or 2 metres high (15 times their body length). They bound many metres in seconds and hop like kangaroos on flat surfaces. They eat insects as well as carbohydrate- and mineral-rich acacia gum, which they scrape off branches with modified lower front teeth. They forage alone but, except for the males, sleep together in family groups inside nests or tree cavities, interacting and grooming with a special 'toilet claw' on the second digit of the hind foot. The gum-scraping toothcomb is also used for grooming and kept clean with a sharp fleshy comb under the tongue.

Males defend territories and scent-mark by 'urine-washing', urinating into a hand and then rubbing their feet, chests or females, and leaving the scent as they move. To chase away intruders, they hold their fists up to 'box' and will wrestle and bite ferociously, skills they hone from just 6 days old. Urine-washing is also used for communication in conjunction with a repertoire of more than 25 clicks, grunts and chatters. Babies are carried around in the mother's mouth so that they are not left unattended and vulnerable to predators such as owls, snakes and genets. She 'parks' them on a branch while she feeds nearby.

Greater galago (Thick-tailed bushbaby)

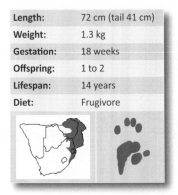

Galago crassicaudatus

Length:	72 cm (tail 41 cm)
Weight:	1.3 kg
Gestation:	18 weeks
Offspring:	1 to 2
Lifespan:	14 years
Diet:	Frugivore

The greater galago is a larger species with similar adaptations to the lesser galago but differs in lifestyle and behaviour. It has dense woolly fur, especially the fluffy tail from which it gets its alternative name, and resides in dense riverine or evergreen forest where it has access to large fruiting trees. While fruit is the mainstay of its diet, greater galagos also eat gum, nectar, seeds and small quantities of insects.

Large trees offer these slower moving galagos broader branches on which to walk or run, as they do not bounce in the manner of lesser galagos although they can jump if necessary, usually downwards. They also sleep in the forks or interweaving branches of large trees amongst tangled vegetation. Greater galagos walk on all fours when on the ground. Females live in individually defended areas with their young offspring and several of these ranges overlap with a single territorial male, although mixed sex sleeping groups do form. This is the most social of the bushbaby species, probably as a result of its diet and larger body stature. Groups typically disperse to forage alone but congregate in fruiting trees or at established gum lick sites.

While greater galagos that encounter one another may fight, they do also take opportunities to groom socially. A bare patch on the chest is underlain with glands and used by both sexes for scent-marking territory, as is urine-washing. Long-range wailing calls sound remarkably child-like and these vocally advertise territory; a repertoire of about 10 varied noises constitute the rest of this galago's vocabulary, including a shrill alarm call.

Greater galagos fall prey to larger owls, leopards, caracals and pythons. They have well-developed sight and hearing to discern threats and their slower movements are believed to help them avoid detection. Both sexes' genitals change during the mating season, the female's becoming red and swollen while the male's enlarges and becomes exposed from his fur with a patch of pink skin. Copulation lasts hours and twins or triplets are usually born. The female moves these around with her, carrying them in her mouth or clinging to her back.

SS

123

Where avifauna is concerned, there is much at which to marvel. A myriad body, beak and feet designs suit these feathered wonders to the plethora of habitats in which they are found – from the plentiful pantries of forested glades to the merciless surfaces of barren, rocky ground, and every arboreal nook and cranny in between. Birds are resourceful beyond measure in their pursuit of food and mates, thanks to their ability to fly and their well-developed senses of sight and hearing. They are also of the most extraordinary homemakers and parents on the planet. When it comes to communication, little compares in the audible realm, to the musical tunes and tones piped from their intricate syrinxes, with each species producing more than one if not several different vocalisations, each with its own purpose, and often paired up with visual displays fit for Broadway. While there are an impressive 900 bird species in southern Africa to potentially identify, as with the observation of any animal, it is what the creature is doing and how it does this, that proves more interesting than the mere identification of the critter and this section gives wings to learning such things about birds.

Feathers

Strong yet light and flexible, feathers are a bird's key to flight and the feature that makes birds unique from all other groups in the animal kingdom. Feathers are believed to have evolved from reptilian scales and from a necessity to colonise habitats.

Feathers are made from the tough structural material keratin and comprise a horny, hollow shaft supplied with blood and a vane of softer barbs that zip together with tiny barbules. They are not all identical but modified to perform different functions:

- The **remiges and retrices (1)** are the strongest and usually strengthened with the black pigment melanin. The former make up the wings, including primary and secondary flight feathers and the latter are tail feathers used for steering and stabilisation.
- **Contour feathers or tectrices (2)** streamline the body to make it move effortlessly through the air and at the base of these, soft fluffy **down feathers (3)** insulate the bird.
- Between the contours are long, filamentous sensory feathers called **filoplumes** that are sensitive to fluctuating air currents.

SS

Feathers may be specialised for different purposes. The **barn owl's** feathery facial disc acts like a parabola to collect sounds and augment the owl's acute hearing. Sandgrouse have special water-carrying feathers on their breasts to transport water to chicks on exposed nests in arid areas. **Nightjars** and other insectivorous birds have rictal bristles around their gapes, which help to direct prey into their mouths as well as having a sensory function. Woodpeckers and oxpeckers have retrices with reinforced shafts that help these birds to prop themselves up. In addition, feathers provide for the functions of insulation, waterproofing and camouflage.

Marabou stork

Depending on the species, different birds put different emphasis on their appearance, some prioritising colour and attractiveness in courtship over camouflage while others prefer to blend in, using displays and song rather to attract mates. Some birds have modified feathers and take courtship to the extreme, for example the long streaming tails of the **whydahs** that grow each new breeding season and are shown off to females in elaborate aerial displays to infer genetic superiority. Rollers also perform elaborate and raucous air shows to put their dazzling plumage on show.

Feathers are replaced annually, sometimes more than once, in a process called moulting to ensure that the instruments of flight remain in perfect working condition. Damage may occur through wear and tear and particularly the flight and tail feathers need to be in shipshape. Some birds will shed all their feathers at once, such as female hornbills do during breeding but most lose and replace a few feathers at a time so that flight is not impeded. Feathers are also maintained through rigorous grooming and other hygiene practices.

Pin-tailed whydah

SS

Flight

Flight is achieved through the forces of lift and airflow over an aerodynamic surface, in the case of a bird, its wings. The wing is wider on the leading edge and tapers off causing the air to deflect off the upper surface, creating lower pressure and therefore lift from below. Wing loading is important because a broader surface (i.e. the wing) allows for more lift, depending on the mass of the object it is lifting (i.e. the bird's body). Feathers provide the aerodynamic shape and surfaces of the bird. The shafts give structural support but the tips remain flexible for movement. A bird jumps and flaps to generate momentum, air movement and ultimately lift.

Apart from the feathers, other adaptations are also key to effect flight. Birds have very light skeletons with hollow bones reinforced with a honeycomb structure for strength. Their skeletons typically weigh less than all the feathers. Well-developed shoulder blades provide the surface for wing attachment and a large, keeled breastbone forms the point of attachment for powerful flight muscles. Birds have just a single ovary to reduce their body mass and the pelvic girdle is strong to absorb the shock of landing. Eggs develop overnight and can be laid in morning before flying. Birds concentrate wastes as uric acid instead of heavy urine.

SS

SS

Airflow moving over the leading edge of a wing creates an audible swish sound, but **owls** have mastered silent flight. They have very large wings relative to the size and mass of their bodies, which allows them to fly without having to flap excessively. The feathers on the leading edge of their wings are 'frayed' to divide the passage of air hitting the edge and this also reduces the sound of the airflow over it. Silent flight is essential so that owls can hear their tiny prey as well as remain unnoticed while hunting it.

Some species have developed techniques to save energy in flight. There are many different strategies but by way of example, the woodpeckers use bounding flight. Bouts of flapping allow the bird to gain lift and momentum at which point they close their wings and 'free-wheel', descending for a short distance before flapping some more.

Because flight requires much energy, birds typically consume high-energy foods or foods that digest quickly. The avian heart beats rapidly circulating nutrients and oxygen throughout the body. This generates much heat, which is dealt with through a system of air sacs over and above lungs. The air sacs also facilitate breathing during flight, assisting with the provision of oxygen throughout the body, and at high altitudes, and making the bird's body substantially lighter.

Some species are super-aerobatic, like **bee-eaters**. They have long narrow wings, forked tails and small streamlined torsos, which facilitate their acrobatic hunting manoeuvers. Rictal bristles on the face channel food into their mouths and protect the eyes.

Some birds have mastered the art of hovering flight. By using a figure-of-eight wing stroke and thus effectively reversing the wing beat on the up-stroke to remain in the same position, **pied kingfishers** have honed this ability in order to catch fish effectively. It is, however, an energy-expensive form of flight and cannot be sustained for long periods. The pied kingfisher essentially practises aerial perching, as true hovering involves the ability to move forwards and backwards (like the hummingbird) which the kingfisher cannot do.

The birds on this spread:
Main *Bearded vulture*
1 *Barn owl* (SS)
2 *Carmine bee-eaters* (SS)
3 *Pied kingfisher* (SS)

Pigmented plumage for a purpose

There are two kinds of pigment in birds' feathers. The main one is melanin, responsible for the spectrum of black and brown colour. It has a structural function too, strengthening the feathers. The other pigments are the carotenoids, responsible for the spectrum yellow through to red. Examples of birds with yellow feathers are weavers, canaries, bush-shrikes and orioles. The golden-breasted bunting has a bright splash of yellow on its breast. The red of some bee-eaters and the head of a red-headed weaver is also caused by carotenoids. A red pigment called turacin is unique to the turaco family.

The colour blue in birds is not from pigment. Blue is caused by a trick of light known as Tyndall scattering. The layering of the structural material of the feathers, keratin, interspaced with air, reflects and scatters particular wavelengths of light, resulting in the gorgeous blues of birds such as rollers, kingfishers and blue waxbills.

In the absence of airspaces between the layers of structural keratin, the effect created by the reflected light from the feathers is iridescence. Depending on the angle of the light, feathers may look blue, green and mauve and in the absence of light, black. **Glossy starlings** are classic examples of birds with iridescent feathers while many **ducks** have an iridescent window, or speculum, on their wings used in breeding. The **hadeda ibis** also has a glossy sheen.

Green feathers are a combination of pigment and light-effects that create the bright greens of bee-eaters and parrots. The mixing of the primary colours yellow and blue creates green therefore, in the presence of carotenoids (yellow), Tyndall scattering (blue) produces the green feather colour of all green birds except **turacos**. Turacoverdin is a green pigment unique to the turaco family. The more olive green colour of some of the **thrushes** and bush-shrikes comes from a combination of yellow and black pigments.

The grey of the **grey go-away bird** and other grey-feathered species like doves is caused when light scatters off feathers containing small amounts of melanin. If there is a complete absence of pigment in feathers, all light scatters and features look white.

The birds on this spread:
Main *Red-winged starling* (ME)
1 *Golden-breasted bunting* (ME)
2 *Blue waxbill* (ME)
3 *Black-headed oriole* (SS)
4 *Southern red bishop* (SS)
5 *European roller* (SS)
6 *Yellow-billed duck* (ME)
7 *Hadeda ibis* (SS)
8 *Cape glossy starling* (SS)
9 *Livingstone's turaco* (SS)
10 *Kurrichane thrush* (SS)
11 *Grey go-away bird* (ME)
12 *Cattle egrets* (ME)

Keeping feathers healthy

Birds preen to keep their feathers healthy. This involves drawing a feather through the bill to re-zip the barbs on the vanes dishevelled from wear and tear or weather. During preening, birds coat their feathers with preening oil from the uropygial gland on the lower back to make them supple and to protect them from bacteria and fungal infections. Preening also removes excess fatty residue from the plumage and waterproofs feathers. Many birds allo-preen one another to ensure the hard-to-reach head and neck areas are cared for. This behaviour is especially typical in monogamous pairs.

Some birds have powder-down feathers that fray into a talc that is applied in addition to preening oil during preening. Waterbirds like egrets and herons do this to rid themselves of the grime from fishing. The powder absorbs the dirt and the birds can then strip the dirt off with a comb-like, pectinate claw. Feathers are coated in preen oil after the feathers have been cleaned.

Many birds enjoy water and bathe regularly. The extent of soaking needs to be balanced with the ability to fly away as heavy feathers could slow a bird down just enough for it to be caught by a predator. Birds that have weak perching legs, like swifts and bee-eaters, cannot as readily jump into flight as other birds so instead of bathing, they dip-dive into the water. After washing, birds will shake their feathers to dry them. By rousing the feathers and shaking vigorously, the bird not only gets rid of moisture after a bath but also dislodges dust and parasites. They will then apply preen oil and preen.

Birds will assume a variety of poses to expose their feathers to the sun. Sunbathing dries feathers, softens grease and dislodges parasites at which point birds start preening. UV light also kills bacteria and helps to restore the shape and structure of feathers.

Some birds enjoy dust bathing, writhing in patches of loose soil and flicking it over their bodies with their wings. Dust dislodges parasites, sticks to grease and creates a muck that is easier to preen away. Hoopoe chicks are raised in very unsanitary nests, a deterrent to predators, so when they leave the nest on fledging, they immediately take a dust bath. Spurfowl, francolin and guineafowl dust bathe frequently.

Anting is understood to play a part in hygiene and preening whereby formicide ants are actively or passively encouraged to squirt formic acid on a bird's feathers. Birds may pick up an ant and rub it on the feather or allow ants to crawl over it, stimulated by the shaking of the bird's wings to squirt acid. Formic acid may help get rid of old preen oil or act as a pesticide. It may also have a soothing effect on the skin during moulting.

The birds on this spread:
Main & 1 *African darter* (SS)
2 *White-faced whistling ducks* (SS)
3 *Greater flamingo* (ME)
4 *Blue crane* (ME)
5 & 6 *Speckled pigeon* (ME)
7 *Spoonbill* (ME)
8 *Ostrich* (SS)

Pairing or pooling?

Survival is about more than just staying out of harm's way or finding the next meal, it also involves finding a mate and keeping the family genes alive. Most birds form pairs when they breed, a system known as monogamy. However, there are several unique systems at play amongst birds.

The majority of birds form monogamous pairs for breeding purposes with both sexes investing equal time and energy into the relationship and cooperating with parental duties. Birds need to catch food to nourish their chicks and as a pair they are more successful at doing this and thus more effective at rearing offspring. Pairing may happen once off, e.g. African fish eagles pair for life; annually, e.g. owls; or seasonally e.g. with migratory species. Monogamous pairs defend a territory together and much energy is invested in maintaining pair bonds by singing, displays, preening and nuptial gifting.

Some birds choose to consort with many mates, known as polygamy. In this instance, male birds spend much time and energy attracting potential female mates and convincing them of their superior genes. In this case, physical appearance and showy displays are useful. The red-crested korhaan has an elaborate display, taking off from the ground and flying to the skyline where he stalls, flashes his black belly and drops. At the last minute a graceful landing is executed. The whydahs exhibit their long tails and attractive breeding plumage in their flashy display flights. The 'handicap hypothesis' suggests that avoiding predators while handicapped with a weighty tail must infer genetic fitness to females. Weavers build nests to attract females into mating. The male's skill at weaving offers females an indication of their fitness and also offers some form of parental provision for the chicks as the male will play no further role after mating.

The birds on this spread:
Main *Long-tailed widowbird*
1 *African fish eagles*
2 *African jacana*
3 *Yellow-billed stork*
4 *Golden weaver*
5 *Lesser spotted eagle*

Polygamy can take on a male and female expression. When the male bird has more than one mate, the breeding system is called polygyny, i.e. 'many women'. When the female has more than one mate, it is called polyandry, i.e. 'many men'. In the case of the African jacana, the female mates with and lay eggs for several males in a season. Each male constructs the nests, broods and raises the chicks himself.

Generally, monogamous birds look alike, or are monomorphic. In the case of a breeding pair, the emphasis is on maintaining the territory and raising chicks. Both the male and female are equally vested in the brooding process and both need to be camouflaged, for example doves. Storks, cranes and ducks also have little to no sexual dimorphism and will rely on showy displays rather than bright colours to attract partners.

When male and female birds look significantly different to one another, we say they are sexually dimorphic. Polygamous birds are generally sexually dimorphic. Typically the male bird plays no

role in brooding or raising young, which then doesn't necessitate the duller, less conspicuous colours of their females. Birds such as weavers and whydahs exhibit great sexual dimorphism and also spend a great deal of energy enhancing their appearance through display.

Reverse sexual dimorphism occurs when the female of the species is more conspicuous than the male. In raptors, the female is usually larger than the male in spite of them being monogamous. This is because she must produce eggs and then incubate them while her partner's role is that of provider and his smaller size renders him more agile to catch prey to feed to his mate and chicks.

Teamwork

If working in pairs renders benefits for the breeding effort, then breeding cooperatively must also do. Cooperative breeding occurs when a flock of birds help a breeding pair (the dominant or alpha pair) to breed successfully. Typically, these species have learned that they breed better cooperatively than if pairs attempt it alone. 'Helpers' collect nesting material, incubate eggs, protect the nest, assist with finding food and provide extra vigilance.

Cooperative flocks first form when a pair of birds integrates their offspring into a group or when two single-sexed groups of dispersing birds meet and join up. A representative from either sex will become the dominant breeding bird. In both scenarios, the principle of kinship-selection is at play and since the 'helper' birds are related, they essentially assist with perpetuating their own genes.

The **pied kingfisher** practises a form of cooperative breeding and, unlike other kingfishers, is found in more gregarious groups. A breeding pair may have a number of mostly male helpers aiding with food provision and incubation. Offspring from a previous breeding season that do this are known as primary helpers, but secondary helpers are birds unrelated to the dominant pair and consequently allowed to do less for them. Secondary helpers seem to simply be learning from the breeding efforts of others, possibly to improve their own chance of breeding in an upcoming season, potentially even with the current breeding female.

White-crested helmet-shrikes have an alpha pair that bond for life. The dominant pair selects a nesting site in the fork of a tree and the whole flock then constructs the nest with thin strips of bark bound with spider's web collected on the modified, erectile head feathers. Supplementary cobwebs are added throughout the nesting process. The helpers take turns to incubate and when the bird on duty is ready to be relieved, it calls to the flock that flies around and settles collectively near the nest site as a distraction. The incubating bird then swaps out with another member and the flock moves off again. Helmet-shrikes remain together outside the breeding season, roosting together, defending a common territory and feeding as a group.

Green wood-hoopoes maintain a hierarchy with the oldest male and female assuming the role of the breeding pair. Males dominate over females and older birds dominate over younger ones. This rank is maintained by mutual feeding and grooming and determines the next in line to breed. Green wood-hoopoes nest in natural tree cavities with narrow entrances. The entire flock prospects for the nest but only the dominant female incubates the eggs, fed by the male and helpers. Fledglings are attended to by the helpers that vie to feed, preen, guard and lead them to the roost sites at night. Green wood-hoopoes practise allelomimetic behaviours for group cohesion, cackling compulsively and displaying as a group, swaying their bodies and flicking their tails. One of the dominant birds may 'flagwave'-picking up a twig in its bill and waving it at a predator or neighbouring flock while its own flock calls loudly.

Arrow-marked babblers are another common species that practises cooperative breeding and allelomimetic behaviour.

Foster families

About one percent of all birds are brood parasites that leave the brooding and rearing of their chicks to a foster family. Using host families reduces the amount of energy required to breed successfully and allows the brood parasite to produce several broods in a season. In southern Africa five different groups practise brood parasitisms, i.e. cuckoos, honeyguides, indigobirds, whydahs and the cuckoo finch.

Brood parasites use different techniques to ensure success. The parent bird or newly-hatched chick may evict the host's eggs or chicks (for which some cuckoos have specially concaved backs) to reduce competition and gain the undivided attention of the host. Sometimes only a single egg is removed to mask the addition of the parasite egg, which is typically camouflaged in the same colours and patterns as the host's eggs. Brood parasites' chicks outgrow and outcompete their host-siblings, as they are

usually larger from the start. In some cases, the host's brood is trampled and smothered as a result of the larger chick in the nest. Indigobirds and whydahs have smaller offspring and these are usually reared successfully alongside the host's chicks. Honeyguide chicks have a sharp bill hook when they hatch which they use to destroy their host-siblings. In addition to these techniques, the brood parasitic chicks are further benefitted by their immunity to host-specific nest parasites.

To induce the host bird to feed the brood parasite chick, the chick has a similar coloured gape with matching palatal spots to the host's chicks. The gape is exposed during food begging and is unique for each species.

Host birds recognise and spend much time and energy chasing adult brood parasites away. Some species have developed avoidance techniques, e.g. the girth of some weaver nest-tunnels accommodate the weaver adults but not necessarily an adult cuckoo that may get wedged and even die in the tunnel. But while hosts develop tactics to avoid being exploited by brood parasites, these are often countered by the brood parasites' own tactics. Remarkably, brood parasites never meet their own parents yet their species songs are inherited genetically so that they can attract mates later in life.

Brood parasites may be generalist or specific in their choice of host species. The purple indigobird only parasitises the Jameson's firefinch, mimicking its call to get close to the nest and laying a perfectly matching egg. The scaly-throated honeyguide uses several hosts but all are hole-nesting species like woodpeckers or barbets. The greater honeyguide uses 36 different species.

GM

Cape robin (left) feeding a red-chested cuckoo foster chick (right)

Chicks

Birds' chicks are born altricial or precocial. Altricial chicks are blind, naked and immobile. Precocial chicks, on the other hand, are covered with down, have their eyes open and as soon as they dry after hatching, they can move around and even swim. The bird kingdom is divided into three groups partly based on whether the chicks are altricial or precocial, i.e. passerines, non-passerines and near-passerines.

Passerines are the largest order of birds and include mostly small, perching birds that have three toes facing forward and one facing backwards. These birds typically nest in trees or holes, which provide shelter for the chicks. As a result, passerines usually produce altricial chicks. The chicks need warmth and protection from the parents to develop fully and the nesting period is somewhat protracted. While the adults spend time foraging to cater to the growing chicks' needs, they can be left in the safety of the nest.

Non-passerines are usually ground or water-dwelling birds. Nests are constructed on the ground, if at all, and are susceptible to many predators. Because it is vital for the chicks to be able to escape danger as soon as they hatch, these chicks are born precocial. To accommodate for more advanced development at hatching, precocial species have longer incubation periods. Being more developed at hatching has the additional benefit that they can regulate their body heat and are less reliant on the parent for warmth. Finding food is thus the priority.

An intermediate group known as the near-passerines produce altricial young in nests but do not have perching feet. These birds have modified zygodactylous or syndactylous feet for clinging or other functions. Zygodactylous feet have two toes facing forward and two backwards, allowing birds like woodpeckers and wood-hoopoes to cling to upright tree trunks while foraging. Owls have a toe that they may direct forwards or backwards as required. Syndactylous feet have the second and third toe fused and are found in kingfishers and hornbills.

Raptors are the exception, as their chicks hatch fully coated in down and with their eyes open but they are nonetheless helpless, nest-bound and rely on the parents for food. This is called semi-altricial and is also a trait seen in herons and egrets.

Precocial: Crowned lapwing and chick

Altricial: Collared sunbird feeding chick

Making music

Birds vocalise to communicate; many in very harmonious, musical ways, others in less than melodic tones but all species do so uniquely. Birds call in different ways and for different reasons. They may sing alone, in duet or in chorus. The passerines are typically the songbirds and have the broadest range with some species boasting up to 15 calls.

Birds sing using the syrinx, a boxy, cartilaginous organ at the base of the windpipe but just above the lungs. A bronchial tube from each lung feeds into the syrinx, the opening controlled by fleshy membranes that alter pitch and tone. By contracting its lungs, a bird shoots a spurt of air through the syrinx, which creates sound. More intricate melodies are produced by using both tubes concurrently and generating different sounds from either side. The **crested barbet** can produce its incessant call by vocalising with one tube and breathing with the other. Other species make their uninterrupted calls by taking shallow breaths and expelling air from each side of the syrinx while the other side continues singing.

Different species make multiple sounds and each has a purpose. Usually birds sing melodically to advertise their territories, display and attract mates or reinforce pair bonds. The same song may send a different message to a female as compared to a male intruder. Birds use contact calls to maintain communication while foraging or between family members. Individuals are recognisable from their calls. Alarm calls are harsh rasps that are made in response to danger. Birds also use flight calls, aggression calls and young have begging calls.

))) The dawn chorus is the first and most intense burst of collective birdcalls made in the day by diurnal species. In the early morning the air is still and sound travels best. The dawn chorus is a time of territorial advertisement and neighbours are reminding one another of their presence and ownership of an area.

))) Another time of collective vocalisation takes place pre-dusk as a final statement of territorial ownership before dark falls.

Crested barbet

Many monogamous birds reinforce their pair bond by duetting. Duets are usually so exquisitely antiphonal that the song appears to come from just one bird but is actually made by two. The **black collared barbet,** crested francolin and southern boubou are all examples of regular duetters.

White-browed robin-chat

Black-collared barbets

Sounds are also produced non-vocally. Bill-snapping is a common form of communication in mating rituals and used by marabou storks and **black-backed puffbacks** for example. Woodpeckers tap hollow logs, drumming out a signature rhythm to advertise territory, the sound resonating far and wide. Wing-claps produced while in flight by a few species also serve as audible communication and are used in displays, e.g. flappet larks.

Some birds are experts at mimicking others' calls. They duplicate sounds or even whole phrases of song belonging to other species as a means of expressing gene superiority. The more complex and extended the arrangement, the fitter the individual is presumed to be. A strong mimicked song may also intimidate rivals. **Robin-chats** and fork-tailed drongos are mimickers. Brood parasitic indigobirds mimic the calls of their firefinch hosts to locate their nests.

Black-backed puffback

Bokmakierie

Bills for banqueting

The bird beak is comprised of keratin, which regrows as it is worn down. It is a sensitive apparatus and supplied with nerve endings so the bird can taste and feel. Beaks come in a diversity of shapes and sizes, each style a modification to utilise a particular habitat and a diversity of foodstuffs. Birds are so successful as a group because of resource partitioning whereby each type of bird makes use of a different food source or a different part of a food source. Birds eat seeds, nectar, wax, insects, microscopic organisms, succulent plants, fish, carrion and every kind of small to medium vertebrate.

Filtering bills

Spoonbills have spatulate bills that terminate in a spoon-shaped disc, which are used to filter mud to capture small fish and invertebrates. Spoonbills sweep their bills from side to side, keeping it slightly submerged in the water as they move slowly along the shallows. Flamingoes also have unique filtering bills. Lamellae run along the sides of the bill and filter microscopic algae and other small animals from the water that is pumped into the bill by a strong tongue. The head is held upside down while feeding.

Fish eagle

The fish eagle is a specialist feeder focusing its diet on fish and aquatic reptiles like monitors. Long, sharp talons and spicules under the feet help it to grip its slippery prey. Fish eagles hunt from a perch, swooping down low over the water and throwing its talons forward to snatch quarry off the surface before returning to its perch. Very heavy prey is paddled to the edge. Fish eagles are also accomplished pirates and rob other birds of their food or harass them into disgorging their crop contents, especially other piscivores. They catch trapped fish in drying puddles and pull weavers nests apart to get to the nestlings.

Lesser flamingo

African fish eagle

Probing bills

There are two designs for probing bills, decurved and straight. Birds with probing bills are usually insectivorous and use their bills to extract food in various ways. Sunbirds use their bills to access nectar from flowers. Bee-eaters have thin, tweezer-like bills with wide gapes to snatch air-borne insects on the wing. Hazardous prey like bees are held in a vice grip at the end of the bill and beaten against a perch until the sting comes free.

Green wood-hoopoes are voracious, using their long, curved bills to harvest beetles, termites, grasshoppers, caterpillars and millipedes off the trunks and branches of trees. While they do so, they clamber awkwardly using their zygodactylous feet to cling and their tails as props. Waders like sandpipers have long, straight bills to probe for invertebrates in mud. Waders' bills vary in length and shape to access food at different levels.

Orange-breasted sunbird

Swallow-tailed bee-eater

Chisels and spears

Reinforced, straight bills work well to chisel away wood in the case of woodpeckers making holes or foraging for grubs; and they are efficient spears in the instance of piscivorous kingfishers or herons. The long, sharp, sturdy beak allows kingfishers to grip their prey tweezer-like at the tips. Herons spear fish, patiently standing still as statues for ages to allow the prey to come within reach. The flexible, muscular neck then powers the strike to spear the fish with power and speed.

Striped kingfisher

Scavenging bills

Marabou storks have straight bills and opportunistically scavenge meat worked free by vultures. These bills do not cut but are adept at monopolising trapped catfish in drying pools. With their feet they stir up muddy water, disturbing the fish that are then found by sight or feel, and stabbed. Fish are swallowed headfirst so that scales and fins align with the digestive tract. Vultures have tough, curved bills that grow continuously to replenish the bill from wear and tear. They are adapted to tearing tough flesh, prying smaller bits off bones with their serrated tongues.

Fruit-eating bills

Thick, sturdy bills are adapted to deal with hard-shelled fruits, e.g. parrots and turacos, and are thinner in birds that use softer fruits. The frugivorous dark-capped bulbul uses its bill for plucking and cutting fruit, sometimes supplementing their diets with nectar. Some frugivores get protein into their diet by eating insects occasionally. The gut of fruit-eating birds is short and seeds pass rapidly through their systems facilitating seed dispersal. Fruit is seasonal and frugivores have nomadic, gregarious lifestyles as a result.

Marabou stork

Meyer's parrot

Hooked bills

Hooked bills are for tearing and usually belong to carnivorous species – either flesh- or insect-eating birds – albeit there are exceptions. These come in a range of sizes. Shrikes simply have a hook at the end of their stout bills, toothed for catching insects and small vertebrate prey. Smaller raptors have a notch behind the tip of the bill, specifically designed to cut through the spines of their prey. The sharply hooked bill of parrots is modified to process hard nuts, seeds and fruit. Parrots can conveniently lift their feet to their mouths. Raptors use their powerful, sharp, hooked bills for tearing the flesh of their prey. Some birds, like crows, have multi-purpose bills which effect the processing of animal flesh, fish and insects as well as fruit and seeds.

Red-backed shrike

Specialist bills

The **hamerkop** specialises in eating frogs and tadpoles, particularly platannas, using its sturdy bill. They wade and stir the shallow, muddy water with their feet, probing until a frog moves and can be captured. Hamerkops also eat some fish and invertebrates. The **openbill stork's** bill is another unique creation, being open between the upper and lower mandibles. The bill only connects at the tip and the base and gapes about 6 mm in the middle. The design offers structural support for eating molluscs and mussels. Once probing with the bill ajar proves fruitful, the openbill pins down the prey with the upper mandible and expertly uses the lower one as a blade to remove the soft tissue from inside the shell.

Hamerkop

Openbill stork

Duck bills

Ducks have flat, filtering bills for straining edible items out of the water. Many ducks dabble, partially submerging their upper body while foraging. They eat aquatic plants, insects, detritus, algae, crustaceans and other invertebrates. **White-faced whistling ducks** may also dive under the water to access food. They are also fairly unique among ducks because they feed at night on grass, seeds, grain and fruit and their whistled call is regularly heard as they fly over on their way to feed. Egyptian geese are true grazers, flying to open areas to feed on grass, seeds and grain, leaves and even young crops early in the morning or late afternoon.

Seedeaters

Seedeaters have short, conical bills that are the perfect design to crack open seeds. **Waxbills**, canaries, sparrows, weavers and doves are common seed-eating birds. They are often found foraging on dirt paths or tracks where seeds have been knocked to the ground by passing animal or human traffic. The dry nature of their food dictates that seedeaters must drink water regularly.

White-faced whistling duck

Violet-eared waxbill

Bird defences

Birds are preyed on by a diversity of predators and not just avian predatory species. As a result, birds have an arsenal of different defence strategies that can be deployed to ensure their survival in both adult and juvenile stages of life.

Birds have exceptionally well-developed vision. To hunt on the wing, acute vision is imperative, as it is for survival generally. The size of birds' eyes relative to the size of their heads is a good indication of this. The larger the eye, the larger the imprint on the retina, the better vision. Large eyes do pose a problem with mobility but birds have flexible necks to compensate for this. Predators have more forward-facing eyes to provide binocular vision to gauge depth and distance. Vegetarian birds have side-positioned eyes for better peripheral vision. Birds can see in colour and can see more of the colour spectrum than people, including ultra-violet light. A nictitating membrane moves sideways across bird's eyes to keep them clean and moist and for protection.

Hearing in birds is advanced and they can perceive a range of infrasonic sound as well as the same frequencies humans hear. Their ears are internal so that they do not impede flight and are positioned behind and below the eyes. Some species have asymmetrically placed eardrums, which allow for determination of direction, as sound is received split seconds apart. Smell in birds is less developed than sight and vision but varies in acuteness between species.

Very often, the best port of call is to hide away from a predator when one threatens. For this reason, many birds have cryptically coloured feathers with earthy colours, intricate patterns and delicate markings that all work to break up the bird's outline. Once nestled into the mottled background of undergrowth, uneven soil or dense vegetation, the bird can become invisible to the eye, providing it remains still. Scops owlets and nightjars are masters of cryptic camouflage. Cryptically coloured eggs are easily concealed while adults are off the nest and cryptic chicks enjoy better concealment if danger threatens.

RF

Birds tend to respond to one another's alarm calls and a distressed call results in a number of birds from different species flocking to investigate the hazard. Very often, in the case of a snake or predatory bird in a tree, the birds will mob it, diving at the intruder frantically to dissuade it from hanging around. Sometimes the offender is actually attacked and hit but mostly the birds veer away at the last moment. Small birds like drongos are known to mob predatory birds in flight. The cocky little birds are more agile than the predator, which is why it is safe to do so. Plovers and lapwings may dive bomb predators out of the sky while calling loudly and even make contact with beak and claws to wound it.

In conjunction with cryptic colouration, many birds employ a strategy of simply living secretive lives. They avoid trouble by avoiding detection of any kind, skulking in the undergrowth or deep under the cover of thick vegetation. Many will use discrete foraging methods and move carefully.

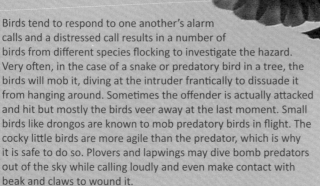

Brightly coloured birds that live active lives have to rely on speed and agility to evade their enemies.

4

The birds on this spread:
Main *Fork-tailed drongo mobbing a Wahlberg's eagle*
1 *vOstrich*
2 *Helmeted guineafowl*
3 *African scops-owl*
4 *Carmine bee-eater*

The green wood-hoopoe has an arsenal of defence strategies, including chemical warfare. A foul-smelling secretion is produced by the preen gland and can be sprayed at offenders in conjunction with a squirt of liquid excreta. Inside the nest cavity, chicks will sway and hiss in the dark to mimic snakes if disturbed. They also jab their long, sharp beaks menacingly at the source of the disturbance. The southern black tit female also makes a snake-like hiss to put predators off that approach her hole.

Some species use poor nest sanitation as a predator deterrent. Hoopoes are notorious for using this technique, with chicks defecating against the sidewalls of the hole to create a mucky, smelly environment. They keep their feathers sheathed until they depart the nest to protect them and their first priority on leaving the nest is always to take a dust bath. Malachite kingfishers are another species that allow their tunnel nests to become totally soiled to the point that smelly matter oozes out the front entrance.

Chicks use a variety of safe havens. At the adults' alarm, jacana chicks will submerge below the water with just the beak protruding. Sometimes, parent birds transport their young carrying them under their wings or on their backs as with grebes. When warned, many chicks respond by taking cover and crouching motionless. The nests of most bird species are cleverly designed or chosen to ensure maximum safety for the chicks. Parent birds typically approach these cautiously to not draw attention to them and defend their nests vigorously if need be.

4

SS

5

The lapwings derive their common name from their propensity to perform 'broken wing' displays although they are not the only birds to feign injury. If a nesting site is threatened, a crowned lapwing, for example, will drop its one wing down as if injured and in zigzag movements, with quick steps, will lure the predator away from the nest. Once the lapwing is satisfied that it is far enough away, it will take off, leaving the predator without nest or adult bird to pursue. Some species mimic rodents to achieve the same effect, darting rat-like in front of the predator to lure it away.

Many birds use startle displays to intimidate predators. Some species may open their wings aggressively and, usually accompanied by loud noises, they attempt to scare away the threat. Some species have bright colours or black and white patterns that are employed to distract predators. The red flash of a turaco's wings is obvious in flight but once the bird has landed, it is difficult to locate it.

Many bird species live together in flocks or have crèches for their chicks. Sometimes different species congregate together in bird parties. The presence of numerous pairs of eyes and ears enhances the chances of detecting danger early on. In a group there is also less chance that a particular individual gets targeted and birds can also collectively mob threats.

The birds on this spread:
1 *Green wood-hoopoe in nest*
2 *Malachite kingfisher*
3 *African paradise flycatcher female at nest*
4 *Blacksmith lapwing*
5 *Spotted thick-knee*
6 *Sociable weaver nest*

6

Bird homes

Birds build nests in which to breed and shelter from the elements. The passerines are particularly reliant on nests to protect and insulate their under-developed offspring. Birds build and utilise a diversity of homes made from a variety of materials, including cup-nests, woven domes, large and small platforms, holes in trees or banks, stick or grass or mud structures and those built with cobweb, saliva, lichen and feathers. Some birds use no nest at all, laying eggs in a rudimentary scrape or directly onto the ground. No matter the kind of nest, they are normally all carefully located to reduce the chances of predation, whether built on a steep cliff, in a thorn tree, at the end of a branch stripped of leaves or to float on water.

Tunnels

Most kingfishers are tunnel nesters, as are bee-eaters and they excavate holes into riverbanks or other earthen verges. They use their bills to dig and then, supporting themselves on the bill and wings, they kick dirt backwards with their feet. Some tunnels penetrate 30–60 cm into a bank or nearly two metres in the case of the giant kingfisher. Usually the tunnel terminates in a small, unlined chamber where the eggs are laid. Some bank-tunnellers like carmine and white-fronted bee-eaters live in colonies due to the scarcity of suitable nesting sites and for communal vigilance.

White-fronted bee-eaters

African hoopoe

Natural cavities

Green wood-hoopoes make use of natural cavities in trees for both nesting and roosting at night. They are territorial about their roosting sites because appropriate holes with the required narrow entrance to exclude predators are hard to come by. Entering the nest in the evening is ritualised and some members of the flock create a decoy at a different site while the rest slip quietly and unnoticed into the actual cavity. If cavities are especially rare, birds may have to travel further from their nests to find food and flocks then tend to be larger, as young birds are less inclined to emigrate. Other birds that use natural tree cavities include African hoopoes, oxpeckers, starlings, hornbills and rollers.

Holes

Few birds are able to make their own holes in trees and must rely on those with sturdy bills to provide for their needs. Woodpeckers, barbets and tinkerbirds are adept at making holes and do so each new season, usually in dead wood. The entrance is usually sized to narrowly accommodate the adult birds and may be built on the underside of a branch for cover from rain and reduced access by predators. Barbets are monogamous and both sexes take turns to excavate the hole, which penetrates about 8–10 cm into the wood before taking a downward turn for 30 cm and then terminates in a cavity lined with woodchips where birds roost and eggs are brooded.

Bennett's woodpecker

Woven nests

Many birds weave a ball-shaped nest out of grass, twigs or bark strips with a side or bottom-placed entrance. Sparrows, cisticolas, sunbirds, queleas and weavers as well as more than 100 other species employ this method. Male weavers are the experts in the field since his construction determines whether a female will mate with him or not. Each species of weaver has a signature design. Once complete, the brightly dressed male flags down females with energetic displays. Females inspect nests to check the weave and freshness of material, and then begin lining the interiors to show their approval where after the birds mate. A nest repeatedly rejected by females will be destroyed and the male will begin anew. Some species of weaver nest in colonies over water for added predator avoidance.

Lesser masked-weaver

Stick constructions

Raptors, herons, storks and several other species make use of stick platforms, which may be lined with fresh leaves for insulation and comfort. Red-billed buffalo weavers make large, sturdy, long-lasting stick nests on the northwestern side of large trees, in which they live communally. Tunnels from the outside lead to individual chambers occupied by different females but each nest has just a single dominant male. If the male's display of fluttering his drooped wings results in a mating, a female will line her quarters, and produce and raise her brood on her own but with the benefit of shared vigilance from her neighbours.

Yellow-billed stork

Hamerkop

Stick castles

Sometimes one comes across enormous piles of sticks in the fork of large riverine tree, resembling flood debris. These are the gigantic constructions of the hamerkop and they contain a variety of materials, including sticks of up to 1.5 m long, can measure 2 m high by 1.5 m wide and weigh 25–20 kg once complete. The roof may support the weight of a grown man. The epic creation is a territorial beacon and reinforces the bond between the pair that cooperates to build it. An internal chamber is mud-lined for insulation and can simultaneously house both parents and the chicks. The mud-lined upward-facing tunnel leading to the centred entrance makes it inaccessible to predators but many other creatures do usurp the nest once the hamerkops are done with it (and sometimes while they are still using it) including barn owls, eagle owls, Egyptian geese, comb ducks, tree squirrels, genets, monitor lizards, snakes and bees.

Saucers and cups

Smaller bird species tend to make use of a simple cup-shaped nest to house their eggs. These they line with finer materials than those used to construct the nest. Usually these nests are built in inconspicuous settings and in the case of species like batises, may be camouflaged further with materials like lichen. Many birds make use of spider's web as a binding agent for their nests. The paradise flycatcher builds a tiny cup-shaped nest from pliable inner bark fibres and binds it together with spider's web and then also decorates it with lichen. The white-crested helmet-shrike plasters the outside of its cup with cobweb until it is smooth and also joins the nest to the branch. Doves make rudimentary stick saucers, allowing the nestling's excreta to accumulate and act as the gluing agent.

Penduline-tit nest

African paradise flycatcher

Purses

Crombecs and penduline-tits make bag-like nests or purses, also using spider's web in the weaving process. The crombec builds its seasonally reused nest at the end of a branch using grass, sticks and cobweb and decorating it with leaves. Penduline-tits create felt-like bag nests using soft fibres like bits of wild cotton or sheep's wool, which they knit together with cobweb. They also build false-entrances, which act as a deception to predators.

Floating nests

Some birds such as jacanas and the red-knobbed coot build floating nests from aquatic vegetation. These are usually not anchored, to prevent flooding. Eggs are covered with plant debris while adults are away from the nest.

Red-knobbed coot

White-throated swallow

Special considerations

Some birds have been particularly creative with their nesting strategies. The palm swift breeds in palm trees and because of its weak legs, uses sticky saliva to glue its feathery nest and eggs to the underside of the leaves, incubating by clinging to the leaf. Blue waxbills generally nest in thorn trees, not unlike other small species, but they also do so in the proximity of active wasp nests, which act as an additional deterrent to predators. Birds like plovers and coursers that nest directly on the ground produce incredibly **cryptic eggs** that blend in perfectly with the ground. Nightjars nest on the ground but produce white eggs instead concealing the eggs with their superbly camouflaged bodies. There are numerous species that don't build nests at all but rather take over other birds, nests, nest holes or even other holes or burrows in the ground, e.g. owls and ant-eating chats.

Mud nests

Swallows and martins are renowned for their ability to build with mud collected as pellets from beside waterholes, and inevitably construct the nests on flat surfaces around human habitation or on the undersides of bridges where they are isolated from predators. Mud hardens to provide a robust shelter and elaborate tunnels further eliminate unwanted disturbances. Inside, the nest is usually lined with softer material before the eggs are laid.

Fiery-necked nightjar

Raptors

Raptors are predatory birds that eat flesh that they tear off prey with their sharp, curved bills. They have sharp talons for capturing prey and strong feet with vice-like grip for holding and crushing it. Raptors have exceptional sight with which to hunt and a variety of energy-efficient flight patterns, i.e. riding thermals. True eagles have feathered legs that extend all the way down to the feet. All the eagles belonging to the genus Aquila are true eagles. But raptors come in different sizes, shapes and forms, from the enormous martial eagle to the tiny pygmy falcon. Many raptors practise siblicide, otherwise known as cainism. Adults typically lay two eggs staggered over time, so the first to hatch is larger and has outgrown its sibling by the time it hatches. The older chick pecks the younger one to death, eliminating competition for food or attention. The second egg appears to simply be insurance if the first does not hatch.

Snake-eagles

Snake-eagles are relatively common large raptors easily identified from their square heads and large yellow eyes. They have naked legs armed with tough scales for handling their serpentine prey. Poorly executed hunts can leave snake eagles at risk of becoming the prey if the venomous snakes they pursue turn on them. Generally, snakes are struck behind the head to crush head and spine with the talons and beak. Snake-eagles swallow their snake prey directly into their stomachs, not storing them in their crops first. Other prey may be stored in the crop like lizards, rodents, insects, birds or fish. Nestlings are fed snakes partially swallowed by the adults barring a bit of tail. The chick pulls out and swallows the snake, contorting its neck to accommodate its food. Snake-eagles are solitary and can be seen prominently perched at the top of a tree or soaring and aerial perching.

Brown snake-eagle

SS

Bateleur

These are striking black eagles with short tails and bright red bills and feet. The bateleur's Latin name describes it well, *Terathopius* meaning 'marvellous face', and *ecaudatus* meaning 'without a tail'. *Bateleur* is a French word that refers to a tightrope walker or acrobat – the eagle rocks in flight like these performers balance on a rope. The short tail reduces stabilisation in flight. Young birds learn the art of flying with a short tail by starting off with a slightly longer one. It takes seven years for a bateleur to fully mature and with each successive moult, the tail become shorter. The short tail helps them to fly low and to manoeuver themselves when hunting or fighting. It also reduces drag while they are covering vast distances foraging. Bateleurs scavenge or feed opportunistically, hunting just a third of their time. Bateleurs pair for life, defending a territory year round and diving at or attacking intruders. Courtship involves dramatic aerial acrobatics during which the male dives headlong at the female who rolls onto her back and shows him her talons. The bateleur is easy to identify in flight. It has tapering black and white wings and up-turned primaries. The black trailing edge is much broader in males than females. A grey window on the wing below the grey shoulder is visible on female birds when perched.

Martial eagle

The martial eagle is a large and powerful predator that hunts on the wing, soaring for many hours each day over distances of 100–1 000 km². Prey is spotted from 6 km away and using cover, the martial drops upon it stealthily. They also use ambush techniques, waiting in a leafy tree at a waterhole or near frequented game paths until an opportunity presents. They specialise on catching monitor lizards but martial eagles also hunt mammalian prey, which can be large, including hares, warthogs, smaller ungulates, primates, small carnivores, polecat, hyrax, pangolin and bats. They easily carry a few kilograms of weight back to a perch but can lift prey up to 8 kg, feeding on very large kills where they were made.

Wahlberg's eagle

A widespread small brown eagle with a long, square tail in flight and perched, that migrates to southern Africa in summer to breed. Typical of eagles, a pair constructs a platform of sticks below the canopy in a tall riverine tree and lines it with green material. The same nest may be used for up to 28 years successively but some pairs have a selection of about five nests in their territories. Pairs remain together over successive seasons too. Wahlberg's eagles are conspicuous, perching in evident places and soaring within their territory regularly. They also perform spectacular aerial cartwheeling displays and are very vocal. A brown and a pale morph also occur.

Tawny eagle

The tawny eagle is a common and widespread brown eagle present in southern Africa year round. It is larger than the Wahlberg's and different to other brown eagles because its gape only extends to the middle of the eye. Tawny eagles can be very variable in colour, from dark brown to pale beige. They are successful scavengers and pirate food from other raptors or ground hornbills, but they hunt efficiently and catch other birds in flight.

African harrier-hawk (Gymnogene)

This is an attractive and bold raptor that is slate grey with yellow facial skin and long yellow legs. The legs are modified at the tarsal joint to bend in all directions and they use this function to grasp at prey that lives in holes or crevices, such as birds and reptiles, and also readily dismantle birds' nests. The head is also small to fit into narrow spaces in pursuit of prey. Birds live in wooded areas and use various foraging methods, clambering on tree trunks, searching on the ground or soaring to locate prey. During courtship, the facial skin becomes red and pairs perform an aerial display in which the female turns on her back to touch talons with her mate.

Verreaux's eagle

This is a huge, jet-black eagle with a distinct white V on its back and a propensity for mountainous terrain. It specialises on rock hyraxes, which it hunts by surprise, often knocking them off the mountainside and picking the dead animal up below. They are usually spotted in pairs using thermals to glide along rock faces in search of their prey but they may also perch on covered ledges for hours at a time.

Secretary bird

Characterised by the plume of feathers that protrude past its head, this bird is tall with long legs, grey feathers and an orange face. Secretary birds are found in pairs or groups and stride intently through the bush at quite a steady pace, catching large grasshoppers, other insects, reptiles, young birds or eggs, and rodents in the grass. Although snakes only form a part of their diets, secretary birds are adept at trampling them with their strongly clawed feet, which is impressive to observe. They may also stamp their feet to flush out prey. Secretary birds do not fly readily, taking a run-up to take off and landing again with a short run, wings open. When they do fly, they fly high, using their broad wings to soar in the manner of vultures.

Pale chanting goshawk

An upright bird with grey feathers, barring on the belly and a bright orange beak and legs. The legs are long and the pale chanting goshawk is obvious where it perches atop trees for long periods. It gets its name from the repetitive, piping sound it makes, WIP-pi-pi-pi-pi-pip gaining volume and pitch towards the end of the phase. They live in arid savanna areas across the western half of southern Africa and are replaced in the east by the dark chanting goshawk. Pale chanting goshawks typically hunt lizards, insects and small birds and mammals, often from a perch but also on the ground where it follows honey badgers to catch fleeing rodents.

Steppe buzzard

Steppe buzzards have very variable plumage but as rule, this is a medium-sized, brown raptor that has streaking or barring on its underside and naked, yellow legs. It is a non-breeding migratory bird that visits southern Africa in summer to avoid the cold conditions in the northern hemisphere, some birds coming all the way from Russia. They occupy open habitats and primarily hunt insects from a perch, and are found alone or in groups where good food sources occur. Steppe buzzards are frequently spotted perching on telephone poles. A luckier sighting may include its impressive aerial dive-bomber display.

Pygmy falcon

The pygmy falcon does not even measure a full 20 cm and weighs under 70 g. It looks much like a shrike, has grey upper parts, is white below and the female has a chestnut-coloured patch on her back. The black tail with white spots is diagnostic. An orange ring encircles the eye and the cere and legs are also orange. Pygmy falcons are arid zone birds and make their living catching small lizards and large insects, roosting in sociable weaver nests. Although they may be found alone or in groups, birds that pair up tend to engage in much vocalising and displays involving head-bobbing and tail-wagging.

Owls

There are just a handful of bird species that are active at night. Owls and nightjars are the two major groups of nocturnal birds having taken the opportunity to exploit rodent and insect populations that are plentiful under the cover of darkness. These niches are occupied during the daytime by raptors and insectivorous bird species respectively. Being active at night means that nocturnal bird species have little use for coloured feathers and rather make use of cryptic colouration to remain undetected while resting during the day. Sight and hearing are finely honed and calls are usually adapted to carry over long distances to allow communication in a sightless realm.

The birds on this spread:
Main *African scops-owls*
1 *Pearl-spotted owlet*
2 *Spotted eagle-owl*
3 & 4 *White-faced owl*
5 *Barn owls*

An owl's eyes are its most obvious adaptation to life in the dark, being huge with widely dilating pupils. The eyes are designed to collect light and are therefore able to enhance vision in low-light conditions although no bird can see in absolute darkness. They are well supplied with light-sensitive rod cells and consequently are exquisitely movement sensitive. Owls' forward-facing eyes provide them with brilliant binocular vision, a result of 70 degrees overlap. The enormity of their eyes poses some challenges with both their mobility in the skull and the total field of vision being limited. To compensate, owls can flex their necks to turn their heads 270 degrees. An artery on either side of the neck prevents blood supply from being restricted while the neck twists. Owls also bob their heads to determine the relative positions of objects and gauge distance.

Owls have excellent hearing to complement their eyesight. They can hear the tiniest, ultrasonic sounds made by their prey. Asymmetrical positioning of the ears in some species accommodates for a slight difference in the reception of incoming sound, allowing them to isolate the direction accurately and consequently operate in even total darkness. Ears are located on the edges of the dish-like facial disc, which directs high-pitched sounds into the eardrums. Soft feathers around the ear openings ensure that incoming sound waves

are not interrupted. Barn owls have a movable flap that can even direct sounds coming from behind.

Some owls have ear tufts which are merely feathers on the top of the head that can be erected to look like ears but which have a camouflaging purpose, helping owls to blend in with their environment during the day. The tufts break up the shape of the animal – the African scops-owl is a specialist in this regard, looking more like a piece of bark than an owl while resting up. Nesting owls also employ their ear tufts to help conceal themselves and brood.

Owls have zygodactylous feet with two toes facing forwards and two facing backwards. This arrangement assists with clinging to awkward perches or prey. Owls can lift their feet up to their beaks, a useful trait when dismembering prey that cannot be swallowed whole. Bones and other indigestible matter can pose an obstruction in the digestive system and is therefore regurgitated as a mucous-covered pellet.

Not all owls are nocturnal, some are crepuscular becoming active in the early morning and late afternoon to avoid competing with other species. The pearl-spotted owlet is an example and as a result is less dependent on its hearing to detect prey.

This owlet also employs a startle display to deter its own predators – two eye-spots on the back of its head mimic real eyes and confuse predators with regards to where the bird is really looking. If a predator believes it has lost the element of surprise, it usually will not attack.

Owls are either hooters or screechers. The Strigidae family has huge yellow eyes, stout bills and no pectinate preening claw. The members of this group croak, whistle or hoot their calls, for example the eagle-owls. The Tytonidae family, which includes the grass and barn owls, are screechers. These owl species have long slim beaks, small, dark-coloured eyes and a pectinate claw. Owls vocalise to advertise territory or to communicate and many species do so as a duet.

Owls are nest-generalists and usually do not construct their own nests but simply take over suitable platforms made by other large species or, in the case of spotted eagle-owls, use the ground. Smaller owls move into natural tree cavities and lay white eggs in the dark where no egg-camouflage is necessary. Barn owls frequent human habitations. Owls typically lay two eggs and raise one chick but barn owls are unusually fecund, laying up to 20 eggs in a season depending on food availability, and accommodating various sized chicks within the same nest.

Nightjars

Built for aerodynamics, nightjars are often called 'swallows of the night' and are exquisitely adapted for their role. From the open terrain of roads or other exposed areas nightjars identify insects against the sky and hawk them on the wing before alighting once more. Nightjar species all have intricate cryptic colouration and as a result look very similar, barring slightly different white markings on the wings and tail. Each however, has a unique, night-piercing call, the most iconic of which is the fiery-necked nightjar's 'Good Lord, deliver us...'

Fiery-necked nightjar

Hawking insects on the wing requires a modified bill and nightjars have broad, squat bills with very wide gapes into which insects are almost sucked. Special modified sensory feathers on the face, called rictal bristles, help to channel food into the wide gape.

Nightjars have enormous eyes relative to the size of their heads and these allow large amounts of light to enter the eye in low-light conditions. Behind the retina is a layer of reflective cells which also enhances improved nocturnal vision, giving the eyes a red shine in the wash of a spotlight or headlight. During the day, nightjars close their tell-tale eyes to conceal them and prevent them from betraying the owner's otherwise well-disguised position.

Nightjars have a specially adapted comb-like pectinate claw – the middle claw of both its feet – for preening and scratching. This helps to rid the bird of parasites and to smooth out the vital rictal bristles.

Nightjars have stippled brown cryptic patterning that disguises their location during the day where they rest motionless. Nightjars even rely on their body camouflage to conceal its creamy white egg, unusual of a ground-nesting species. The eggs are laid on bare earth without the addition of any nesting material and are incubated by the female bird by day and the male by night. The adults keep their eyes closed to conceal the shiny eyeballs and the body is flattened to eliminate shadows.

Nightjars have flattened, narrow wings tapering at the tips to enable the rapid flight required of a wing-hunter. Flapping generates momentum and lift and their aerodynamic shape adapts them to migration, critical for when aerial-borne insect populations begin to diminish into winter.

Vultures

Vultures are ecological waste-removers, cleaning up carcasses and potential centres of disease. They are often perceived as undesirable and their use in traditional African medicine for their supposed powers of foresight has led to their demise. Four species are common in southern Africa and fulfil different roles. White-backed vultures are numerous, frantic, noisy feeders arriving with wings and neck outstretched and skipping from leg to leg, wings out, to dominate a kill. They may attempt to feed even while predators are still on a kill and they feed right inside the carcass, shearing meat from the bone with their strong bills. If a predator has not opened a carcass, the lappet-faced vulture is most adept at tearing the skin with its huge bill. It generally feeds on the intestines, tougher skin, tendons, hair and ligaments. The white-headed vulture is solitary, remaining one side and taking bits to feed on further away. It has a powerful bill to twist meat off bones. The hooded vulture eats the softer eyes or intestines. It also stays on the periphery, snapping up scraps and using its smaller bill to probe into crevices after the carcass has been abandoned. The endangered Cape vulture is also encountered in the region and fulfils a similar niche to the white-backed vulture.

Because vultures insert their entire head and neck into bloody carcasses, they lack feathers in these areas. Preening the head and neck is difficult for birds at the best of times so avoiding soiling is the healthier option. Vultures bathe regularly to rid themselves of dirt. The more social white-backed vultures may group together at favoured waterholes and spend an entire afternoon there, sunning themselves and preening. Their naked heads and necks pose a problem with insulation while in flight and to keep warm while circling high up where temperatures are chilly, they erect the ruff of feathers around the base of the neck that acts like a scarf. They also pull their necks into their bodies to prevent heat loss. On hot days, the exposed head and neck help to dissipate heat.

Cape vulture

Vultures circulate on thermals to effect low-energy flight facilitated by their enormous wingspans. By using pockets of heated, rising air to gain elevation, vultures omit the need to flap, saving more than three times the energy they would otherwise need. They use thermal flight to forage and cover vast areas this way, slipping from thermal to thermal. They can soar at altitudes up to 12 000 m, covering thousands of kilometres and gliding at 60–80 km/h. White-backed vultures forage in a grid formation so that birds can watch one another. If a bird breaks formation, the others follow – made easier by the obvious white back of the descending bird. Vultures also watch lower-flying scavenging raptors like the tawny and bateleur eagles and can dive on a meal at up to 120 km/h. At night and on overcast days, vultures find themselves grounded and to take off requires excessive amounts of energy.

Vultures have excellent eyesight and can spot even small kills from high altitudes. Their eyes are large relative to the size of the head, which provides them with more detail on the retina. The eyes have a fisheye lens to view the wider landscape as well as a lens to magnify objects. Strong, curved bills grow throughout life and are adapted to tearing tough flesh. Smaller bits of meat are pried off bones with the rough, serrated tongue.

Vultures spend much time on the ground and being heavy, need to run to take off. They thus have flat feet with claws less curved than eagles. When

White-backed vulture

they perch, they do so on solid posts devoid of entangling vegetation, like the dead branch of a leadwood tree. At night, vultures usually roost in the large trees that line river courses.

Vultures are long-lived species that breed slowly. They may breed in colonies or alone, either on cliffs or in trees. The white-backed vulture forms loose colonies, usually in large trees along a river. They build their nests at the top of tall, thorny trees, 15–25 m above ground. A robust platform of sticks is constructed to support both adults and chick and the same site is reused seasonally. Cape vultures breed socially on cliffs in colonies of between six and a hundred pairs. They build grassy nests on ledges with protective overhangs and nests may contain a few tufts of straw or be stick masterpieces. Cape vultures also reuse their breeding sites and cliff faces develop whitewashes from their droppings.

Vultures are scavengers and can fill their crops with over a kilogram of meat in mere minutes. The crop is a distensible 'sock' in front of the oesophagus that stores undigested food until the vulture can process it in peace. Vultures regurgitate putrid meat from their crops if they feel threatened, as this helps the bird to escape faster and is off-putting to a predator.

Cape vultures

White-backed vultures

Lappet-faced vultures

Ostrich

Ostriches are the largest and heaviest birds on the planet. They are flightless, lacking a keeled breastbone where flight muscles might attach. They also have soft, loose feathers that do not zip together. They can reach 2.5 m tall and a large male may weigh 150 kg. They are gregarious, flocking in groups for shared vigilance and separate flocks may keep their chicks in communal crèches for better safety in numbers. Ostriches are long-lived, surviving for 40 years. Males call with a deep lion-like booming sound.

The ostrich is the fastest running bird and might reach a speed of 70 km/h and cover 4–7 m per stride. They not only run quickly but can also sustain this gait for long distances. Their unique two-toed feet assist with running, their primary escape mode. Their sharp-toed feet are also on the delivery end of a powerful kick. In addition to kicking, an ostrich might jump and flail its strong wings frantically and aggressively.

The ostrich has excellent vision due to its huge eyeballs, the largest of all birds. A large degree of detail can be detected due to the broad area on the retina where an image falls. This sense is critical in detecting predators, including lions, hyenas and cheetah. Predators such as jackal, caracal and raptors catch ostrich chicks. To avoid detection, the chicks are cryptically coloured in mottled browns from hatching. Nonetheless, many do not escape predators as young birds.

Ostriches are communal breeders. The male has a group of females, including one major hen and several minor hens. A courting male has a red beak, forehead, neck and shins. He chases other males and dances to attract females. Males prance around females with their feathers lifted up and then drop to their knees waving their wings and corkscrewing their necks. The major hen and the male incubate the eggs. The major hen lays 8–10 eggs to which the minor hens add theirs until the two-metre wide nest contains up to 40 eggs. The adult birds can cover about 20 eggs. Many of the minor hens' eggs are shifted to the sides and sacrificed to keep the rest of the eggs safe as these may roll out the nest or be stolen by predators.

Ostriches lay huge white eggs, which the parent birds conceal with their bodies. The female bird is paler brown so she incubates by day, blending with the earth and lowering her neck or flattening her body if necessary. The black male incubates at night. Eggs are laid in rudimentary ground nests in exposed areas so the white colour protects unattended eggs from the heat. Ostrich eggs weigh 1.5% of the female's body mass and are the largest eggs in the world with the capacity of 24 chicken eggs. The shell is 2 mm thick and eggs weigh 800 g to 1.5 kg.

Ostrich chicks struggle to free themselves from their hard shells at hatching but this serves the vital process of drawing the yolk sac into their bodies on which chicks subsist for the first 24 hours of their lives. Thereafter, chicks eat whatever they can swallow, including stones which aid with mechanical digestion of food in the gizzard. The ostrich's diet includes succulent plants, grass, berries, seeds, insects and small reptiles.

Ostriches are adapted for life in arid areas. They obtain most of the moisture they need from the food they eat. Their long necks make drinking difficult so to conserve water they do not exhale moisture-saturated breath like most other creatures. The long trachea and wide nasal passages cool the air being breathed out, subsequently reducing the water vapour content. Ostriches gular-flutter on hot days, shivering the blood-rich gular skin at the rear of the mouth with beak ajar to create a cooling draft over the capillaries. This is less energy expensive than panting. Ostriches use their wings like umbrellas, lifting these slightly to allow air movement against their naked thighs. They also shade their chicks with their wings. When it is cold, ostriches use their loose feathers to insulate their bodies while lying down.

Helmeted guineafowl

Birds that have adapted to live on the ground share a few common traits. They are usually cryptically coloured, produce cryptically coloured eggs (mostly) in basic nests on the ground and have cryptically coloured chicks. These birds belong to the non-passerines and do not have feet adapted to perching but rather have large feet with widespread toes that help them to move and run around in their habitat. Species that don't perch at night lack the fourth, backward facing toe present in perching birds and reduced in ground birds that perch. The young are born precocial and ready to leave the nest as soon as their feathers dry.

Guineafowl do not fly readily, covering short distances if threatened or flying into trees to roost at night. They roost from sunset each evening coming down again at dawn whereupon they usually drink, lining up in a long row to walk to the water. Social activities and personal hygiene are the first priorities of the day. Males also use this time to chase one another, a ritual to maintain flock hierarchy. Guineafowl will repeat the morning programme before roosting again in the evening.

Guineafowl separate into pairs to breed and the pair nests alone. Male guineafowl chase around madly to gain a mate and then he defends her and performs the hunchback display, bringing her nuptial gifts of insects to fatten her up. The male birds hardly feed

during courtship and may lose 85% of their body mass. The females, however, increase theirs by 15% prior to laying. Guineafowl lay the thickest shelled eggs of any equivalent sized bird.

The basic nest is hidden on the ground. Large clutches of up to 20 eggs are laid but females may dump their eggs in another female's nest, increasing the brood up to 50 eggs. The eggs are pyriform so that they roll in a circle and not away. The female keeps the creamy eggs concealed with her body, lying still to avoid discovery. She does all the incubation during which time she does not feed so she needs to do so urgently when the chicks arrive. Consequently, the male cares for the chicks initially. Guineafowl chicks are known as keets. They hatch precocial and leave the nest soon after. The parent birds feed, keep them warm and defend the brood, even charging at offenders. By two weeks old, the keets can fly and family groups begin joining up again for safety in numbers.

Another guineafowl species also occurs in southern Africa, the **crested guineafowl**. This bird is blacker but also has fine spots and instead of the casque on the head, it has a crown of curly black feathers. The crested guineafowl prefers forested areas and dense woodland, foraging in the leaf litter or following troops of monkeys to peck at scraps of fruit they drop. Like the helmeted guineafowl, they also live in flocks, separating into pairs to breed during summer.

Helmeted guineafowl are comical yet attractive birds that typically move in noisy flocks of up to 40 birds and are hard to miss. Easily recognised by the bare casque or 'helmet' on the head, red wattles and flecked plumage, these are very successful birds and are common in most open habitats. Their diet includes bulbs, seeds and sedge stems as well as invertebrates when they are breeding. Occasionally flocks may aggregate in good feeding areas in their hundreds. It is hard to distinguish the sexes but male guineafowl are slightly larger and perform a humpback display.

Crested guineafowl

Francolin and spurfowl

Francolin (below left) and spurfowl (below right) are very similar in appearance and habit but are otherwise not thought to be very closely related. As a rule of thumb, francolins are smaller with yellow legs, a musical call and flush when disturbed from their open habitats. Spurfowl are larger with orange, red or black legs, raucous, harsh calls, they hide or run away when disturbed and roost in trees at night. The 'spurfowl' is named for the backwards-facing spurs on its heels, believed to be for competitive duelling between males. Groups of francolin and spurfowl are called coveys and males of some species are usually much larger than females.

Coqui francolin

Swainson's spurfowl

Francolin and spurfowl have broad diets including both plant and animal material. Food may include insects, molluscs, seeds, berries, shoots and bulbs, which they scratch around in leaf litter to find. Their droppings are large and smelly from the omnivorous diet. Many species prefer to forage under the cover of vegetation but are regularly seen feeding on grass seed along road verges. They frequently disassemble elephant and rhino dung to access seeds and insects. Their loud vocalisations and noisy foraging habits betray their presence, as do their breeding antics that involve chasing one another. Francolin and spurfowl nest in simple nests on the ground relying on their cryptic feathers to hide the eggs.

A covey usually consists of a breeding pair and their chicks. Young are precocial at birth and cryptically coloured so they can hide by lying still.

The young can fly within ten days so that they can roost in trees at night. Usually an alarm results in the covey flying up or scattering, accompanied by loud vocalisation. They do not fly far and hide in thick cover. The covey reunites after dispersing by contact calling to one another.

Orange-river francolin

Some common francolin and spurfowl species include:

Crested francolin: A small bantam-like francolin with white streaks on the head and a white stripe above the eye. It often cocks its tail. Crested francolins are common in bushveld areas and their rhythmical call is conspicuous. The pair duet with a repeated 'kee, kik, kerrik' so in tune it sounds like one bird.

Crested francolin

Coqui francolin: These are the smallest francolin in the bushveld but have a loud, diagnostic call announcing 'Co-qui...co-qui...co-qui'. They are quail-like, cryptically coloured and males have a mustard face with dark chestnut crown. They climb onto termite mounds or tree stumps to call and eat more fruit than other francolins or glean ticks off grass stalks.

Shelley's francolin: A species that occurs in the eastern parts of southern Africa and has an obvious white throat and thin black necklace. The lower breast feathers have bold black and white bands. It is a sedentary and relatively scarce species sensitive to the degradation of its grassland habitat; its presence in an area betrayed by

a repetitive 'go drink your beer... go drink your beer' call.

Shelley's francolin

The Shelley's francolin is replaced in the more arid western areas by the very similar **Orange-river francolin**.

The **red-winged francolin** resembles both these species but has a broad bill and resides in pristine highland grassland in the eastern half of South Africa.

Grey-winged francolin: An endemic species to the highland grasslands of South Africa and Lesotho. It is cryptically coloured with distinct grey freckling on the throat and no red on the wings. This species occurs in high numbers because it thrives in habitats modified by stock farming and is the only southern African species suitable for commercial wing shooting.

Natal spurfowl: These are plain coloured spurfowl with bright orange beaks and legs. They congregate at areas of good feeding but scatter readily if under threat. The Natal spurfowl has a very harsh call and

Natal spurfowl

vocalises noisily at dawn and dusk. A mewing contact call is uttered to reunite individuals. Males have formidable leg spurs.

Swainson's spurfowl: This is a large, dark brown spurfowl with bare red skin on the neck and face and black legs and upper bill. The call is a harsh 'krrraa, krrraa, krrraa' usually given by males at dawn and dusk from atop termite mounds. Unlike other spurfowl or francolin, Swainson's may feed on warm, moonlit nights. They are fond of foraging in agricultural lands for waste grain.

Swainson's spurfowl

Other red-faced and/or legged spurfowl include:

Red-billed spurfowl: has red legs and a red bill and is common in the drier, sandy parts of southwestern Africa.

Red-necked spurfowl: very similar to Swainson's but it has a completely red bill and occurs in high rainfall areas.

Cape spurfowl: has orange-red legs; lower bill is dark orange; no bare skin on the face; fynbos and karoo habitats.

Sandgrouse

Sandgrouse are arid habitat specialists and their appearance and lifestyles are fine-tuned to accommodate the drought, excessive summer heat and freezing night conditions. They have short legs, a small seed-eating bill and long, pointed, pigeon-like wings. The feathers are densely packed with thick under-down and their feet are reinforced with thickened skin and scales. To reduce the production of excessive body heat, sandgrouse metabolise at a lower rate than would be expected of a bird its size. They are gregarious birds and usually occur at high densities.

Sandgrouse have modified feathers on their bellies that are able to absorb water. Males will wade into the shallows, raise the feathers and soak their bellies when they drink. They then flatten the feathers to hold the water and fly back to their flightless chicks that suck the water directly off them. Males may fly 80 km between nest and water supply to provision the chicks. Sandgrouse usually drink just after dawn and aggregate in large flocks to do so. They are particular about where they drink, preferring waterholes not too susceptible to ambush by raptors and avoiding sites with brackish water. They draw water into their beaks and then lift the head to swallow. Double-banded sandgrouse visit waterholes at sundown, zigzagging through the trees to avoid detection until reaching the water's edge.

Sandgrouse are elaborately decorated in different dull colours including yellows, greens, browns, white and black, which render them cryptically camouflaged. Females have more streaking than males. The birds rely on their cryptic plumage to escape detection in the arid, open areas where they live. They spend much time on the ground and move effectively in spite of the short legs. They rest in open sandy habitats punctuated with sparse vegetation and they seem to go to great lengths to match the substrate on which they rest to their body colours. They nest in a scrape on bare ground and eggs are also cryptically coloured so remain hidden when the parents are away. Parents share incubation.

Burchell's sandgrouse

Burchell's sandgrouse

Namaqua sandgrouse

Sandgrouse are seedeaters and chicks eat hard seeds from hatching, the only birds in Africa to do so. Sandgrouse monopolise on the abundance of seeds produced by annual plants sporadically. Often these are no larger than the sand grains amongst which they fall. The seeds are rich in protein and an enlarged oesophagus means that the birds can store thousands of these in their crops. It is also possible that sandgrouse play an important ecological role in dispersing seeds in the desert. Sandgrouse are migratory or nomadic, moving in response to resource availability.

Namaqua sandgrouse

Burchell's sandgrouse

SS

Four species are encountered in southern Africa:

Namaqua sandgrouse: This species has long, pointed tail feathers and resides in the southwestern portion of southern Africa.

Burchell's or spotted sandgrouse: A Kalahari basin species especially in Botswana and northeastern Namibia. Recognised by its pink and yellow underparts spotted with white. Males have grey faces and throats with obvious yellow eye patches. Females have yellow faces.

Yellow-throated sandgrouse: The largest African species that uses short open grasslands near swamps or rivers. Occurs in Limpopo in South Africa and predominantly in northern Botswana spilling over to countries on either side.

Double-banded sandgrouse: A species that prefers woody habitats and rests by day, flying to water at dusk. Widespread across the savanna. Males have a black and white band across the breast and forehead from whence its name comes. Females are more cryptic.

SS SS SS

Korhaans and bustards

These are medium to large ground birds with robust bodies and long legs and neck. They live alone or in small groups in open terrain and are cryptically coloured above but usually have bold colours below, playing a role in displays.

Finally an urgent high-pitched series of 'pippity' notes results. To display, the male takes off from the ground and flies a diagonal projectory to just above the skyline. Here he stalls and drops, flashing his black underbelly as he commences the downward plunge. Just before connecting with the ground, he opens his wings and lands elegantly.

To impress his females, the **black-bellied bustard** produces a deep 'quark' sound from within his upright, distended neck that shows its black and white colours. He then suddenly withdraws his neck into the shoulders and then straightens it again while producing a 'pop' like the crack of a champagne bottle.

The **red-crested korhaan** is a polygynous species and attracts females using a vocal repertoire and an extravagant display. Hidden amongst his cryptic plumage is a red crest the feathers of which are erected in courtship. But first he must win the attentions of a mate. He begins by making throaty clicking sounds that progress into rhythmically whistled notes that increase in volume.

The **kori bustard** is the world's heaviest flying bird. These are large, gregarious birds that live in open and more arid areas, feeding on insects, small vertebrates and even rotting meat, and pairing up to breed. To do this, males gather in loose lek formations to perform for the females. They can inflate the oesophagus to four times its normal size and cock the tail-feathers to show the white feathers underneath while drooping the wings down to almost touch the ground. During direct courtship with a particular female, a male will bow to a female with his neck inflated, snapping his bill and making a booming sound. Copulation lasts just a few seconds before the male leaves to attract another female. The female lays cryptically coloured eggs directly on the ground and the male plays no role in incubating or raising chicks. The kori bustard can use its inflatable neck to startle predators too, making itself look more intimidating in this way.

Cranes

These are large, attractive birds with long necks and bills and known for their elaborate breeding displays. They are monogamous when breeding and territorial. Three species may be found in southern Africa, namely wattled, blue and grey-crowned cranes. Cranes are endangered by the fact that the grassland and wetland habitats they inhabit are constantly being transformed for other uses like agriculture, afforestation or development. Cranes are susceptible to poisoning and are often electrocuted on power lines. Nests and eggs may be destroyed inadvertently by agricultural activities.

Wattled crane

This large crane has a distinct white head and neck with wattles dangling from its chin and bright red around the bill. It lives, breeds and roosts in wetland areas and feeds in open grassland and in agricultural fields. Its range is very restricted and in southern Africa these birds are critically endangered. Wattled cranes breed in winter. They construct mounds from wetland vegetation and keep predators out by surrounding the mound with a moat. They call in unison with strangled bugles. Conservation efforts see crane minders dressing up as wattled crane parents in order to rear chicks without imprinting them. Second eggs are collected from wild birds and incubated artificially. The chick is taught to feed and fly before being released. Only one chick is typically reared by the parents in the wild.

Blue crane

A large bird with blue-grey plumage and elegant, long, curving tertials that look like tail feathers. The tail is black. Blue cranes may form flocks of hundreds of birds outside the breeding season. They feed on frogs, reptiles, insects, fish and grain or green shoots and roost in shallow water at night. Blue cranes soar well and may call while doing so. They make a distinctive, loud, guttural croak. They breed between October and February at which time birds pair up and share parental duties. The blue crane is South Africa's national bird.

Grey-crowned crane

An attractive crane with grey body, white wing patches and a spiky, blonde crest. The head is black with white cheeks and red wattles. It too lives in grasslands and wetlands and is gregarious when not breeding. They roost communally at night in trees. Grey-crowned cranes perform elaborate, dance-like displays, in pairs or communally. They eat frogs, reptiles, insects and grain. They breed in summer on a mound of reeds in a marsh and hidden by vegetation.

Hornbills

Hornbills are conspicuous birds both because of their enlarged bills and because of their comical mannerisms and vocal repertoires. The enormous bill is used for both specialised feeding and to resonate their unique calls. The enlarged portion on the upper mandible of the male hornbill's beak is known as a casque.

Hornbills (specifically the common species, namely yellow-billed, red-billed and grey) use their bills in the pursuit of insects, their primary prey. Dung beetles are a favourite. The beak proves a useful shovel for digging but objects can also be expertly manoeuvred in it. Because their prey is large and potentially hairy or flailsome, the long bill helps to keep prey away from the eyes. Hornbills have a broad diet, including lizards, nestling birds, bats, rodents and berries.

African grey hornbill

Red-billed hornbill

Hornbills form monogamous pairs and build their pair bond through elaborate and noisy courtship displays. Pairs typically feed together and the male lavishes the female with nuptial gifts to build up her reserves before nesting. The pair pauses frequently during activities to call and display. Red- and yellow-billed hornbills raise their wings above their backs, bowing down to each other and vocalising in an increasingly urgent manner. This is usually performed from a prominent perch atop a tree.

Yellow-billed hornbills

The common hornbill species have a remarkable nesting strategy. The female bird is sealed into a mud-lined natural cavity in a tree by the male that uses mud and excreta to close off the entrance excepting for a slit through which to feed her. She lines the nest with feathers, which she moults to free up space inside the nest. The male is solely responsible for provisioning the female and the chicks in the nest but once the youngsters are half grown the female breaks out, resealing the chicks in, and she helps the male to feed the chicks. Inside the nest, the chicks keep their tails erect to make space and to protect their feathers from damage. When the chicks fledge, they remain together for a time and the adults continue to feed them but after three weeks they become independent.

Hornbills nest in holes about 4 m above ground. The specifications dictate that the cavity must be 20 cm wide with the entrance about 10 cm above the main area. The entrance itself should be 2.5 cm tall. A chimney is required as a hiding place for the chicks should danger rear its head. Good nest sites are hard to find and hornbills reuse nest sites in successive seasons. To prevent the nest from becoming squalid, the chicks and female climb up and forcefully defecate out of the entrance.

Female hornbills use the opportunity of being safely sealed in the nest to moult their feathers, particularly flight and tail feathers. This serves the dual purpose of rejuvenating the female's feathers while she is incarcerated and making space in the confined cavity to accommodate eggs and chicks. When the female is ready to leave the nest, her new set of feathers have grown.

Yellow- and red-billed hornbills are often found around dwarf mongoose that live in small groups and forage by overturning stones or digging to find invertebrates. Prey that escapes or is in excess to what an individual mongoose can grab is quickly snapped up by the hornbill, which eats similar foods. Hornbills give the alarm to warn the mongoose of imminent danger while they feed. This relationship is so effective that the hornbills will even wait for dwarf mongoose outside their burrows in the mornings, calling to rouse them.

Ground hornbill

Ground hornbills are large, black, ground-dwelling birds with striking red wattles that live in family groups of between four and nine birds. A single dominant pair within the flock breeds, the alpha female being identified by a patch of blue on her red throat patch. At maturity, female birds leave their natal flocks and form a new flock with a group of males. The flock defends a territory of about 100 km², which is advertised with a booming hoo-call that travels over 4 km. Juveniles have drably coloured faces that turn red at about 3 years old.

Ground hornbills are an endangered species due to several reasons. They have very specialised breeding needs, requiring large cavities, 4–7 m above the ground and about 40 cm wide, in big trees like jackal berries and baobabs, which are often hard to come by and becoming scarcer due to wood harvesting and elephant destruction. Breeding is irregular probably due to rainfall and ground hornbills only mature at six years old. Flocks only successfully produce a chick once every six years and as a result, viable populations can only be sustained if birds survive for a minimum of 28 years. People feed ground hornbills inappropriate foods in game reserves and kill birds that peck at windows, which further compromises their survival.

When ready to breed, the female goes into the chosen cavity and lines it with material brought by the male and the helpers who also bring her food throughout the nesting period as she only leaves the nest to defecate once the eggs are laid. Incubation takes 40 days and one or two eggs are laid but the second chick usually dies as it is smaller than the first and easily outcompeted, often trampled by the adult and first chick and somewhat neglected by the adult. The second egg is really just produced as an insurance policy should the first not hatch. The nestling period may continue for more than 85 days. Chicks start to feed themselves at 6–12 months old and are supplementary fed by the flock for two years at which point they become helpers themselves.

With their long, sturdy, sharp bills ground hornbills are voracious predators specialising on tortoises that they are well able to break open with their bills, as well as killing venomous snakes. Hornbills scout through the veld to discover and overcome any manner of meaty creature, from chameleons and lizards to small mammals and birds or insects and snails. In the nest, the chick is force-fed large prey including tricky things like scorpions. It is believed that enzymes dribbled into the chick's beak from the mother assists with digestion and seems to prevent compaction occurring in the chick's stomach as a result of the force-feeding.

Ground hornbills are revered and thought of as 'wise spirits' in African culture. If a bird is harmed, one must sacrifice a calf to compensate. The ground hornbill is not spoken of in conversation for fear of retribution. Their distinct call is said to predict rain and in some countries their skulls and bills feature in hunters headdresses.

Kingfishers

Kingfishers are vibrantly coloured, active and noisy birds that are easily spotted. There are ten species in southern Africa varying from the minute 12 cm pygmy kingfisher to the large 45 cm giant kingfisher. In spite of their name, not all kingfishers are piscivores (about half the species) but rather eat insects, other invertebrates and vertebrates like lizards, frogs and even rodents. Whether kingfishers are piscivorous, e.g. malachite kingfisher, or insectivorous, e.g. pygmy kingfisher, influences whether they migrate or remain resident since fish are in relatively constant supply all year while insects diminish in winter.

Malachite kingfisher

Most kingfishers live in pairs. Males defend a territory and bond with a female using visual displays and nuptial gifting. Nuptial or courtship feeding is the process whereby males prove their ability to provide for their mate by bringing her food. In the process, the female builds up reserves needed for reproduction and brooding. Most conspicuous of the kingfishers' displays is that of the woodland's kingfisher that pivots open-winged on a branch alternately showing off the white and blue sides of his wings. The exhibit is accompanied by loud, characteristic 'chipp-whirrrrs'.

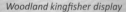

Woodland kingfisher display

Pied kingfisher display

Kingfishers usually live in well-wooded areas near water where insect prey is common. Kingfishers also have a stringent hygiene regimen. Many species nest in tunnels in earthen banks and allow their abodes to become fouled to deter predators. The malachite kingfisher's nest, for example, often has faeces leaking from the entrance. Adult birds typically engage in dip or plunge bathing as they emerge from their tunnels. To protect their feathers from the grime, chicks have spiky sheaths over them while in the nest. Striped and woodlands kingfishers do not nest in tunnels. They use cavities in trees such as disused woodpecker holes.

Striped kingfishers ▲   *Malachite kingfisher* ▼

Woodland kingfisher at nest

Kingfishers, like hornbills, have syndactyl feet meaning the second and third toes are fused together but the reason for this is not clear. While hornbills spend much time on the ground, kingfishers do not because they have weak perching legs and are consequently slow to become airborne if danger threatens. This is also why kingfishers bathe by plunging from a perch and do not allow themselves to become waterlogged while stationary.

Pied kingfishers

Piscivorous kingfishers are superbly adapted to catching fish. The long, sharp, sturdy beak facilitates fishing, allowing birds to grip their prey tweezer-like at the ends. Apart from the pied kingfisher that hovers, most dive from a perch. The pied kingfisher's eyes can correct for the refraction of the water so it can pinpoint the exact position of the fish being pursued. Other modifications such as a tough cornea and sac in front of the lens allow the eyes to remain open during the dive and further assist with clear vision. Prey is taken to a perch and beaten to immobilise and soften it for swallowing. This takes place headfirst so that the fins, scales and tail align with the bird's digestive tract. Kingfishers regurgitate pellets of indigestible material in the manner of owls.

Oxpeckers

Oxpeckers are noisy, conspicuous birds that live with medium to large mammalian herbivores eating parasites out of the pelage of their hosts. Southern Africa is home to two species, the yellow-billed and the more common red-billed oxpecker. The red-billed oxpecker has a narrower bill and manipulates the hair of its hosts with a scissor-like beak action. The yellow-billed oxpecker has a stouter bill and pecks to glean ticks. This species usually frequents larger mammals like giraffe, buffalo and hippo. Red-billed oxpeckers may also use smaller hosts, including warthog, impala and other antelope.

To assist oxpeckers in navigating around on their moving hosts, they have very sharp claws and feet that cling tightly to the animals' fur. Specially stiffened tail feathers help to prop the bird up and stabilise it while it feeds.

Blood loss to parasites constitutes the loss of vital energy necessary for the survival of a mammal species. For this reason herbivores tolerate the often-annoying activities of oxpeckers on their faces and coats. Oxpeckers do not remove all the ticks on an animal but they help to control infestations and prevent overspill into the environment from where secondary infestations can occur. In habitats with high tick loads, oxpeckers can be the difference between life and death if other circumstances have already created stress for the host species, e.g. competition or food availability.

The association between bird and mammal is a mutualistic symbiosis whereby both species gain advantage from the relationship. However, oxpeckers can also become almost parasitic when they irritate wounds and scars on their hosts or peck open lesions caused by skin parasites. The birds do this to drink small amounts of protein-rich blood but simultaneously aggravate wounds, making them susceptible to secondary infection and ultimately weakening the host animal.

Oxpeckers live in family groups of about five birds and employ a cooperative breeding strategy with just one pair breeding. Courting and mating takes place on a host animal. The dominant pair encircles one another, shivering their opened wings and holding beaks ajar. Oxpeckers nest in tree cavities lined with fur plucked from host animals once any cracks in the hole have been sealed with host dung. Oxpeckers make inspection flights to scout for appropriate nesting holes. Once approved by the entire flock, a fitting nest site may be used for consecutive years. The dominant pair incubates the eggs while the other birds, usually all relatives, help to feed the brood and remove eggshells or faecal sacs.

Oxpeckers offer an early warning system flying up noisily if disturbed. They make a loud hiss-rasp call to which their herbivore hosts quickly respond. Oxpeckers can also alert humans to the presence of a large herbivore. Not only do they fly up off the backs of their hosts if startled but also descend nosily onto their hosts, betraying the presence of a potentially dangerous rhino or buffalo. The oxpecker's dipping flight accompanied by the characteristic chip-chip-rasp call is distinctive.

Yellow-billed oxpecker

Red-billed oxpeckers

Woodpeckers

Woodpeckers have unique lifestyles and physiognomies amongst birds to peck or chisel living and dead wood in order to find food, excavate nest holes or to communicate with one another.

Cardinal woodpeckers ▼

SS

SS

Golden-tailed woodpecker

Golden-tailed woodpecker

Drilling is actuated by a long, powerful bill that grows continuously to compensate for considerable wear and tear. Despite the shock involved in using their heads to chisel into solid wood, woodpeckers do not suffer concussion. Modified frontal skull bones at the base of the bill absorb much of the shock and the brain is suspended in a jelly-like protective layer. The tongue muscle extends from behind the eye and over the bird's skull to the mouth cavity and may also play a role in cushioning the skull and brain against shock. Woodpeckers' neck muscles are very strong, driving the drilling strokes of the head and beak.

Woodpeckers have a zygodactylous foot structure – two toes face forward, two backwards – which secures them while they cling to tree trunks in various positions. Reinforced

shafts in the tail feathers or retrices assist with propping the bird up while it forages and clambers around.

Woodpeckers have exceptionally long tongues, measuring up to 15 cm in some species. The tongue is extendible outside the mouth and is sticky or barbed at the end to probe and extract insect larvae from under bark or inside cavities. The Bennett's woodpecker has very gluey saliva to assist with ingesting termites. Holes are often left behind on the branches where woodpeckers have been foraging.

The ground woodpecker feeds exclusively on the ground or among rocks.

Ground woodpecker

Each species of woodpecker has a call and some of these allow for individual recognition, useful in declaring territory. Some species, like the bearded woodpecker, also employ drumming. Drummers tap

out a fast-paced rhythm against a hollow log with good resonance and this sound is loud, more coordinated than normal pecking and travels over distance. Individual birds may even have diagnostic drumming signatures.

Many bird species nest in cavities in trees but few are able to drill out their own holes like woodpeckers do. Construction takes two to six weeks and is done as a pair. Dead trees are used most often and to deter predators, the round entrance is made just wide enough for the adults to enter and is usually excavated on the underside of a branch. Woodpeckers make new nests annually, surrendering the old ones to other hole-nesters like starlings and barbets.

Bennett's woodpecker

Cardinal woodpecker

Bearded woodpeckers

Sociable weavers

Sociable weavers construct the enormous grass-packed nests that drape thorn trees or even telephone poles in arid areas like the Kalahari. These are the largest nests in the world. Straw-like grass is gathered and knitted together in a complex structure that accommodates multiple chambers. These line the bottom portion of the nest to make them inaccessible to predators. The nests can weigh a ton and a single entity can provide homes for up to 300 birds. They are long lasting and provide shelter from the extreme elements of the desert, being well insulated against temperature fluctuations and remaining in a range of 15–31 °C, never less or more. The structures are typically positioned in as shaded positions as possible and the choice of host tree inevitably includes camel thorns, armed with defensive thorns, or shepherd's trees, both species excluding other plant growth below and offering natural firebreaks for the dry straw structures.

Sociable weavers are cooperative birds and young stay on with the colony after reaching maturity to assist with subsequent broods and communal life. Pairs will mutually help one another to brood and raise chicks and build or repair chambers simply because survival is enhanced in such harsh conditions when birds cooperate. Sociable weavers are able to minimise their food, water, energy and thermoregulatory requirements by living together in their super-insulated abodes. They are insect eaters.

Cape cobras climb into sociable weaver nests during summer and steal chicks and adults, potentially wiping out entire colonies at a single sitting. Honey badgers also raid weavers' nests, pulling them apart to access the birds. Genets and wild cats may also visit the colonies for food. Fortunately, sociable weavers breed with great success, laying eggs a mere six days after the rains arrive and, if good conditions prevail, they may produce up to four broods in a season.

Pygmy falcons monopolise on the sociable weavers' home modifications, making use of the nests to survive the freezing winter temperatures. It takes over a chamber in the colony, which is evident from the whitewash at its entrance. Pygmy falcons have been known to eat weaver chicks, but as a rule stick to lizards and insects and live peacefully with their hosts. Raptors and geese have been known to take up residence on top of the sturdy nests.

Sociable weavers have developed various strategies to manage the hot, desiccating conditions where they live. Their body temperature exceeds mammals' by 3°C, meaning that they experience less thermal stress provided the air temperature is lower than 40°C, as heat automatically flows out of the body. Birds perform wing-drooping to allow heat to dissipate by revealing the sparsely feathered skin under the wings to the breeze. If the air temperature exceeds that of the body, birds huddle together and fluff out their feathers to diminish heat gain. Gular fluttering can keep the body temperature below 42°C even if air temperatures reach up to 50°C.

Reptiles and frogs are not everyone's cup of tea but they too are intricately suited to their lifestyles in a myriad fascinating ways. Summertime pulses with life in the wild and much of the activity at this time of year is reptilian or amphibian in nature so it's enriching to be able to decipher some of the behavioural traits and adaptations exhibited by these perhaps more primitive but no less interesting creatures. The ectothermic nature of reptiles means temperature regulation is a high priority and many species are spotted during the important daily task of basking while with frogs, breeding is the most pressing activity as evidenced by the cacophony of calls once the rains begin. There are 500 species of reptile and 130 amphibians in southern Africa and as with any part of the ecosystem, they play a multitude of essential functions in the ecology and do so each in a unique fashion influenced by where they occur. In this section, the life histories of some of the most common species are unpacked.

REPTILES AND AMPHIBIANS

Nile crocodile

🔊 *Crocodylus niloticus*

The largest of southern African reptiles, the robust Nile crocodile is unmistakable and common in many water bodies. The Nile crocodile is the only species in southern Africa. Its body is covered in thick, horny plates as insulation for aquatic life, and the laterally flattened tail is a powerful propeller. The tail stores fats for times of dietary stress. Its sides expand to allow for breathing and for when females are gravid. Jaws are long with obvious teeth and the skin has sense organs believed to react to water pressure changes. Crocodiles spend many hours basking in the sun to warm up and take cover in the water by night. They are often observed lying on banks with their mouths open on both warm and cool days. Males are significantly larger than females. They are territorial and defend harems of about eight females.

Life under water requires a few specialised adaptations. The crocodile has gular flaps at the back of its mouth to allow it to swallow underwater and valved nostrils also prevent water in. They have four-chambered hearts and can control blood flow to accommodate pressure equalisation between the arteries and veins during long, deep dives as well as supplying just critical organs if necessary. They usually only submerge for minutes but can remain underwater for half an hour and if

inactive, up to 2 hours. Stones in their stomachs are believed to act as ballasts for diving and transparent nictitating membranes protect the eyes and enhance vision underwater.

Since crocodiles operate on land and in the water, they have limbs modified for this. Webbed hind feet assist with manoeuvring their bodies to launch well-timed attacks and clawed feet provide traction while walking and the ability to dig. Crocodiles are actually rather nimble when they need to be, walking with a high-legged gait on land and even managing short gallops of up to 13 km/h. A quick belly slide into the water is the usual response to disturbances.

Crocodiles are largely nocturnal and vertical pupils which expand or shrink to adjust to light conditions help them to see in the dark. They also have a tapetum lucidum, a reflective membrane reflecting light onto the retina for improved sight in low-light conditions. This shines in a spotlight.

Crocodiles are aquatic, living and hunting in water bodies. Eyes, ears and nostrils are all located atop the head so that the body remains concealed by the water during prey ambushes. They eat fish chiefly, which is swallowed whole after some softening jaw chomps. Crocodiles regulate catfish populations in many rivers and cooperate to herd fish in shallower water or drying pools. They also ambush any mammalian species that approach the water to drink, being indiscriminate in their choice of prey, and are capable of launching 2 m out of the water to seize animals using a sideways flick of the head. These are dragged into the water and drowned. Crocodiles also take terrapins, birds and carrion. Hatchlings take frogs and insects.

Crocodiles' teeth do not articulate against one another so they cannot bite well and the death roll is employed to free chunks of meat from carcasses, often with several crocodiles feeding simultaneously. Securing a grip on a piece of meat, the crocodile spins lengthways with force freeing its mouthful in the process. A few jaw crunches are then employed to soften the mouthful before it is swallowed with an upward tilt of the head. Teeth are replaced continuously and new teeth appear from below, forcing the older ones out. It is the crocodiles' teeth arrangement that partially separates them from alligators. Closed mouthed, alligators lack the fourth mandibular tooth projecting up on either side of the jaw.

Breeding begins in May and is rather lively. Males compete for dominance by bellowing, bubble-blowing and fighting; older and thus larger animals have the advantage over younger, smaller ones. In July, mating takes place in the water, lasting just a few minutes but is repeated over days and then females are gravid for two months at which time they dig holes in soft, dry riverbanks above the flood line to lay eggs. About 20–80 hard-shelled eggs are laid in a 40 cm deep hole, covered using the hind legs, and the female then guards the site from predators like baboons or leguaans.

High-pitched chirping alerts the mother that the eggs have hatched around December and she uncovers the hatchlings and helps them exit their shells by rolling the eggs between her tongue and palate. Hatchlings are carried in her mouth to the water and released. She guards them for another two weeks after this.

SS

The sex of crocodiles is influenced by the ambient temperature during incubation. Females develop at 26–30 °C and males at 31–34 °C. At hatching, baby crocodiles measure 30 cm and grow by the same amount each year to begin, reaching 1.2 m at 2 years. Growth then slows and 12–15 year-old crocodiles measure just 2–3 m and weigh about 90 kg. They continue growing throughout life, reaching a maximum of 6 m and possibly in excess of 1 000 kg. Typically crocodiles live about 60–80 years but rarely up to 100 years.

Lizards

Lizards are common reptiles closely related to snakes but with shorter, usually limbed bodies. There are different families within the lizards' taxonomical suborder (Sauria) which means a number of different kinds of lizards exist, including chameleons and monitors or plated lizards. As a guideline:

- **Lizards** *usually refer to the Old World lizards. These species have well-developed legs, claws and long tails and they have granular scales on their bodies.*
- **Geckos** *lack eyelids and instead are able to lick their eyes clean. They have fine scales on their skin and they can shed their delicate tails. They have specially adapted feet for climbing vertical rock faces.*
- **Skinks** *are medium-sized lizards that have strong legs and smooth shiny scales that overlap and are reinforced. This facilitates the burrowing lifestyles of some species. They have small heads without a noticeable neck.*
- **Agamas** *are squat lizards with triangular heads and typically have obvious ear discs. They have rough body coverings and cannot shed their tails.*

Common flat lizard

))) *Platysaurus intermedius*

This lizard is most conspicuous due to its vividly coloured males and because they live in colonies, usually in large numbers. Weathering rocks are the favoured habitat and they shelter under the pieces that flake off. There are eight subspecies and each varies in colour.

Bushveld lizard

))) *Heliobolus lugubris*

Adult bushveld lizards are cryptically coloured to match the sand, dashing from cover to catch small insects. Their young are dark with yellowish spots and move with a stiff-legged gait to mimic the 'oogpister' ground beetle known for squirting acid at predators. For this reason many predators, including birds and mongooses, avoid the baby lizards, mistaking them for the foul-tasting beetles.

Barking gecko

⏺ *Ptenopus* species

Barking geckos live on the ground and make extensive burrows in the sand. At sunset the males, identifiable from the distinctive yellow patch under the throat, begin to make their distinctive barking noises like two marbles knocking together. They call from the entrance to their burrows with just head and shoulders sticking out. They bark to ward off other males and attract females. The barking is most intense on warm summer evenings. Insect prey is ambushed from burrow entrances. Unusual for geckos, barking geckos can move their upper eyelids. Most other geckos clean their eyes with their tongues.

Bibron's giant gecko

⏺ *Pachydactylus bibronii*

A large (20 cm long), nocturnal gecko, which is purple-grey with obvious white spots and keeled tubercles on the head, body and tail. The large triangular head has powerful jaws and Bibron's gecko bites readily in self-defence. It also sheds its spiny tail. They form large aggregations among rocks or on walls near lights and are skilled climbers. It ambushes insects and smaller lizards with sudden lunges.

Moreau's tropical house gecko

⏺ *Hemidactylus mabouia*

Pale grey with darker banding and large eyes, this common gecko is often found around lights, attracted to the warmth and to the insects that gather there. Otherwise they are arboreal. Males are territorial and fight viciously. Geckos tolerate lower temperatures than other reptiles and many are nocturnal. Scansors on the toes are made up of rows of tiny hairs, and these in conjunction with kinetic energy between the layers of skin, give the feet traction on the smallest of defects on a surface, allowing geckos to scale vertical walls, overhangs and even glass surfaces. They have huge eyes to see at night and keep their eyes moistened by licking them. They can lose and regrow their tails several times to escape danger. New tails

are thicker and unpatterned. The gecko family is known for its ability to vocalise and the Moreau's tropical house gecko makes a tik-tik-tik sound. They produce hard-shelled eggs and eat old eggshells to boost their calcium intake, storing it in glands in the neck for future use.

Striped skink

🔊 *Trachylepis striata*

A very common reptile in the bush and city easily spotted darting across rocks between patches of sun and shade to thermoregulate. Skinks, like other reptiles, need to warm up sufficiently to have the necessary energy to catch insect prey with an active pursuit. Lithe, flexible bodies covered with overlapping scales facilitate life in rocky habitats. Spiny scales on the soles of its feet also help with grip on rock surfaces. Striped skinks can lose their tails to escape danger.

Tree agama

🔊 *Acanthocercus atricollis*

Found sunning on the trunks of trees, the tree agama is the largest southern African agama, reaching 40 cm in length. The blue-headed males are particularly conspicuous and males nod their heads to attract females. They are very territorial lizards and chase and fight off intruders. They cannot shed their tails, so when threatened they wind around and up the trunk of a tree, keeping the tree between themselves and the threat. If confronted, they open their mouths to startle predators with its bright inner lining and can inflict painful bites with two fang-like teeth. These squat-bodied, rough scaled, brightly coloured lizards are closely related to chameleons. The pineal organ on

the top of its head reacts to changes in day length associated with seasons and the tympanums are obvious on the sides of the head.

Giant plated lizard

🔊 *Matobosauris validus*

Only the monitor lizards are larger than giant plated lizards, which grow up to 70 cm long. They have square plate-like scales that abut one another rather than overlapping, a restrictive body covering compensated for by a fold along their sides made up of smaller scales. This expands to accommodate a fat belly after a good meal or the eggs of gravid females. Large size and comparatively short legs result in a common toboggan-like form of locomotion where plated lizards slide down slopes on their bellies to escape a threat rapidly. Juveniles are striking black with yellow spots and stripes. Males turn pinkish-purple on the chin, throat and sides of the head when breeding. These are omnivorous lizards eating fruit, leaves and flowers as well as insects and small vertebrates. They live in loose colonies on rocky ground taking to crevices

to escape danger. They may inflate their bodies to jam themselves in to avoid being pulled out. They are also able to shed and regenerate their tails. Like crocodiles, plated lizards store fat in their tails.

Monitor lizards

)) Family Varanidae

The monitor lizards are common and widespread reptiles and are the largest lizards in southern Africa. Two species occur: the rock (or white-throated) monitor (Varanus albigularus) and the water (or Nile) monitor (Varanus niloticus). These lizards use a variety of habitats, including the ground, water, trees and termitaria. They are long-lived species and grow slowly, and are active during the day. Male monitors are territorial, establishing dominance through wrestling with their robust bodies. Monitor skin and fat are desirable in traditional medicine markets and the meat is sometimes eaten. Skins were used for leather and led to the listing of monitors on CITES Appendix II.

The **rock monitor** is 80 cm long at full size with an equally long tail. It is dirty grey-brown with some cream blotching on the body and limbs, and a yellowish belly. Older animals are more uniformly drab. The tail is banded brown and cream. Juveniles have a black throat that turns white in adulthood. The rock monitor is less attractive than the water monitor and has a broad, bulbous snout, a well-developed neck and a pink or blue tongue. It often has bits of unshed skin clinging to its body and ticks attached to the soft skin of the face and legs. It spends much time on foraging patrols on the ground and regularly climbs trees or rocky outcrops, sheltering in rock or tree holes or inside termite mounds.

The **water monitor** reaches about 1 m long and its tail is longer than the body length. It has a more slender snout and more vivid colouration than the rock monitor. The body can be almost black with distinct yellow markings on the body and head, and yellow banding on the tail. Young water monitors are striking black and yellow in colour. The water monitor's tongue is dark. Its long tail propels the body while swimming in the manner of a crocodile. Although they live near water bodies, they forage widely and are adept diggers to unearth the eggs of other reptiles like crocodiles or terrapins. They spend time sunning themselves on rocks or climb into the boughs of trees overhanging water from where they can drop into the water if threatened.

Monitor lizards are formidable predators equipped with powerful laterally compressed tails, strong limbs and claws and flexible necks. They hunt any animal prey that they are able to overcome, from small mammals and birds, lizards, tortoises and snakes to snails, millipedes, crabs, mussels, frogs, fish, insects, eggs and even carrion. They have rapacious appetites, swallowing their prey whole or shredding it with their sharp claws. They employ their well-developed eyes and forked tongues to locate prey, the fork directing the animal to where the scent is strongest. The tongue retracts into a sheath on the palate where it makes contact with the organ of Jacobsen.

Powerful predators, including martial eagles, honey badgers, pythons and crocodiles, prey on monitors. Water monitors will escape into water if disturbed but both species have a suite of defences they employ to protect themselves when in danger. The strong tail is thrashed whip-like, and sharp limbs and claws can inflict wounds on a careless predator. Monitors bite readily and do not easily let go. If grabbed behind the head, they evacuate their cloacal contents as a deterrent and even play dead if necessary.

Monitors breed after rain has softened the earth to allow for digging. They nest in holes in river banks or sometimes make use of active termite mounds as egg incubators, laying 10–60 soft-shelled eggs inside the mound and allowing the termites to seal them in so that the temperature and humidity conditions remain constant. Furthermore, the eggs are relatively safe inside the concrete-like structures, which few animals can break open. Ten months later (sometimes even longer), the young monitors break out of the mound once the soil is again softened by rain.

SS

ME

Rock monitor

Water monitor

Flap-neck chameleon

🔊 *Chamaeleo dilepis*

The flap-neck chameleon is the most common and widespread chameleon in southern Africa. They are superbly adapted arboreal reptiles with long prehensile tails and fused opposable, clawed toes with which to grip onto branches. They have laterally compressed bodies covered in granular scales that can measure up to 15 cm; the tail, body and extended tongue are all similar lengths. The prominent occipital flap behind the head gives this species its name but is variable in size depending on the sex, age and geographic location of individuals. Green colouring provides the camouflage it needs for life in leafy trees and its slow, measured movements helps it avoid attention although it can move more rapidly if necessary. Males have a swelling at the tail base and small spurs on the back feet. Both sexes are territorial. In order to grow, chameleons like other reptiles, shed the outer layer of skin, known as sloughing, as the scales make it difficult for the body to expand. They survive in the wild for about 5 years.

Chameleons derive their name from their aggressive forms of display and self-defence – translated, chameleon means 'dwarf lion'. To appear intimidating to competitors and enemies they inflate their bodies, hiss menacingly and even thrust themselves towards a threat. The occipital flap can be lifted to appear larger and the lining of the mouth is brightly coloured and startling when opened. Head butting and biting may be employed during territorial disputes.

Shaped like miniature volcanic craters, the eyes protrude from the head and can be rotated independently. This allows them a collective vision field of 360 degrees except directly behind or below them. The brain switches between two images rapidly to interpret what the eyes are seeing. The eyes can be focused on a single spot simultaneously for binocular vision essential for hunting. Beetles, grasshopper, flies and butterflies make up their diet and are captured with the sticky, telescopic tongue usually via ambush or as a result of foraging patrols. A muscular contraction forces the tongue off the hyoid apparatus at the rear of the mouth where it collapses at rest, and the broad, moist, club-shaped tip strikes and retrieves prey at a speed of 20 km/h or about 25 body lengths per second.

The flap-neck chameleon is green with an orange throat and some white body markings but changes to shades of brown, yellow, black or to almost white. Special cells called melanophores are controlled by nerves and inundated with melanin to manipulate colour. Changes take place in response to temperature fluctuations or prevailing stresses. Chameleons make themselves darker to absorb heat on cold days, even darkening just the side exposed to sun, or when they are anxious. During aggression, they exhibit light and dark colours and when they are sleeping, turn pale yellow. In order to approach a female for mating, male flap-neck chameleons develop grey skin around the throat.

Their normal blotchy green cryptic colouration allows flap-neck chameleons to escape the attentions of predators amongst their arboreal habitats. They move slowly and in a jerking manner like a leaf in the breeze, climbing along flimsy twigs to evade predators. If vulnerable, they may just let go and drop to the ground. Nonetheless, myriad predators eat them, including ground hornbills, raptors and carnivorous birds, vervet monkeys, monitor lizards, spiders, predatory insects and arboreal snakes. Cuckoo hawks specialise on eating chameleons. Flap-neck chameleons are most vulnerable when moving across the ground to reach a new tree.

SS

Chameleons climb onto the ground to seek out mates or to locate nest sites in soft soil. Mating takes place in early to mid-summer and males will fight aggressively for access to mates. Copulation may last half an hour and egg-development and egg-laying is slow. Females are gravid for about 3 months and then lay 20–60 eggs in a hole dug in soft earth. The eggs are arranged in layers and each successive level is covered with soil. This can take the female 24 hours to complete before she fills in the remaining soil and pats her nest down. Eggs hatch after 10–12 months, sometimes more if conditions are unfavourable. The hatchlings dig out and perch on grass stems in small groups for a few days before dispersing from the vicinity of the nest.

Dwarf chameleons

Bradypodion species

SS

This is a group of small chameleons between 4.5 and 10 cm long, adorned with enlarged tubercles amongst their scales and varying designs of casque on their heads. There are 15 different species that are forest or fynbos dwelling and because of their restricted distribution, many species are threatened. While much of their basic biology is similar to flap-neck chameleons, their reproductive strategies differ. While flap-neck chameleons lay eggs in the soil, dwarf chameleons give birth to live young. The embryo comes out encased in a mucus sack from which the tiny chameleon emerges immediately. The mucus facilitates birth and then sticks to the branch where it is laid. Remarkably, after wiping their eyes, the 2 cm long youngsters move off to fend for themselves.

Namaqua chameleon

Chamaeleo namaquensis

SS

These are large, ground-dwelling chameleons that live in arid areas like the Namib desert and make earth-bound burrows. They are voracious predators and eat whatever they can find and overcome, including beetles and other reptiles, gorging in times of plenty to compensate for leaner times. They are diurnally active, even during the hottest times of the day and use their colour-altering abilities to regulate temperature, not being as shade-dependent as other species. Burrows are vacated in the mornings and the Namaqua chameleon changes to black to absorb sunshine, aligning its body broadside to the sun and flattening its sides to enlarge the heat-receptive surface in order to warm up. The same technique is used in reverse to cool down – the colour changes to pale grey to reflect heat and the body's long axis aligns with the sun, diminishing the exposed surface. They pant to cool down further and any water lost in this way is replaced with its food. They fight aggressively when they encounter one another.

African rock python

)) *Python natalensis*

This is the largest snake in southern Africa and is attractively marked. It has a large triangular head and tiny, smooth scales. It grows to about 5.5 m long and can get to 65 kg. Some specimens have tipped the scales at 100 kg and 9 m long. Pythons are long lived and can reach 30 years of age. Not strictly aquatic, pythons take to water readily to hunt, hide or thermoregulate. They spend time basking in the sun to warm up, especially after feeding. Pythons have vestigial thighbones, which are used as charms and medicinal ingredients in cultural rituals. The spinal column, skin and fat are used for a multitude of traditional magical–medicinal applications and pythons are threatened by overexploitation.

Pythons, like other snakes, have modified anatomies. They have very long backbones with more than 200 vertebrae and while the skeleton comprises of skull, spine and ribs, there are no limbs or hip bones. The backbone extends the full length of the body with hundreds of ribs joined to it. Long snakes could have 400 bones. They usually have just one lung, or in some cases, a much reduced second lung, and the liver and kidneys are elongated.

The heart is near the front of the body. Waterproof scales cover the body and protect it from

desiccating. They are tough, but stretching and bending. The scales grow from the snake's skin, hiding it but the skin is visible between the scales when it stretches after a substantial meal.

Pythons are ambush predators using darkness or camouflage to hunt. They prey on large species such as hyrax, small antelope, primates, large birds and reptiles, and kill, using constriction holding the quarry in the coils and squeezing tighter every time the prey exhales. In this way, the prey's chest is crushed, which prevents the heart from beating properly. The prey is then consumed and more than 50 kg can be taken at one sitting. Even antelope horns go down the hatchet. Long periods of starvation can be endured if food is limited, during which time pythons use stored reserves.

Swallowing is a specialised process in snakes and the jaw area is extremely elastic to accommodate large meals that must pass into the digestive canal. The lower jaw connects in the front with an elasticised ligament and jaws can also dislocate from the skull. The stomach and gut are stretchy to hold large meals and the mouthful is transferred here with the help of the teeth and peristaltic movements. The throat stretches to allow food to pass. When snakes swallow prey, the opening of the windpipe is pushed forward from the back of its mouth to allow breathing.

Pythons are large snakes and while they lack fangs and venom, the can defend themselves with bites using the jagged rows of teeth on both jaws. These inflict nasty wounds. Having fed, pythons are temporarily immobile and become vulnerable to attack. Wild dogs and hyenas frequently eat engorged pythons. Large snakes make a good meal for large carnivores like crocodiles, lions and leopards while smaller ones are eaten by raptors, hornbills, small carnivores, monitor lizards and a variety of other snakes. Eggs are taken by mongoose and monitor lizards.

Snakes and lizards have two penises called hemipenes used one at a time for copulation. These are inverted out of the tail base when needed for copulation. Pythons mate between June–September and several males will track a female's scent trail and attend to her simultaneously. Up to 100 (usually 30–60) orange-sized eggs are laid in summer. While they may be deposited in a cavity such as an aardvark hole, pythons do exhibit some parental care and the female may coil around her eggs during the 80-day incubation to warm and protect them. She warms herself in the sun to assist this process and does not feed during incubation. Once the eggs hatch, the young may remain with the female for 2 weeks being warmed in her coil by night and sunning with her by day, before shedding their skins and departing.

SS

Other common southern African snakes

Of the 173 snakes found in southern Africa, only about eleven per cent are dangerously venomous to humans. Below are some of the more common species.

Black mamba

))) *Dendroaspis polylepis*

This is a large, grey snake that reaches 2–3 m long, exceptionally 4.5 m. Young snakes grow 2 m in their first year. It gets its name from the black lining inside its mouth (see photo above), which it exposes when threatened while erecting a narrow hood. It is the largest venomous snake in Africa, administering a serious dose of neurotoxic venom with front-positioned fangs sharp as hypodermic needles. It actively hunts warm-blooded, live prey in trees and its venom quickly paralyses the quarry, arresting its breathing so it can be swallowed whole. Black mambas strike repeatedly until the venom takes effect. They have large venom glands and each bite can inject about 250 mg of venom although only 10–15 mg is needed to kill a human.

A black mamba's bite is a medical emergency and the venom affects the nerves, resulting in paralysis and respiratory failure. It is able to lift one-third of its length off the ground, which it does to make a speedy getaway or change direction throwing its body ahead of itself. They are shy snakes, preferring to retreat from threats even though they are territorial. They retreat into termite mounds or rock crevices.

Green mamba

))) *Dendroaspis angusticeps*

Large, slim snakes with large heads, brilliant green colouring and polished scales. They are agile, arboreal snakes that reach 2.5 m long and live in forested habitats. They are highly venomous with neurotoxic venom, although they are shy and seldom encountered. They hunt arboreal prey like birds, bats and chameleons.

Boomslang

Dispholidus typus

Translated, boomslang means 'tree snake' which describes where it lives and its cryptic colouration, which varies from dull bark-brown (females) to bright green or black and orange (males), and camouflages it in foliage. They may sway to better resemble branches moving in the breeze. They have enormous eyes with round pupils and excellent binocular vision to identify immobile prey. They hunt chameleons and birds actively during the daytime, chewing down with short back fangs to administer haemotoxic venom. An envenomated human requires monovalent anti-venom, as polyvalent used for most other venoms

is ineffective against haemotoxins. Symptoms may be latent for up to 24 hours but fortunately these snakes are shy and bites are very rare. The boomslang startles its own predators by inflating its neck to expose vividly coloured skin.

Brown house snake

Boaedon capensis

A common, non-venomous red-brown snake about 1 m long with two creamy stripes on either side of the obvious head. It is widespread using many habitats, including human habitations, and feeds on rodents offering useful control of these pests.

Common egg-eater (Rhombic egg-eater)

Dasypeltis scabra

A common, slender-built snake that measures 40–70 cm and has attractive grey chequerboard patterning. It uses multiple habitats and feeds on birds' eggs. The throat and gut are so elastic that the thin body stretches enough to swallow eggs whole and strong muscles in the throat force the food down into the stomach. Shells are ejected. It has no teeth but strikes and hisses in defence, and reveals a black mouth lining.

Puff adder

))) *Bitis arietans*

A master of camouflage, the puff adder is handsomely coloured and patterned to blend with its mottled ground habitat and effectively ambushes rodents and escapes from its own threats this way. It is easily trodden due to its crypsis and habit of lying on roads to warm up, and causes many snakebites in southern Africa. While sluggish to move, it strikes lightning fast and deep, painful bites result from the long, hinged fangs.

The cytotoxic venom causes cell damage and tissue necrosis. The name comes from the tendency to puff or hiss if disturbed at which point the snake rears up and is poised to attack. It uses rectilinear locomotion – lateral muscle contractions that cause it to inch directly forward worm-like, the underbelly scales gripping the ground and leaving a straight track in the sand through which the thinner tail drags. Young are born alive and covered in a fine membrane, after about 30 eggs have been carried inside the female to avoid predation and desiccation. Puff adders hold the world record for producing 156 young at one time. Newborns have fangs and venom.

SS

Peringuey's adder (Sidewinder)

))) *Bitis peringueyi*

A desert endemic and dune-dwelling snake, it is well known for its unique form of locomotion whereby only two parts of the body touch the ground at any one time as the snake throws itself sideways. In this way the snake minimises contact with hot surfaces and best negotiates the unstable dune sands. It is sandy coloured to blend in with the desert and typically buries itself leaving just the upward-facing eyes exposed. In this way they evade heat and predators, and can ambush prey luring it into striking range with their black tail-tips.

SS

Snouted cobra

》 *Naja annulifera*

A huge, thick bodied snake typically measuring 1.5–2 m but occasionally up to 2.4 m. It is yellowish in colour becoming blue-black in maturity and often banded with paler bands. This is a bushveld snake that frequents human habitations. It hunts at night for small vertebrates but can be seen sunning outside its daytime retreats, e.g. hollow logs, rocky habitats and termite mounds. It has strong, combined neuro- and cytotoxic venom, and like other cobras it rears and spreads a large hood to intimidate threats.

SS

Mozambique spitting cobra

》 *Naja mossambica*

Pink-grey to olive snake, which can exceed 1.6 m in length, with bands on the throat and notorious for spitting venom over two metres at its enemies. Forward placed, hollow fangs with grooved openings on the front surfaces accommodate the spitting of venom. Venom is cytotoxic. These cobras also bite readily, causing severe tissue damage that requires skin grafts to heal. A spitting cobra warns of its presence by rearing its head and fanning its hood, often in itself adequate to scare off threats.

SS

Rinkhals

》 *Hemachatus haemachatus*

A large snake reaching a maximum length of 1.5 m with a wide head and a stout body. It has a single or double pair of light throat bands visible when the snake rears up. It spreads a hood like the cobras. It lives in grassland habitats and retreats into rodent burrows or termite mounds. The venom is both neuro- and cytotoxic (mainly cytotoxic) and used for hunting mice, birds, toads, lizards and other snakes, and it spits venom in defence. It also plays dead to avoid the attentions of its own predators.

SS

Herald or red-lipped snake

》 *Crotaphopeltis hotamboeia*

A small (50–80 cm) olive green snake with white speckles and a glossy black head with bright red lips. It lives in open woodland habitats and hunts in marshes for frogs and toads at night. It is an aggressive snake, striking and biting readily but is harmless to humans.

SS

Spotted bush snake

Philothamnus semivariegatus

A slim and attractive snake that is green for its arboreal lifestyle with dark blotches. They are expert climbers and hunt in low plants for tree frogs, geckos and chameleons but are harmless to humans. Keeled belly scales give them traction against the bark of trees, they have good eyesight for hunting and they blend in well, swaying their heads and necks deceptively like branches while keeping the remainder of the body still.

Vine snake (Twig snake)

Thelotornis capensis

These skinny snakes with long tails and grey-brown bodies, resemble twigs or the branches of vines and use their cryptic colouration to blend into their arboreal habitats. The top of the head is green with darker markings and the twig snake inflates its neck intimidatingly when threatened. It uses slow movements to blend in and ambush prey, such as lizards, frogs and other snakes, which is swallowed while hanging down. It has large eyes and excellent stereoscopic vision to discern prey. No anti-venom exists for twig snake bites and a blood transfusion is the only option to replace the clotting agents destroyed by this haemotoxin, but even this may not treat cases of severe envenomation adequately.

Leopard tortoise

Stigmochelys pardalis

Leopard tortoises are the most common tortoise species in southern Africa and also the largest. Some individuals have tipped the scales at 0.7 m long and 40 kg heavy. More usually, adults measure about 40 cm and weigh about 10 kg. Leopard tortoises' shells vary considerably in colour, pattern and shape but overall are brown with dark specks on the scutes and sometimes even bolder spotting. The scute flecking gives it the resemblance of a leopard's coat, after which it is named. Between different geographic locations, populations' colours vary too. Leopard tortoises are diurnal and have well-developed eyes to help them see. They spend time sunning to warm up first thing in the morning and when it is cold do not emerge from their hiding places, possibly for weeks. They take shelter in holes or under vegetation and may dig a shallow scrape for comfort. The leopard tortoise is the only tortoise that can swim and utilises a home range in excess of 80 ha. Reports on lifespan vary but it is believed to be between 30–75 years old.

The rectangular shaped head terminates in a horny, beak-like upper lip, which is usually serrated but can be smoother. Equipped with an efficient feeding apparatus as well as an acute sense of smell, the leopard tortoise forages for vegetarian food items, varying from flowers and fallen fruits to grass, the young leaves of small annuals and succulent plants. The tortoise's skeleton imposes high calcium requirements on it. To supplement calcium in their diet, they regularly chew bones and consume hyena and other carnivore scat to extract the calcium excreted by these bone-devouring predators.

SS

The bursa sac is a water-storage organ that leopard tortoises use during droughts or to moisten soil for digging egg-laying pits. Tortoises may evacuate the liquid in the bursa sac if disturbed, urinating profusely too as a deterrent to carnivores. During times of water shortage, tortoises risk desiccation if threats require them to empty their bursa sacs.

Many predators eat tortoises. Larger leopards and hyenas crush the shell with their strong jaws and ground hornbills use their strong bills. Rock monitors consume juveniles. In many parts of Africa, tortoise meat is eaten by people as a delicacy. This practice and an unimpeded pet-trade have led to the endangerment of wild leopard tortoises.

By seven years old they weigh just 1 kg but body weight subsequently doubles every other year in favourable conditions.

Females are larger than males and have shorter tails. The male's plastron has a concave shape to facilitate mounting while females have flat plastrons. Tortoise sex is determined during incubation. The temperature differs at different levels within the subterranean nest – at 26–30 °C hatchlings develop into males while at 31–34 °C, hatchlings become females.

Scutes are the horny scales that cover the shell. Tortoises develop rings as they grow, indicating the age of the reptile. Scutes do get rubbed smooth and very old tortoises tend to be plain brown so ring aging is not especially accurate. Growth slows in winter or during dry times. Their strong legs are also armed with horny scales and feet are strongly clawed, five each on the front feet and four on the hind ones.

Leopard tortoises are slow growers reaching sexual maturity only after 10 years. Breeding is comical and lively. Males use shell butting to both convince females of their intentions and repel competitors, the latter being treated with more aggressive rams. They mate from September to April laying eggs between October and May. Females smell out nest sites, usually under loose sand and rotting vegetation, and dig a 25 cm deep pit with the hind feet after urinating to soften the soil. They deposit up to 18 hard-shelled eggs, 4.5 cm wide, into the hole and pat down soil on top of them. Incubation can take more than a year and hatchlings may have to wait for rain to soften the soil enough to allow their escape from underground. Juveniles are pale yellow with a big, dark spot on the scutes.

Other southern African tortoises

Geometric tortoise

)))) *Psammobates geometricus*

This species is endangered with few remaining in the wild. It lives in coastal renosterveld in the southwestern Cape. Measuring 12 cm, this tortoise has bright yellow and black radial markings on the scutes making eye-catching geometric patterns. The shell has a slightly upturned margin at the back and raised scutes. Females are larger and have smaller tails than males.

Kalahari serrated (or tent) tortoise

)))) *Psammobates oculifer*

This species is found in dry and desert habitats. It reaches just 12 cm in size and has an attractive browny-yellow shell decorated with brown and yellow stripes radiating out from the middle of each scute. The carapace is low, has a serrated, spiny trim and raised, pyramid-like scutes. It feeds on succulents and grass and burrows into loose earth below plants to escape detection. Just two eggs are laid.

Karoo tent tortoise

)))) *Psammobates tentorius*

Endemic to the dry regions of the Karoo, western and northern Cape and southern Namibia, this tortoise is dark coloured with a geometric pattern of orangey stripes on its carapace. They reach about 12 cm in size and the shell may be either domed or flat. It feeds on succulents and acquires moisture from its shell by lifting its hind legs and lapping water from condensation that flows out of the grooves in the shell and onto the front legs. It lays three eggs.

Speke's hingeback tortoise

)) *Kinixys spekii*

A bushveld tortoise found in the north of South Africa into Zimbabwe, it has a flexible hinge at the rear of its carapace to seal off the back of the shell and protect its posterior. It has a flat shell, which is plain brown, and a spine on the tip of its tail. It grows to about 18 cm. Speke's hingeback tortoise has an unusual diet, readily taking snails, beetles and millipedes as well as fungi and plants. It shelters in hollow logs or between rocks.

Angulate tortoise

)) *Chersina angulata*

This attractive tortoise with a zigzag pattern to the edge of the shell reaches about 25 cm long and around 1.5 kg. It is endemic to the Cape region of southern Africa but frequents various habitats, from fynbos and succulent karoo to semi-desert areas. It is unique for the unpaired protruding gular shield that is especially enlarged in males and used to ram and overturn rivals. This species may occur at high densities where they are found and are relatively generalist in their habits albeit somewhat fire sensitive. They may drink water through their nostrils.

Padlopers

)) *Homopus* species

These are of the smallest tortoises in southern Africa with some adults weighing a mere 70 g. **The speckled padloper** (*Homopus signatus*) is the smallest tortoise in the world. Padlopers (meaning road-walkers) have a flattish, rectangular carapace with scutes that are sunken in the middle. They are usually found in stony areas on ridges or plateaus, taking refuge in horizontal rock crevices. They navigate very successfully amongst rocks and up slopes. They feed on grasses, shrubs and herbs, get moisture from succulents and take insects from time to time.

◀)) Terrapins

Two kinds of side-necked terrapins occur in southern Africa, namely the marsh terrapin (Pelomedusa subrufa) and hinged terrapins (Pelusios species). These terrapins withdraw their heads into their shells but cannot retract them straight back like tortoises and rather the neck is turned to one side. Terrapins are aquatic and they have webbed hind feet to help them thrust through the water. They are strong swimmers but spend much time basking on the banks of water bodies, perched on rocks, logs and occasionally hippos' backs. They overstay dry periods by burrowing into mud and aestivating until the rains return. They are long-lived with marsh terrapins living 16 years and hinged terrapins up to 29 years.

The **marsh terrapin** has a wide, flat shell that cannot be closed off so one eye is visible on the sideways-retracted head. They reach up to 32 cm in length and 2.5 kg. They have large heads with big eyes and two large nostrils at the tip of the snout. These terrapins are adaptable and use a variety of ephemeral or permanent water bodies with slow-moving water.

Marsh terrapin ▲   Hinged terrapin ▼

Hinged terrapins have a hinge on the upper third portion of the plastron, which enables them to close off the front region of the shell once the neck and forelimbs are retracted. Five species occur, ranging from 700 g to 7 kg and 20–40 cm. The **serrated hinged terrapin** (*Pelusios sinuatus*) is the largest in this group. This species has a jagged edge to its shell. The carapace is more domed than in marsh terrapins and has an oval shape from above. The snout is rounder than marsh terrapins. Hinged terrapins frequent permanent and temporary waterholes.

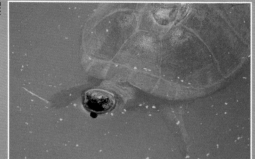

Terrapins are capable hunters and ambush predators and will consume almost anything they can overcome. The menu includes primarily aquatic species like insects, frogs, tadpoles, crabs, fish, mussels and snails but also includes worms, fruit and plant stems. They ambush doves that come to drink or grab ducklings from below the surface. They are partial to carrion, especially that provided by crocodile kills, and hinged terrapins nibble ticks off the rumps of animals that come to wallow!

Terrapins have musk glands on the underside of their shells, which produce a repellent secretion to deter predators. Terrapins also bite readily in defence. They are preyed on by crocodiles and monitor lizards raid their nests.

Terrapins breed in summer, especially after rains have softened the ground. Males court females by rubbing their chin tentacles on the backs of their heads, pouring water from their nostrils over their faces. They mate in the water with the male gripping to the female's shell with the claws of all four feet. Females lay between 10 and 50 soft-shelled eggs in holes excavated in sandbanks. The eggs take 2–3 months to hatch depending on temperatures. Hatchlings measure 3 cm and dig themselves out of the ground over several days.

The terms tortoise, terrapin and turtle are easily confused but denote separate types of Testudines:

Tortoises are terrestrial animals that eat a vegetarian diet. Their shells are domes and patterned and their feet have claws. The head is retracted directly back into the shell.

Turtles are aquatic, marine-dwelling animals that eat a carnivorous diet, mostly squid. Their shells are flattened and may be either patterned or unpatterned. They do not retract their heads into their shells and they have flippers.

Terrapins are also aquatic but they live in fresh water. They have omnivorous diets and webbed feet with claws, as they are more terrestrial than turtles. The shell is flat and unpatterned and they pull their heads into their shells sideways.

Frog breeding and design

There are about 130 species of frog in southern Africa ranging from 20 cm to 12 mm. While the diversity and life traits of each differ, the basics of frog biology and design remain the same. The central focus of the frog life cycle is breeding and the cacophony of calls after good rains is testament to the determined manner in which this takes place. Frogs typically breed in ephemeral pools and inundated grasslands as these lack permanent predators but they use a variety of water habitats. Frogs are amphibians and experience a two-phased life cycle: an aquatic, vegetarian tadpole and the terrestrial, carnivorous adult. They metamorphose from one into the other in response to hormones. Once fully frog, they moult their skins as they grow. Frogs are an essential part of aquatic ecosystems, controlling pest insects and providing food to secondary consumers such as snakes, birds, fish and small mammals. Frogs are often first to disappear if an ecosystem is under stress.

▼ *Mating red toads*

SS

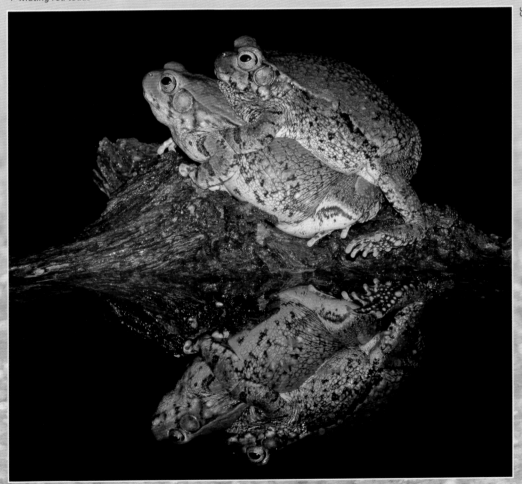

A frog's design suits it to its lifestyle. Eyes and nostrils are high on its head so it can see and breathe when submerged. Large eyes and pupils enhance night-time vision and while eyes are fixed in their sockets, frogs can bulge their eyeballs to see more. Because sound is a primary form of communication, frogs have good hearing and the tympanum, a flat disc-like, membranous eardrum lies directly over the middle ear. Frogs lack teeth and swallow their prey whole after using their long, sticky, front-attached tongues and a well-timed lunge to catch it. The eyeballs assist with swallowing. Well-developed hind limbs propel the frog when it jumps and the shorter forelimbs act as shock absorbers to land upon. The front limbs can manipulate food to a degree and are employed in amplexus.

Frogs are soft-skinned and exchange moisture and gases through their epidermis. Unfortunately this trait makes them especially susceptible to absorbing contaminants too. Frogs have mucous glands in their skin to keep them lubricated since the thin skin dries quickly once they climb out of the water, which impedes gaseous exchange. To conserve moisture, frogs usually remain inactive and shelter in cool, damp places during the day. The occasional swim is necessary to rehydrate. Oxygen intake occurs in the lungs and in the absence of a diaphragm, frogs rely on rapid movements of the mouth floor and the opening and closing of their nostrils.

Foam nest frog

Male olive toad calling

Frogs use a thin balloon of skin under the chin called a vocal sac to call. They create sound by moving a single breath back and forth between the lungs and the vocal sac, which causes the vocal chords to vibrate and the sound then resonates in the vocal sac. Frogs call to advertise to and attract females. Advertisement calls are unique to each species and help individuals space themselves out. Nearby frogs timeshare call, alternating

their vocalisations to help females locate a mate. Aggressive calls are reserved for intruders and are prevalent early on in an evening while males are establishing calling sites. They may even fight to displace each other. Females select mates based on their calling sites and pitch but some males freeload on the efforts of more superior individuals, exhibiting satellite behaviour whereby they remain silent and then intercept females as they approach prime males. Females issue a release call to indicate the end of mating and distress calls are sometimes given by frogs under duress to startle an attacker.

Frogs use an array of techniques to avoid predation. Most are cryptically coloured and rely on their camouflage to hide away. If detected, frogs may employ flash colours, usually bright reds in the folds of their legs, to confuse predators as they hop away. If possible, they may hop into the safety of water and swim away. Some frogs will inflate their bodies to seem more intimidating and others enhance this display with startling distress sounds. Some species go to the opposite extreme, feigning death. Some frogs have toxic or distasteful gland secretions that might cause a predator to reject it as food while others may simply eject water from the bladder when threatened. Only bullfrogs are able to bite in defence.

Reed frog

Rain frogs

Breviceps species

Rain frogs are slow moving, terrestrial frogs that burrow in leaf litter or sand, and breed independent of water bodies. They are odd-looking frogs with cryptically coloured, round bodies and short legs, and a grim-faced flat head almost indistinguishable from the fat body. Rain frogs are endemic to southern Africa and vary from 17–80 mm in size. Of the 14 species, half are forest dwellers but species also occupy deserts and other more arid habitats. Males have black throats. The rain frogs enjoy some creative common names such as the strawberry rain frog or Bilbo's rain frog, named after Tolkien's hobbit character.

Rain frogs are walkers and under duress, runners but they do not hop. Being slow moving has its disadvantages and they have developed some unique tactics to evade predators. Rain frogs inflate their rotund bodies when threatened to apparent popping point. This intimidates some of their predators like snakes, but apparently has no effect on bushpigs that really favour rain frogs. Monitor lizards are also fond predators. Their propensity to inflate earned the rain frog its Afrikaans name 'blaasop' meaning 'blow-up'. Rain frogs may ooze a poisonous milky substance to put predators off and also make distress calls, open-mouthed, in an attempt to intimidate predators. They may also burrow out of trouble.

Rain frogs live deep under humus or in earthen burrows, sheltering from predators and the elements. They are keenly adapted for this underground lifestyle having unwebbed toes and hard tubercles on their heels for digging, which they do backwards. Rain frogs subsist on slower moving insects such as woodlice and have modified eyes to assist in capturing prey. Their small faces support forward-facing eyes that afford the frog good binocular and close-up vision. The face is flat with a bottom positioned mouth.

WMC/BD

WMC

Cape rain frog

AL

Mountain rain frog

Rain frogs make a chirping call and can often be heard calling before the rains begin, probably in response to a change in atmospheric pressure. They usually call from the safety of their burrow entrances and one frog beginning to call elicits a domino effect from others. At a point in the evening, rain frogs abandon their posts and actively search out mates, calling while they move. Males even continue calling while settling disputes with one another using their vocal sacs as bolsters.

Rain frogs practise a unique form of mating called adhesion. This is to accommodate their clumsy rounded body shape and short limbs. To achieve amplexus, the female releases an adhesive substance from glands on her back and the male actually becomes glued to her for the duration of mating, including the burrowing process into the soil. She has to release a solvent once they have completed the process to release the male from his position.

Rain frogs occur in both summer and winter rainfall areas and breed during the rains, emerging from their burrows once the ground is soft enough for digging. The amplexing pair burrows into the softened earth about 40 cm down and lays 20–50 eggs in a chamber. The burrow is typically constructed under the shelter of a log or rock. The eggs have a dense jelly coating and are laid with additional sterile eggs, the jelly of which provides fluid for the developing tadpoles to squirm around in. The eggs are equipped with egg yolk, which sustains the tadpoles while they complete metamorphosis entirely in their subterranean home. An adult remains near the nest until the eggs have hatched.

Bushveld rain frog ▼

WMC/BD

Foam nest frog

🔊 *Chiromantis xerampelina*

Also known as the grey tree frog, the foam nest frog lives in trees but is also a common visitor to human habitations hiding up in the cool of a patio or bathroom to see out hot days. While they do move off to feed or breed at night, inevitably they are back in their chosen 'hide-out' the next morning. The foam nest frog is 50–85 mm long, has a horizontal pupil and rough, grey to brownish skin with faint mottles. It has long, slender, flexible limbs and a prominent pelvis that juts out. Its dry, wood-like appearance is described well by its genus name, xero *meaning dry and* ampelidae *meaning 'of the vine'.*

The tree frog is well adapted for life in trees. The long, supple legs make it a strong climber and the digits of the forelegs are paired and opposed to facilitate grip. They also have broad discs on the toe-tips, which help with grip, especially when the frog jumps. They are able to change the colour of their skin quite dramatically from white to charcoal-grey and adjust this as necessary for cryptic camouflage against the bark of trees. Foam nest frogs vocalise from the trees where they live or move onto long grass overhanging water to do so. They make soft, pretty albeit dissonant squeaks and croaks.

Foam nest frogs are super-equipped to endure dry environments. Their skin colour-changing abilities allow them to become completely white to reflect light during hot times. They hunch up and pull their legs in against the body to avoid evaporative

losses and quickly rehydrate when in contact with moisture through the granular skin. The granulations increase the surface area of the skin to maximise water absorption, especially on the belly and legs. In exceptional heat, foam nest frogs may intentionally excrete water droplets to cool down through evaporation. They economise on water retention by sitting still during the day, by coating themselves with a waxy glandular secretion and by excreting nitrogen in the form of concentrated uric acid.

Breeding takes on a unique expression with foam nest frogs. As their name suggests, they construct foam nests overhanging water into which they deposit their eggs. Males begin calling which attracts other males to a tree. As soon as a female arrives, the jostling begins. Foam nest frog breeding is more collaborative than in other species and while males are not aggressive towards one another, there is somewhat of a scramble to contribute to the breeding effort. The female engages in amplexus with one particular male and secretes a special fluid, which the pair whips up into foam with their highly webbed, disced hind feet. The relatively large eggs are then laid into the mass and all the males begin adding sperm. Some 1 200 eggs may be laid in a single foam nest and fertilised by multiple males. The female climbs down to rehydrate from time to time, amplexing with a new male on her return. Sometimes up to 20 females nest simultaneously, attended by 50-odd males, and the individual foam masses fuse. Females may visit their nests the following day to add more foam.

Frogs breed after good rains have fallen to make use of temporary water that typically lacks an established suite of predators. Foam nest frogs nest in trees or other vegetation overhanging a pool and in the absence of suitable plants will make use of rocks, culverts or bridges. The final meringue-like foam nest is generally melon-sized. A crust forms around the foam, hardening to insulate and protect the developing eggs from the elements and all but the wiliest predators such as birds, monkeys and the leaf-folding frogs that raid foam nests. It only takes 4–6 days before the tadpoles are ready to vacate their foamy premises and they squirm downwards and exit to the water below from the bottom of the nest where the crust becomes soft. The tadpoles are brown and oval-shaped with semi-transparent, grey-speckled fins. They measure 1 cm when they exit.

Reed frogs

 Hyperolius species

Reed frogs are a group of small, colourfully patterned frogs of which there are 16 species in southern Africa. The species name Hyperolius *refers to the smooth skin on the upper side of their bodies. Reed frogs live in warm, wet areas and move freely between the reeds or aquatic vegetation where they call at night, to hiding places in often more terrestrial vegetation during the day. Their webbed legs and digits with terminal discs suit them well to their habitats and reed frogs are accomplished climbers.*

Reed frogs make use of emergent vegetation around pans and other wet habitats to breed. The males return to the same calling site every night, which is defended aggressively from other males. They employ spacing calls in between their advertisement calls to alert other males that they are encroaching too close. Typically, a reed frog chorus is a deafening cacophony of high pitched whistles, chirps or bleats to which females respond by bounding through the aquatic vegetation tilting their heads to the side as they go to navigate to the attracting call. Reed frogs have large vocal sacs and they have to position themselves to accommodate for the inflation of their sacs. They also have protective discs on the front of the vocal sac, probably as reinforcement when they fight.

ME

Sometimes reed frogs can be found in exposed places during the day, probably due to an absence of more suitable hiding places. To avoid the problems associated with exposure, they hunch up their bodies and pull their legs in tightly underneath them to conserve moisture. Some species can bleach their bodies to appear almost white for camouflage and to thermoregulate. If threatened, reed frogs use flash colouration to confuse predators. The skin on the inner parts of the legs is red but exposed only when the frog hops. Predators tend to focus on the bright colour, which disappears as soon as the frog lands again, giving the frog time to conceal itself.

Painted reed frog

))) *Hyperolius marmoratus*

ME

)))

This is probably the most common reed frog occurring in the eastern regions of southern Africa. Despite being a mere 3 cm in size, it is unmistakable for its intricate patterns, likened to marble by its species name *marmoratus*. All reed frogs display variability in colour and morphology with, for example, sex and age classes differing, but this seems to be even more evident in painted reed frogs, display a number of geographical colour forms and subspecies.

221

Bullfrogs

)) *Pyxicephalus* species

Bullfrogs are the largest frogs in southern Africa. Pyxicephalus refers to the box-shaped head but the whole body has a boxy, heavyset appearance. Despite their size they are hard to find as they live underground in deep, sandy soils except during breeding, which takes place only after prolonged heavy rain. A pronounced tubercle on the hind heel is used to dig these large frogs into their 1 m-deep subterranean burrows, which are usually used successively over years. Bullfrogs can endure several years underground if conditions are dry by slowing their metabolism and they overcome desiccation by cocooning themselves in layers of cornified, shed skin from which just the nostrils protrude.

Bullfrogs have unique dentistry. There are serrations on the upper jaw and two tooth-like projections in the front of the lower jaw. These are put to several good uses. Bullfrogs only feed when they emerge above ground during the rains and thus do so voraciously. The teeth-like structures help them to hold large prey, which includes other frogs, small rodents, birds, lizards, snakes and insects. The teeth are also used to bite and pull opponents off females during mating, which they frequently wound and even kill in the process, as well as to defend tadpoles from intruders.

Bullfrogs are the only frogs where the males are larger than the females and this is because of their unique breeding strategy. After heavy downpours in November, bullfrogs emerge from their burrows and congregate in number in shallow pans. The males immediately establish territories and lunge open-jawed at one another to defend these. Females approach cautiously with just their eyes visible above the surface and the first male to spot a female will assume amplexus. Other males then bite and fling to dislodge him. An amplexing pair assumes an unusual stance facilitated by the shallow water in which they breed. The female stretches her legs out and the male plunges her head down and under water forcing her hindquarters above the surface. She deposits her eggs at this point so the male can fertilise them in the air thus enhancing the rate of fertilisation otherwise diluted by the water. After about 15 minutes and 4 000 eggs later, the female shakes her head to be released. Bullfrogs emerge to mate in the morning and are usually done by midday although activity can continue for several days and a second bout of mating may take place under suitable conditions in January and/or February.

Bullfrogs, specifically giant bullfrogs, have very specialised habitat requirements and breeding sites are typically widely separated. As a result of habitat loss mostly due to urbanisation, the giant bullfrog is documented as near threatened on the Red Data list. Bullfrogs use shallow pans filled by the rain that can accommodate their handstand-like breeding

▲ *Giant bullfrog*   *Giant bullfrogs mating* ▼

WMC/BD

Juvenile African bullfrogs

There are two species of bullfrog in southern Africa, the giant and the African bullfrog. The **giant bullfrog** (*Pyxicephalus adspersus*) can grow up to more than a kilogram heavy and over 240 mm long. The species name means 'scattered' and describes the white markings it has on its elevated skin ridges. The giant bullfrog lacks the facial markings of the **African bullfrog** (*Pyxicephalus edulis*) which is half the size of its giant cousin and whose species name means 'edible'. Bullfrogs are fried and eaten by rural people in Africa.

Bullfrogs have large chambered vocal sacs responsible for the deep toned calls they make. The giant bullfrog produces a deep, drawn-out, cattle-like 'wooop' while the African bullfrog vocalises more like a small barking dog, making brief 'whap-whap' calls. African bullfrogs call from the water with just their heads and vocal sacs jutting above the surface. If threatened, the giant bullfrog emits an open-mouthed cough.

method and that are temporary enough to omit most predators but long-lasting enough to support tadpole development. Bullfrogs will typically wait for 4–5 days of rain before emerging above the ground to allow optimum conditions to develop. After breeding is finished, males bury themselves within 100 m of the breeding site while females move about 1 km away and juveniles disperse even further.

Bullfrog development is remarkably rapid. The shallow water of the breeding site accommodates warming by the sun, which hastens hatching and metamorphosis. Eggs hatch within 36 hours and in 3–4 weeks froglets are fully metamorphosed. Swarms of black tadpoles form from the individual clumps and a territorial male stands guard to ensure their safety. These attending parents defend the tadpoles aggressively and ensure they do not become stranded, digging canals to ensure adequate water covers them. After all the effort, it seems unfortunate that the froglets subsequently cannibalise one another.

▲ *African bullfrog*

Giant bullfrog calling ▼

SS

Toads

🔊 *Amietophrynus* species

The difference between a frog and a toad is often queried. Basically 'toads' are a group of stocky frogs belonging to the Bufonid family that have especially granular, glandular skin covered in dark, evenly spaced shapes. Toads have large parotid glands behind the head and secrete a cardio-toxic bufotoxin in response to predators, some of which have learned to eat toads from below. They breed explosively (some species lay 25 000 eggs) and eggs form double-stranded strings, not clumps, which usually become wound around vegetation.

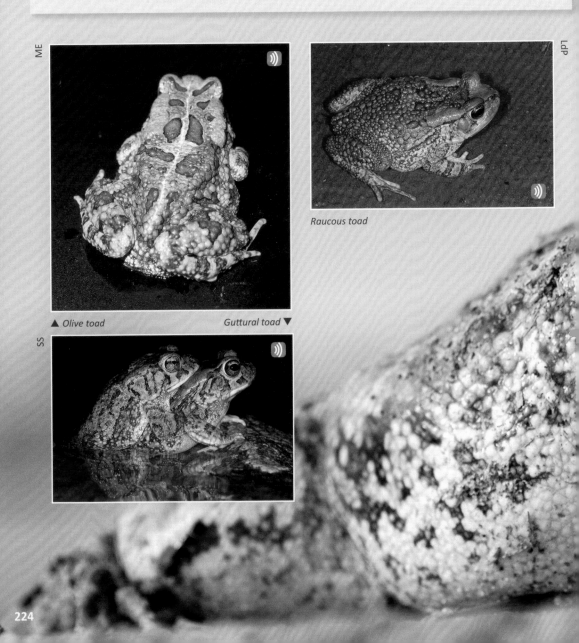

▲ Olive toad

Raucous toad

Guttural toad ▼

Toads are predominantly terrestrial amphibians breeding in water to which they will make long migrations, but otherwise they are more land-living. They are not strong swimmers or jumpers and they rely heavily on cryptic colouration to remain camouflaged. They exhibit flash colouration to confuse predators for which the inner linings of their legs are red. Toads are enthusiastic breeders arriving and vocalising at water long before females appear and then wrestling spiritedly, often a few at a time, to displace individuals that achieve amplexus.

Toads have counter-shaded eggs, the upper section being darker than the lower part. From above the water, the eggs blend in with the dark underwater environment and from below the water the eggs appear pale, blending with the light sky above.

Tadpoles hatch and develop quickly into frogs that reach maturity within 1–2 years and live for up to 40 years.

Similar looking toads can be told apart from the patches on the snout and head. For example, the patches on the head of the **guttural toad** (*Amietophrynus gutturalis*) create a pale cross while the **Eastern olive toad** (*Amietophrynus garmani*) lacks patches on its snout and those behind the eyes are not fused but present two separate patches. The **raucous toad** (*Sclerophrys capenis*) has dark marks on its eyelids, which fuse into a band between the eyes.

The guttural toad snores, the Eastern olive toad makes a quacked bray and the raucous toad quacks incessantly like a duck.

There are eight typical toad species in southern Africa but other groups of toads also occur, for example pygmy toads, forest toads and mountain toadlets. The **red toad** (*Schismaderma carens*) is the only member of its genus and is unmistakable with its entirely red back and lack of parotid glands and warts. It is common in savanna and woodland habitats and frequents human habitations.

WMC/BD

Red toad

Banded rubber frog

🔊 *Phrynomantis bifasciatus*

The banded rubber frog is a unique looking frog with its pear-shaped body and small head, striking colouration and long neck that accommodates a degree of sideways head movement. The rubber frog has two distinct orange-red lines that extend from its snout, over its eyes to the sides of the body, on either side of the spine. This characteristic gave rise to its specific name bifasciatus, *meaning two-banded. The banded rubber frog enjoys several other names, including red-banded frog, two-striped frog and South African snake-necked frog. The frog measures 50–65 mm in length (females are larger), it has a round pupil, red-spotted limbs and is grey spotted below. The marbled and spotted rubber frogs also occur in southern Africa.*

The conspicuous, rubbery black and red skin provides aposematic colouring that warns predators to avoid this frog. The skin secretes potent cardio-toxins that aside from killing other frogs confined near them can make humans ill too. Frogs do not envenomate prey or predators in the manner of reptiles but the poisons on their skin can be absorbed through the mouth, eyes and nose or via open wounds. Recorded side effects from handling banded rubber frogs include skin rashes, sore eyes, a tight chest and other respiratory difficulty, nausea and balance issues.

Banded rubber frogs live in a wide range of habitats from subtropical forests to hot, semi-arid environments, including bushveld and agricultural areas. They spend most of their time ground-bound but they can climb which they need to do to escape daytime detection. They hide in tree cavities or logs and can dig too. They have expanded fingertips and only slightly webbed feet, which facilitates digging. In spite of the lack of webbing, banded rubber frogs are accomplished swimmers.

Frogs are insectivorous but the banded rubber frog is unique in that it eats ants. Other species are typically deterred by the ants' formic acid defences but these do not seem to worry the banded rubber frog. They appear comical while they forage walking on their spindly legs rather than hopping. If threatened, they arch their bodies and inflate themselves rising on the red-spotted legs. This has the effect of alarming would-be predators.

Banded rubber frogs breed in temporary or permanent water bodies, calling from concealed positions along the banks of the pans or pools. They hide in vegetation or cavities, under stones or even in hoof-depressions. Banded rubber frogs make a pleasing 'prrrrrr' call, which is high pitched but harmonious. Each rolling purr lasts 2–3 seconds and occurs at five-second intervals.

A female banded rubber frog produces about 600 eggs after auxiliary amplexus. She deposits her eggs to entangle the eggs in submerged vegetation. When they hatch, the tadpoles are strikingly banded with broad fins and an acutely tipped tail. They cluster together in mid water in thick schools all facing the same direction and filter-feed on suspended algae. Banded rubber frogs can live for ten years.

WMC/BD

Platannas

)) *Xenopus* species

Platannas are primitive-looking, grey frogs quite obviously fatter towards the hind part of the body with enormous hind limbs and clawed feet, and reduced forelimbs. They are essentially aquatic and remain in the water fulltime, unlike other frogs that enjoy both terrestrial and aquatic habitats. The 1930s saw the discovery of this frog as a rudimentary pregnancy test when two South African scientists discovered that injecting urine from pregnant women under the skin caused the platanna to spawn.

Platannas are specialised for their permanent aquatic habits. Because they feed underwater, they have no tongues but rather use their small, unwebbed hands to guide food into the mouth, shredding larger items with the clawed hind feet. They both hunt and scavenge. Platannas are propelled through the water by enormous, muscular hind legs that also boast huge webbed feet. Sensory organs line the sides of the body and function like the lateral line of a fish to detect vibrations and movement underwater essential for hunting. The tympanum and movable eyelids serve no purpose to underwater frogs and so the platanna lacks these. They also lack vocal chords and sacs as they produce their clicked calls underwater. Modified larynx cartilage is rubbed together to produce sound.

Platannas are coated in slippery mucus which makes them difficult to grasp and waterbirds generally beat platanna prey to remove the coating before eating them as it is poisonous. Hamerkops specialise on eating platannas. Presumably, the eyes atop the head and looking upwards assist these frogs with watching out for danger. They retreat to deeper water during the day to escape the attention of predators but they do need to surface to breathe, which they do rapidly, and with gulps.

Platannas practise inguinal amplexus due to the fact that they have such reduced forelimbs. The male grips the female in front of the hind limbs rather than behind the front limbs as in most frogs. Males develop dense bumps on the hands and inner forearms to assist with gripping the slippery female. The tadpoles are free-swimming and filter-feed on plankton. They have flat heads with sensory feelers around the mouth. They typically position themselves with their heads down and pulse the tail to remain in place.

WMC/BG

Common platanna

There are four species of platanna in southern Africa, the **common platanna** (*Xenopus laevis*) being most widespread. They vary in length from 4–10 cm and the Cape species is both endemic and critically endangered. The **Cape platanna** (*Xenopus gilli*) relies on natural wetlands in which to breed, surviving drier times by burrowing into damp earth, but with increased urbanisation and drainage, habitat is quickly being lost. The common platanna migrates overland readily and is also more generalist in its choice of habitats, even using anthropogenic water bodies. The **tropical platanna** (*Xenopus muelleri*) has attractive orange webbing between its toes and on the underside of its legs as well as a noticeable tentacle under its small eyes.

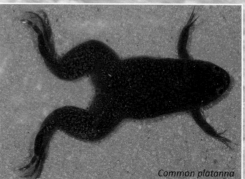

LdP

Common platanna

Other common frogs

Apart from the frogs dealt with in greater detail, there are several common groups of frog in southern Africa. A few common examples are provided for each group.

Ghost frogs

There are six ghost frogs in southern Africa and all are endemic to the Western and Eastern Cape. They live in fast-flowing streams and are strong swimmers. Their flat bodies allow them to escape into crevices. T-shaped adhesive pads give them excellent grip. Ghost frogs have large, asymmetrical markings. The Table Mountain ghost frog is critically endangered as it occurs only in one location, the ghostly Skeleton Gorge.

Cape ghost frog

》 *Heleophryne purcelli*

This species is most common of the ghost frogs, living in streams amidst mountain fynbos and forest. It is 50 mm long, has red patches above with banded legs and is orange on the underside. It makes a single high-pitch ringing note every second.

DH

Shovel-nosed frogs

Three of nine species of shovel-nosed frog are found in southern Africa. These frogs live under the ground and are recognised by their rounded bodies and hard, pointed snouts.

Mottled shovel-nosed frog

》 *Hemisus marmoratus*

WMC/RVH

This frog has a swollen body with a small head and pointed nose. It is mottled grey-brown and yellow above and pink-white below with a yellow chin. It spends its life underground in muddy places near water, and uses the hardened point of its snout to burrow headfirst. The pointed head with its receding jawline and small eyes are modified for a life of burrowing. Eggs are laid underground in a damp compartment and the female couriers the tadpoles on her back to water once they have hatched, after first digging a nearby channel to the water body. Mottled shovel-nosed frogs make an insect-like buzzing call.

Ornate and sand frogs

These frogs have bodies that are square in shape, heavy-set and shorter than their legs. They have a hard ridge on their heels.

Ornate frog

Hildebrandtia ornata

This is an appealing frog decorated in a symmetrical pattern of variable brown patches with banded brown, black or green legs and a prominent green stripe down the back. It has paired vocal sacs used to produce a raucous call during the breeding season once it emerges from the deep sands where it hibernates.

WMC/BD

ME

Tremelo sand frog

Tomopterna crytotus

This is a common sand frog occurring in a variety of habitats. Its body is squat, warty and toad-like with mottled patterns that easily blend in with the environment and there is a pale patch between the shoulders and a stripe all the way down its back from the snout. A granular ridge runs behind the jaw. It has round tubercles on its hands to assist in its burrowing lifestyle.

Tree and leaf-folding frogs

There are five dwarf leaf-folding frog species in southern Africa but although they look similar, they live in different places and make different calls. These little frogs reach a size of 2 cm and live in shallow, grassy pans. They are yellow with dark flanks and the male has a yellow throat patch. Sometimes dwarf leaf-folding frogs have brown stripes or tiny, raised spots.

Brown-backed tree frog

Leptopelis mossambicus

This arboreal frog is brown with a dark 'horseshoe' on its back. It has well-developed discs on the fingers and toes that are very adhesive to facilitate jumping around in vegetation. It calls with a trademark quack-quack vocalisation supplemented with a buzz.

NS

Stream, river and grass frogs

While these groups of frog each belong to their own genus, they are all typically streamlined, smooth-skinned frogs with pointy faces and long legs which effect excellent jumping and swimming ability.

Plain grass frog

)) *Ptychadena anchietae*

This frog lives in flooded grassy areas. It has a sharp snout, long legs, plain pink back and large tympanum behind the eye. The eyes have broken black marks running over them and down the sides of the frog. This is a secretive frog and an adept jumper, which is useful for escaping predators and ambushing prey. The photograph shows it with lateral sacs inflated. Grass frogs are fairly inactive most of the time, waiting for insect prey to pass by whereupon they ambush it. They use their good camouflage to avoid detection and are often only noticed if approached too closely, as they shoot explosively into adjacent water or grass clumps.

Common river frog

Amietia delalandii))

This frog occurs in permanent streams. Typically, it is pale green with dark spots and has a streamlined body with a pointed snout, very long legs and long webbed toes. It calls while partially submerged and escapes into the water if bothered. Males call during the daytime and at night, making rattle-like clicks.

Clicking stream frog

)) *Strongylopus grayii*

A sleek, long-toed frog with a diverse habitat tolerance. They remain active throughout the year and males can be heard calling all day and night from a concealed position near water with a monotonous tapping call. The male has a golden colour on his lower jaw and the usual brown colouring with a scattering of dark patterns, sometimes including a reddish stripe along the spine.

Cacos, puddle and micro frogs

These are small (3.5 cm or less) smooth-bellied frogs bearing white skin with dark marks on their undersides. They lack hard ridges on the hind feet. The micro frog is highly endangered. Cacos are multi-coloured frogs and in fact quite numerous but their tiny size easily conceals their presence.

Snoring puddle frog

Phrynobatrachus natalensis

This squat frog is warty with mottled patches on the body and occasionally a stripe down its back. Its appearance can vary quite a bit. It makes a snoring call early on in the evening. They occur along the edges of both temporary and permanent water but breed in open water.

Common caco

Cacosternum boettgeri

Common cacos measure just 2–2.5 cm and are assorted in colour and pattern. They occur in inundated grassland surrounding temporary pans and produce an insect-like sound that can be ear-piercing at close range.

Kassinas

Kassinas are bullet-shaped frogs with rounded snouts that prefer wetter regions. Of 16 species, two species occur in southern Africa where they breed in both temporary and permanent water. These frogs are not typical hoppers and rather employ a walking-running gait.

Bubbling kassina

Kassina senegalensis

This frog makes the sound of a popping bubble, a high-pitched liquid call that gives it its name. Males call from concealed locations and one call elicits a chain reaction of others. They are ventriloquists. Bubbling kassinas use a variety of habitats and shelter by day in burrows left by other animals, walking down to the water's edge to join the vigorous chorus at sundown. They have dark stripes on their bullet-shaped bodies and dark marks on their vocal sacs to help camouflage them while calling.

Like birds, insects are a group of creatures with the gift of flight at their disposal, a trait which allows them to colonise a diversity of habitats and renders them extremely successful, something to which their ability to breed rapidly as well as an assortment of mouthpart designs contributes. Insects are both food and feeders and as such form a vital role in any ecosystem, providing the life-supporting services of pollination, waste-control and nutrient recycling while they enact their own lifestyles, also spreading and regulating disease. This is the most abundant group of animals on the planet and in southern Africa alone 80 000 species proliferate, so a visit to any natural environment is likely to produce a variety of insects to observe. Also, like birds, these present in a myriad shapes, colours and designs and have a diversity of intriguing survival strategies at their disposal. Other invertebrates, including spiders, scorpions, ticks and mites are abundant in the natural environments of southern Africa too. This chapter addresses the life histories and survival techniques employed by the commonest of the 'creepy crawlies' that travellers are likely to encounter.

INSECTS, ARACHNIDS AND OTHER INVERTEBRATES

Dung beetles

🔊 Subfamily Scarabaeinae

Dung beetles are an essential part of the ecosystem performing the critical role of waste removal and disease control. In the process of consuming animal dung and burying reserves for themselves and their larvae, dung beetles are responsible for reducing the amount of excrement available to pests like flies for breeding, eliminating the eggs of internal parasites, burying seeds and recycling nutrients into the soil. Their ability to shift many times their own weight in dung in each breeding effort, results in many metric tons of waste being buried annually. Many thousands of beetles may colonise a single pile of dung, which is detected and occupied within minutes and disposed of within hours. Southern Africa boasts a little over 10 per cent of the 7 000 species found worldwide, varying in sizes from a few millimetres to almost 5 cm.

Dung beetles are scarabs and members of this group all carry antennae that end in a fan of several joints that are able to fold over one another. They are robust beetles with stout front legs equipped with strong teeth that are used to scoop and rake dung together into balls or to break compacted droppings open. The flattened head is also used for digging and raking dung and patting it into a ball. While most are black or brown, a diversity of colours, including pretty metallic coatings, are to be found.

Different dung beetle species use different kinds of dung. Some species specialise on the rougher material in elephant and rhino dung while others prefer the finer material in buffalo, zebra or antelope dung. Most dung beetles prefer herbivore dung over carnivore scat. Dung beetles also feed in different manners from one another. Many species simply feed on the dung where it is deposited on the surface. These may be referred to as dwellers or **endocoprids**. Others make chambers below the dung pile in which to bury their larval stores. These are tunnellers or **paracoprids**. Many species move their dung away from the pile to reduce competition, usually rolling balls that may be quite sizable. These are the rollers or **telecoprids** and they stand on their front legs while pushing with the hind legs. Occasionally species will monopolise on the efforts of others and steal ready-made balls. These are known as **cleptocoprids**.

Dung balls are rolled as food for the adults or as reserves for larvae. During courtship, the male rolls a nuptial ball, which he and the female feed on together in a hole before mating. Brood balls are rolled for breeding and a single egg is deposited in each ball and patted down by the female in the process of burying. Once it hatches, the larva feeds on the material in the ball while enjoying the safety of its hardened outer shell and

subterranean chamber. Some species of dung beetle exhibit basic parental care, remaining with the ball while the larva develops. Dung beetle larvae pupate underground and emerge as fully developed adults. Certain species lay up to 100 eggs per season.

Adult dung beetles have a lifespan of two years or more if they can escape predation by honey badgers, baboons, civets, hornbills and other birds. Honey badgers, mongoose and civets also dig up the balls to harvest the grubs. Robber flies and wasps catch smaller species of dung beetle.

A flightless dung beetle is found in Addo Elephant National Park. The fused elytra (wing coverings) restrict the ability of these insects to disperse to new regions and as a result, the population is endangered. A desert-dwelling flightless dung beetle species is believed to eat fungus that it grows on vegetable material and dry dung pellets buried in moist soil.

Dung beetles Down Under

The native Australian dung beetles are adapted to processing kangaroo dung and in the past have proven ineffective at cleaning up the copious cattle dung in which plague proportions of flies breed. In an experiment, African dung beetles were translocated to Australia but failed initially as the beetles had to be sterilised for immigration. Subsequently it was discovered that a symbiotic microscopic organism facilitates the dung beetle's navigation ability. Without sterilisation, the African dung beetles did the job brilliantly, except where invasive cane toads inflict heavy predation on the beetles.

Ants, bees and wasps

)) Order Hymenoptera

This order has in excess of 6 000 species and the insects in this group have enormous value to man. Hymenoptera also exhibit very advanced social structures although there are some solitary species too. Bees, wasps and ants all tend to make use of nests in which to deposit their eggs. They have waisted bodies with a distinct constriction between the thorax and abdomen and while only the reproductives in an ant colony have wings, bees and wasps have two pairs of membranous wings. Mouthparts are modified primarily for biting and the well-developed ovipositor is often used to sting.

Ants

Ants come in many different shapes, forms and sizes. Their choice of food varies from grains and vegetable matter to carnivorous items or honeydew farmed from aphids. The array of nesting sites used by different species includes underground, hollow twigs, thorns and reeds, aerial structures, leaves bound with silk and the burrows of other species. The entrances to many ant nests belie the impressive structures spreading out below the ground (up to 6 m down) and a humble pile of soil to divert rainwater or a heap of grass (in the case of the harvester ant) is all that is visible above the surface. Many ants hide the entrance to their nests under rocks or by sealing them up with grass. The ant's nest is its castle and colonies are aggressively defended. A

Harvester ants

threat is met with an arsenal that includes painful biting or squirted formic acid. The alarm is raised by the release of pheromones or in some species with sounds that emanate from moving body parts. Ants use pheromones copiously, leaving scent trails when they forage and strike a food source so other members can find it, and when directing the colony to new nesting sites.

Ants practise a caste system and are socially extremely advanced. A colony usually comprises a queen that becomes an egg-laying machine after mating, but there is no king. Wingless workers and soldiers perform their relevant functions and are all sterile, adult female ants. Unlike termites that have a hemimetabolous life cycle that produces nymphs (no pupation takes place), ants are holometabolous so their eggs hatch into grubs that cannot contribute to colony

life and depend on the workers to feed them. The colony reproduces through winged castes that make a short nuptial flight, mate and die in the case of the male, or become queens in the case of females and start new colonies.

Cocktail ants

Cocktail ants cock their tails (abdomens) when they are threatened. They cannot sting but the pose is intimidating nonetheless. They also secrete an irritant. Cocktail ants farm aphids for the honeydew they produce, sometimes causing population explosions of these pests. Cocktail ants make carton nests in trees with plant fibres and saliva (see below).

Cocktail ant

Matabele ants

Matabele ants are predators and form raiding parties consisting of lines of these large, dark ants that can be 150 cm long and several ants wide. Two size classes are present and perform different roles, the larger measuring 17 mm and the smaller 10 mm. A scout locates a food source and then lays an odour trail for the raiding party to find it. Breaches in termite mounds left by foraging aardvarks are ideal access points for Matabele ants that collect the termites by stinging and paralysing them. These are carried back to their own nests as food. Matabele ants respond to a threat by falling out of formation and moving around wildly, making a hissing sound and biting whatever gets in the way. They also have a distinctive, offensive odour, the colony is often smelled before observed. The Matabele ant gets its name from the Matabele tribe (native to Zimbabwe).

ME

Bees

Bees need little introduction: most people are familiar with **honey bees** and their helpful role in pollinating plants as they gather nectar to eat and pollen to feed their brood, but there are many lesser known bee species. Some species form highly coordinated colonies with division of labour while others are solitary. All lay their eggs in nests, usually natural cavities but sometimes homemade, and feed their young pollen and nectar. **Carpenter bees** are conspicuous as they are large and males patrol zones around particular flowers or bushes. They drill holes into wood and construct elaborate nests, using wood chips and saliva to compartmentalise them. **Leaf-cutting bees** use materials ranging from plant fibres to resin, mud and gravel to make cells in wood or ground cavities.

Mopane bees

This is a tiny, 4 mm, stingless bee sometimes called a mopane fly because of its pesky habit of trying to get at the moisture in people's sweat, eyes and mouth. Mopane bees make honey which is sought after by people but due to their size, they produce only small amounts.

PW

Mopane bee

LS

Honey bee

Carpenter bee

Wasps

Wasps are diverse in both species and survival tactics. The majority parasitise other insects' eggs or offspring in the process of reproducing and in this way perform the ecological function of regulating population numbers. Two broad types occur, namely internal parasitoids and external parasitoids. With the former, the wasp larva develops inside the host species, and with the latter the wasp larva develops by feeding on the outside of the host. Sometimes the withered remains of an unlucky caterpillar can be found bearing the silky cocoons that the parasitic wasps have spun in which to pupate and complete their life cycle.

Kleptoparasitism occurs when a wasp species takes advantage of a nest already provisioned by another species and its larva then feeds on both the provisions and the host species' larva. The small, bright green cuckoo wasp is an example of this, as is the ichneumonid wasps that also use their long threadlike ovipositors to pierce the bags of bagworms and lay their eggs inside the worm.

Many wasp species paralyse caterpillars and other insects

with which to provision their nests. These are dragged down holes or into mud chambers with remarkable dexterity. The mason and potter wasps are construction experts and use mud to build a range of mud homes, from single-cells to complex structures. The paralysed caterpillars they capture are then sealed into the mud vessel with their eggs. Spider-hunting wasps follow a similar tack but target large spiders on which they lay an egg and incarcerate them in underground chambers. These are some of the larger wasps and are often noticed because they make a noise with their wings.

Paper wasps

Paper wasps are social. Once they have mated, the male dies and the queen begins to build a paper-like celled nest with chewed up wood and saliva. She is soon joined by other females that add additional cells to the nest. Eggs are laid at the bottom of each cell and larvae are fed chewed up caterpillars. Different age classes assume these tasks, with younger wasps hunting for food while the older ones lay eggs. The nest is assertively protected by the newly formed colony and where the nest attaches by a robust stem to its

Paper wasp

sheltered position, the wasps coat it with ant repellent to keep these pests at bay. Cells are sealed when larvae pupate. When the new wasps emerge from their pupas, males are fed and retained for the purpose of breeding while females integrate with the colony.

Velvet ants

Velvet ants are maroon with a black abdomen spotted in white or yellow dots and covered in soft hairs. The aposematic colouration is an indication of its nasty sting, as this insect is in fact a female wingless wasp.

Velvet ant

She measures about 18 mm. While the female is wingless, the male is not and on finding a mate he will airlift her to mate with her. Velvet ants parasitise ground-nesting bees and wasps amongst others, laying eggs inside the larvae of their hosts. On hatching, the larva eats the host insect's larva, including the provisions stored up for it by the host adults. Velvet ants are busy insects and move quickly in their search for hosts to parasitise and often enter human habitations in the process.

Fig wasps

))) Family Agaonidae

Fig wasps are of the tiniest members of the insect world. They fulfil a vital function in the pollination of fig flowers. The relationship is an obligatory mutualistic symbiosis, as the fig wasp is the only insect small enough to crawl through the fig opening to reach the tiny flowers encased inside and pollinates them, and the wasp requires a safe breeding ground to perpetuate its own genes. The wasp could not reproduce without the tree and the fig could not reproduce without the services of the wasp. Certain species of fig wasps are specific to different fig species.

The fig is both flower receptacle and fruit to the tree. It is a hollow, thickened stem with a tiny opening at one end encircled by small bracts. Female wasps lay their eggs in the female flowers' ovaries depositing pollen they collected from another fig in the process. Once fertilised, the ovaries of the minute flowers ripen and become the flesh of the fruit. Every species of fig tree has just one or a few species of fig wasp that can fit through the fig opening. The system works like a lock-and-key.

Female fig wasps hatch and depart from the figs where they were brooded shortly thereafter. Before leaving, she gathers pollen from male fig flowers that cluster around the small exit. She then finds another fig on the same or on a different tree and enters it. Before selecting a female flower in

which to lay her eggs, the female first deposits the pollen she has brought along with her.

Male fig wasps remain inside the same fig life-long and for this reason are wingless. The males bore into the galls containing new females before they hatch and mate with them. To enhance oxygen availability in the fig, the males bore holes into its external walls, helping to dissipate carbon dioxide simultaneously. The improved ventilation stimulates both the development of the female wasps and the development of fig fruit.

Also known as 'fairy flies', some species of fig wasps measure just 0,2 mm. Many animals, including monkeys, baboons, bushpigs, warthogs, civets, bats, porcupines, antelope and frugivorous birds, relish figs and fig wasps are consumed inadvertently by these animals.

WMC/JMK

Fig wasps associated with the broom cluster fig (Ficus sur)

WMC/JMK

Termites
)》 Order Isoptera

Termites descend from a type of cockroach and are not related to ants even though they look similar. They eat decaying organic material and live underground, foraging in tunnels or consuming wood from the inside out because they do not have well-pigmented bodies. Termites break down wastes, recycle nutrients into the soil, aerate the soil through burrowing and bring moisture and minerals to the surface from deep underground. Termite mounds are usually fertile and seeds germinate readily and once trees establish, thickets may form and provide microhabitats to many animals. Termites are social and use a caste system and division of labour. Each member of the colony is genetically identical, having been produced by a single king and queen and individuals cannot survive without the colony. The colony reproduces itself through winged alates that emerge after rain, simultaneously providing a nutritious food source to myriad creatures. Colonies live for decades or occasionally centuries.

Only the king and queen breed. After mating for the first time, the queen's body swells grotesquely and she begins laying eggs, sometimes tens of thousands in a day. The royal chamber is just below the ground in the centre of the mound and she becomes too large to move from here. The small king remains with the queen to keep her fertilised. The queen is long-lived, surviving for up to 50 years in some species. Sometimes colonies persist if the queen dies and a nymph is fed a chemical which stimulates her to assume the role of queen. This new queen will be winged, having never completed a nuptial flight.

The winged reproductive alates are released from the mound just once a year after good summer rains. After a short nuptial flight, a female lands and releases pheromones by wiggling the tip of her abdomen to attract a mate. Opposite sexes from different colonies pair up, shed their wings and in tandem they seek a nest site. They dig themselves under the surface, mate and begin producing a new colony.

The blind, sterile workers are the most numerous castes and they collect food, construct the mound, tend the eggs and nymphs, and care for the queen. The soldiers are larger than the workers and have huge heads and strong mandibles to deal with intruders. They also squirt an irritant. Soldiers constitute just 5 per cent of the colony and rely on the workers for food.

The queen runs her colony by chemical communication. In exchanging food, saliva and excreta with the queen, and in turn all other members of the colony, the workers circulate pheromones. Changes in colony composition are remediated by chemicals the queen releases and receives. If there is a shortage of soldiers, for

ME

Harvester termite nymph, worker and soldier

the main chimney and cools at the surface, the cooler air sinking down the side vents. This creates a constant circulation of air. Moist vanes below the central nest cavity also cool the air. Workers tunnel down to the water table to access water.

Old or broken termite mounds, especially ones that are raised and offer some relief from floods, are often taken over by burrowing animals that modify them for their own purposes. Mounds are insulated and ideal for raising young. Almost 30 species have been known to make use of aardvark burrows after they have vacated them. Dwarf mongooses use smaller mounds and cavities.

example, the queen will produce more soldier eggs. Pheromones fed to the nymphs triggers the production of winged alates at the right time of the year. Workers use chemicals to lay scent trails to food sources. Soldiers send up the alarm by tapping on the walls of the tunnels.

With the activity of thousands of termites below the ground, heat and carbon dioxide build up especially if ambient temperatures are also hot. Termites create air conditioning systems to combat this, generally maintaining a constant temperature inside the mound. Some species use their spired mounds for ventilation building a central chimney up the centre and side vents radiating off this to just below the external surface. Hot air rises up

Harvester termites (*Hodotermes* species) are large and have well pigmented bodies so they are able to forage above the ground. As a result, they also have functional eyes. They cut off pieces of grass and other vegetation and stockpile it before carrying it back to their underground homes. Tunnels lead from their piles of cut grass to temporary storage shelves below the surface and then down to their spherical hives where they store the grass in chambers. Harvester termites can remove 1–3 metric tons of forage per hectare and in high concentrations can damage veld and lead to erosion.

The **snouted harvester termite** (*Trinervitermes trinervoides*) is another common species but is not related to the harvester termites. The snouted harvester termite belongs to the Termitidae family and gets its name from the long, thin protrusions they carry at the tip of their faces. They also forage on grass but do so under the cover of darkness via underground passageways. The snouted harvester termite constructs smooth, domed mounds that stand no taller than 1 m. They have very hard outer walls and various cells and galleries internally. Soldiers spray enemies with a sticky, repellent liquid.

The **fungus-growing termite** (*Macrotermes natalensis*) builds huge, spired mounds that contain tons of soil carried particle by particle from below as it is displaced during foraging. Mounds may tower up to two metres high. To digest the structural cellulose in their plant food, these termites cultivate fungus gardens. They lack the single-celled organisms in their digestive systems other termites have. Workers chew and swallow food they find but then when they return to the colony they excrete it in neat piles and fashion it into combs on which miniscule white dots of fungus begin to grow. The workers then eat the combs once they have been digested by the fungus and regurgitate some for the soldiers. The queen and nymphs are fed the fungus directly. The fungus gardens are tended constantly to ensure the colony is fed and spores may even be cultivated outside the mound at times. The thick-walled royal cell is at the heart of the nest, below the shelves where the fungus gardens are cultivated and above the brood galleries where the eggs are kept. The primary nest cavity is at ground level, is spherical and compartmentalised and measures about 80 cm wide.

Dry and damp **wood termites** have simple nests comprising galleries in dead branches in trees or in timber. These termites can be pestilent if they get into homes and furniture.

Harvester termites

Snouted harvester termites and nest

Fungus-growing termite nest

Butterflies and moths

)) Order Lepidoptera

The transformation of leaf-chomping caterpillar to sap-sucking butterfly or moth fascinates us from the earliest age. These are a popular group of insects because of their beauty. As a rule, butterflies are diurnal, fold their wings together when at rest and have antennae that terminate in a bump. In contrast, moths are typically nocturnal, keep their wings spread open when at rest and have fanned antennae. The adult form of most species of butterfly and moth a have long, curled proboscis for sucking sap and nectar. Some species do not feed at all as adults. Caterpillars take on a variety of colours, shapes and forms.

Butterflies and moths have four-stage life cycles known as holometabolous and complete metamorphosis occurs. Females lay their eggs on a species-specific larval food plant and when the caterpillars emerge they begin eating, growing and fattening themselves for pupation. Once ready, caterpillars spin cocoons attached to a branch by a silk thread and they pupate. Inside the pupa it is understood that the larvae liquefy. Bundles of suspended cells that express both the butterfly and the caterpillar form are present from the start. While in the pupa, the cells that express the butterfly form increase while the others decrease. The mass then takes on the form of the butterfly cells and some weeks later, the adult butterfly emerges from its cocoon.

Caterpillars use an array of defence strategies to avoid becoming food to predators. Some feed on poisonous plants and assimilate toxins into their bodies, which they advertise with bright colours. Others may be covered in prickly hairs and deliver painful stings. The citrus swallowtail's caterpillar remains unnoticed by because it mimics a bird's dropping. It can also give off offensive smells. Some species develop elaborate protuberances to resemble bark or highlight the wrong end of the body as the head. Some species are gregarious and use their communal habits to hide their identity.

Citrus swallowtail pupa

Citrus swallowtail later stage larva

African monarch butterfly

This is a widespread and common species of butterfly attractively coloured black and orange. The colours are aposematic to warn predators that the species is unpalatable. African monarch caterpillars feed on toxic milkweed and they assimilate the poisons into their bodies, which then offer them some immunity from predators. Adults retain the toxicity after pupation and sometimes give off an offensive brown fluid. Other butterfly species, the female common diadem for example, freeloads on the monarch's survival tactics by mimicking the appearance of the monarch and thereby enjoying immunity from predators even though they are not poisonous.

Other common butterflies and moths

Some other common butterflies include the fast-flying foxy charaxes (1); citrus swallowtail; brown-veined whites (3); acreas (2); broad-bordered grass yellow; and yellow pansies (4).

Some common or obvious moths include owl moths (8); the lunar moth (5) – a green, swallow-tailed moth that is often found on marula trees; hawk moths (9); maidens (7); and crimson speckled footmen (6).

WMC

LS

RF

LS

Mopane worms

Attractive black, red, white and yellow mopane worms may occur in plague proportions in summer months and feed with loud crunching on the widespread mopane tree, the leaves of which are high in protein. The worms, themselves high in protein, are harvested by many different African communities and dried or cooked and eaten. The mopane worm is the caterpillar of the **emperor moth** (*Imbrasia bellina*) a large, pinkish-brown moth with orange eyespots on its wings.

SS

ME

Processionary worms

The small cream and brown processionary moth is not terribly conspicuous but its caterpillars are. Processionary worms, as the caterpillars are known, are gregarious and move about in a procession, imperceptibly slowly, and in the process mimic a stick or larger creature such as a snake, thereby avoiding the attentions of predators. A leader lays down a fine silk trail, which is followed by the other caterpillars, each placing its head adjacent to the rear of the preceding member. The caterpillars pupate together with as many as 600 individual cocoons in a communal purse-like 'bagnet'.

ME

Bagworms

The bagworm moth's caterpillar encases itself in a 'bag' of plant materials, often acacia thorns, which is fastened with strong silk. The bagworm transports its bag wherever it goes so that it is able to retreat into the shelter if needed in the manner of a tortoise and its shell. Most bagworms enjoy a degree of camouflage because of the cryptic appearance of the natural materials used to construct the bag. The adults are inconspicuous and short-lived.

Dragonflies

)) Order Odonata

Dragonflies are well-known and popular insects because they are brightly coloured and conspicuous. Found in the vicinity of water, they are territorial insects and active hunters. They are unmistakable for their slender bodies, powerful wings and flight, enormous compound eyes and forward-placed legs modified into a foraging basket that is used to scoop up aquatic prey while in flight.

Dragonflies have four, evenly sized, gauzy wings that move independently and effect both forwards and backwards flight. The wings are palaeopterous and cannot be folded away. They are large and enable the powerful flight required of a predator but disadvantage the insect as it cannot hide in crevices or under objects from its own predators.

Consequently, dragonflies usually land on the tip of a reed or piece of grass that accommodate for the spreading wings which are held horizontally at rest or folded down and forwards. The similar albeit more delicate **damselfly** folds its wings together and over the abdomen or holds them half open when at rest.

Dragonfly breeding is elaborate and unique. The territorial males mate with females that enter their stretch of river protecting the female afterwards from the attentions of other males. The pair flies in tandem with the male gripping the female behind the head with the claspers on the end of his abdomen. The pair then come to rest at which time the female arcs her abdomen into a wheel position coming into contact with a special repository on the male's second abdominal segment. He transfers sperm here early on, freeing up his abdomen to clasp the female. Once copulation is complete, the pair fly in tandem once more so the female can lay her eggs which she does by dipping them lightly into the surface of the water.

▲ Damselfly   Julia skimmer ▼   ▲ Red-veined dropwing   Dorsal dropwing ▼

Adult dragonflies and nymphs live very different lifestyles. While the adults are terrestrial, the nymphs, known as naiads are aquatic. Both are predatory however. The naiad's labium is modified into an extendible apparatus called a mask and this is used for grabbing prey. The naiads hide in the sand on the bottom of water bodies and create intricate patterns there from their foraging activities. They hunt insects, tadpoles or small fish. The nymphs have gills in the anus through which they breathe. Dragonflies have hemi-metabolic lifecycles with no pupa phase and the naiads grow through ecdysis (shedding of exoskeleton).

More common dragonflies include the Julia skimmer, red-veined and dorsal dropwings. These dragonflies all have a wingspan of about 6 cm and settle on reeds and grass along the water's edge from where they hunt. The males are colourful while females are duller. The **Julia skimmer** male is powder blue and rests with its wings down and forward. **Red-veined dropwings** have bright red bodies and red-veined wings while the **dorsal dropwing** male has a dark blue body with transparent wings paneled at the ends in dark brown. The dorsal dropwing female is pale blue and yellow, and also has brown panels on her clear wings. These dragonflies settle with wings up or down.

Dragonfly nymph or naiad

Naiad mouthparts

Other common insects

Antlions

Antlion adults resemble dragonflies and may have wingspans of up to 16 cm but they are more delicate and flimsy. They are part of the lacewing family, Neuroptera. The larva has a round abdomen and large pincer-like mouthparts, can be tiny or measure up to 2.5 cm. They are predatory and live in conical pits on the ground, although some kinds are free-living on bark or vegetation. Some species build pits with collapsible sides in soft soil by rotating backwards, anchoring themselves at the bottom with rear-facing hairs and there they lie in wait to ambush ants that fall in. They flick sand over captured prey to confuse it and prevent its escape and then suck it with the pincer-like mouthparts. The larval antlion has a blind intestine but drops a stored pellet of waste when it metamorphoses. Adults do not feed.

Horn moths

The larvae of a ceratophagic or horn-eating moth produce the protuberances that resemble grey worms on old horn sheaths. Horns are comprised of keratin and it is this material that the larvae consume reinforcing the growing tube with their excrement as they go. The tube protects the developing moth larva from the elements and from predators until it pupates. It can take up to two years before larvae pupate.

Fireflies and glow worms

Fireflies and glow worms attract mates by flashing light in their abdomens. Most firefly females are wingless and resemble worms while winged males more closely resemble flies. Light is emitted by special cells on the abdomen wherein a layer of reflective uric acid crystals intensify the illumination caused when chemical luceferin is oxidised by the enzyme luciferase. The pulses are regulated by nerves, which can be contracted at will to increase or decrease oxygen supply to the cells. Different species have different pulse patterns by which they recognise their own kind.

Cicadas

Cicadas are responsible for the incessant buzzing heard in the summer months. Male cicadas make these calls to attract cicadas of both sexes to a central get-together. The sound is produced by convex tymbal membranes located one each in a ventral cavity on either side of the abdomen. Contraction or relaxation of muscles causes the tymbals to flex in and out, resulting in the high-frequency noise. The sound resonates in the cavities, augmented by folded membranes and a structure called the mirror. Cicada nymphs feed on root sap underground and sometimes enjoy a very protracted instar phase. They ecdyse for the final time when they emerge above ground in early November.

Spittlebugs

Spittlebug nymphs have sucking mouthparts and draw sap from trees, which they excrete at a similar pace to that which they take it in. Excreted liquid is frothed up into a protective jacket known as 'cuckoo spit' that shields the nymphs from both the sun and predators. Drops of fluid may drip off the insects and first gave trees like the rain tree or weeping wattle their names.

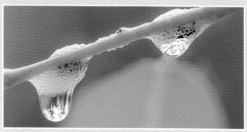

SS

ME

Blister beetles

The blister beetle releases the chemical cantharadin from its leg joints when it is threatened, which causes blisters on human skin. Blister beetles are also called CMR beetles after the Cape Mounted Rifles whose uniform is black and yellow like the beetle. The colours warn against their chemical defences. They are just under 3 cm in size and fly with their wings held above the body, which appears to hang down. The adults feed on flowers and the young on the egg pods of grasshoppers and locusts. Cantharadin was traditionally used in southern Africa to produce the aphrodisiac Spanish fly but actually just causes irritation to the urinary tract.

Assassin bugs

These bugs have a large, recurved proboscis, which they use to pierce their quarry and can deliver a very painful bite to humans. The assassin bug has legs modified with tiny suction organs for gripping its prey. They are ambush predators and once they have secured a meal, they jab it with the proboscis, which has four sharp lancets, and inject toxic saliva to dissolve the innards that are subsequently sucked out. Some assassin bug species exhibit basic parental care and males guard the eggs until hatching, or even longer. Nymphs cover themselves with soil and other debris to hide away. Adults have pinkish bodies with dark brown, membranous wings that show when the insect is at rest. The shield has characteristic darker pink and grey patterning.

Bombardier beetles

Bombardier beetles or bombardier ant's guest beetles are identifiable from their wide, flat antennae. They use corrosive hydroquinones, stored in specialised partitions on the end of the abdomen, to produce small yet audible explosions of irritant liquid in self-defence. Bombardier beetles live amongst ant colonies and produce sweet-smelling secretions, which the ants consume. In turn, bombardier beetles and their brood feed on the ants' larvae.

Tenebrionids (Toktokkies or Darkling beetles)

These are large, black, mostly flightless beetles, the latter a consequence of fused wing covers. They live on the ground and scavenge fungi and dead plant or animal material. Males tap their abdomens on the ground to attract mates and feign death if threatened. Tenebrionids are found in a variety of habitats but are especially successful in arid areas where they fog-bask to collect dew and fog moisture on their backs, which they then drink. They have well-developed legs and are fast-moving insects covering a metre in less than a second. Many species are nocturnal.

Ground beetles

Ground beetles are very active, large, black predatory beetles that have strong, sharp jaws to catch prey or defend themselves. They are also able to squirt strong jets of formic and other acids from glands on their abdomen and wear colourful yellow or white spots to warm of this ability. They can spray the irritant about 30 cm and are particularly accurate in doing so. They are flightless.

Stick insects

Stick insects are the longest insects in southern Africa and can reach up to 25 cm long. They are masters of camouflage and use very convincing mimicry to resemble sticks or bark to avoid detection. They have other defence mechanisms at their disposal too and might suddenly flash open their brightly coloured wings to startle a predator or they might play dead to ward off attention or have the ability to shed a limb to escape capture.

Mantids

Mantids are ambush predators that use various guises to escape detection mimicking flowers, leaves or bark. The praying mantis holds its front legs poised ready to attack looking as though it were in prayer. Equipped with a huge moveable head, big compound eyes and spiny legs with enlarged coxa, the mantis is an effective predator and dispatches prey quickly, shredding it with mandibles modified for chewing. Female mantids are notorious for biting off the male's head while mating, depending on how hungry she is but this does not prevent transfer of sperm. Eggs are laid in a frothy, creamy-white, individually celled oothica. New hatchlings may feed on one another.

ME

Grasshoppers and katydids

Grasshoppers and katydids are best known for the noises they produce. The process of stridulation involves the rubbing of body parts together and this generates sound. Some species rub the edges of their wings together, others rub a leg against a reinforced surface on the forewing. The **rain locust** is common and sounds like garden sprinklers when it stridulates. Like most katydids and grasshoppers, the rain locust also has brilliant cryptic colouration resembling bark.

ME

Rain locust

The **leaf katydid** has leaf-like venation on its wings and legs to make it look as close to a leaf as possible. Katydids have extremely complex unidirectional hearing, their tympanal organs being situated in slits on the front legs. They employ their highly accurate sound receptors to detect danger and track down calling males.

PW

Leaf katydid

The **elegant grasshopper** is widespread throughout southern Africa and feeds on milkweed and poison apple. It is not cryptically camouflaged but rather its bright colours indicate its chemical abilities, which include the dispatch of a foul-smelling yellow fluid. Eggs are laid communally in the ground and may not hatch for six months. Wings are seldom functional.

Elegant grasshopper

251

Jewel beetles

This is a group of very attractive torpedo-shaped, brightly coloured beetles that contains many endemic species. They vary from 2 mm to 5 cm and have tough bodies painted with metallic coppers, blues and greens. So attractive are the beetles that their wing covers have been used in jewellery in some countries. Some species have tufts of yellow or red waxy setae on their bodies. They have large eyes with good eyesight and are strong fliers, surviving in hot locations and moving around flowering bushes in the sun when other creatures would be under cover. Adults eat pollen, nectar and foliage and are short-lived. The juveniles, however, are extremely long-lived, some species taking up to 35 years to reach maturity. Eggs are laid in cracks in bark or softer stems and the larvae make galleries between the bark and wood. They do not have legs but use a hugely enlarged flat head to burrow.

Fruit chafers

This is another group of vibrantly coloured beetles that are part of the same family as dung beetles (see page 234) and share with them the trait of clubbed antennae with moveable plates that fan out. Adults are flat, square-shaped and robust, and the males of some species are adorned with imposing horns. They fly strongly, not lifting the wing cases when they do. Adults feed on fruit, flowers, sap and gum while larvae typically use manure or compost for their lifestyles. Fruit chafers have been noted in a few unusual places, including inside birds' nests and bee hives and in association with wasp nests on which they feed.

Ladybirds

A popular and well-loved insect, ladybirds have shiny, round, domed bodies hardly showing head or legs, are coloured black, red, orange or yellow and decorated with spots and stripes. They are small, measuring 0.5–10 mm but have healthy appetites and play a vital role in dispatching pestilent species like aphids, their primary food source. Both adults and larvae are carnivorous and eggs are laid on plants already plagued by aphids so the young have a food source as soon as they hatch. They set to spearing the aphids with sharp, sickle-shaped jaws and sucking them dry. A ladybird's colours warn predators of its unpalatability and it secretes unpleasant, yellow fluid from its leg joints when disturbed. Predators tend to ignore them and ladybirds are usually conspicuous. A few duller, herbivorous species do occur. Large groups of ladybirds may amass to oversee the dry season.

Longhorn beetles

This is a very successful group of insects. Longhorn beetles are most notable for their exceptionally long antennae that measure at least half, but usually more, of the length of the body. These are filamentous and can be pointed up or back and folded parallel to the body. The beetles themselves vary in size from 3 mm to 10 cm but include some of the largest beetles in southern Africa. They have long, tubular or flat bodies and colours vary from brown on nocturnal species to cryptically marked diurnal species to many species with bright metallic colours or warning colours. Males, particularly, have enormous mandibles. Longhorn beetles are typically woodborers and lay their eggs in cracks of tree trunks or in the roots of woody plants. As the larvae feed, they burrow into the wood where they mature. Grubs can reach large sizes and are

sometimes eaten by people. Some species make holes in herbaceous plants or are seedeaters. Adults feed on pollen and nectar or on leaves, roots and wood.

Armoured ground crickets

These peculiar looking, lumbering crickets are also known as long-horned grasshoppers and are endemic where they occur in more arid locations. They have strong jaws and can bite painfully and although they release yellow-coloured repellent fluids from the thorax when alarmed, they are not toxic. They typically drop off vegetation if they feel threatened. Most species are herbivorous with more omnivorous tendencies showing if the opportunity to scavenge presents – even the dead of their own kind. They, in turn, are eaten by jackals, bat-eared foxes and large birds. The males attract mates by calling at high pitches using the stumpy, membranous residual wings that sit beneath the shield and are fitted with file-like teeth to produce the rasping noise when rubbed together. The female locates him using the tympanal organs on her front legs. Egg hatching is rain related and eggs may lie dormant for a year.

Anopheles mosquitoes

This mosquito holds its abdomen at a 45° angle when at rest. The mosquito is the host to the often-fatal disease malaria, which manifests as headaches, fever, nausea and flu-like aches. Males suck nectar but females suck blood, thereby spreading the disease. Mouthparts are modified to pierce and suck and an anticoagulant facilitates the free flow of blood while feeding, leaving an itchy, red bump behind. Malaria takes 10 days to 6 weeks to incubate and is treated with a 10-day course of quinine and antibiotics.

SS

Baboon spiders

🔊 Family Theraphosidae

Baboon spiders belong to the same family as tarantulas and are large, heavily built, hairy spiders that vary in colour from light brown and yellow to silvery grey or black. They measure 3–9 cm but the spread of the legs can mean they are about 12 cm in size. The legs are thick and the pedipalps are long and resemble an additional pair of legs. The spinnerets extend beyond the end of the abdomen. These are long-lived spiders surviving about 20 years in captivity and there are 162 African species in this family. They typically inhabit warm, arid areas and may be found in the vicinity of houses.

Baboon spiders earned their name from their hairy appearance and because the pads on the ends of their legs (tarsi) are a similar colour and texture to a baboon's footpads. The last two segments on the spider's leg also resemble a baboon's finger.

The baboon spider lives on the ground, is sedentary and nocturnal. It constructs a silk-lined tunnel about 40 cm deep under the ground or makes a silk-lined chamber in which to hide, seldom straying away from its burrow except when males are seeking mates.

Adult spiders lack the group of teeth on the head of the chelicerae, called the rastellum, which are used for digging. These are present in young spiders to construct burrows. Consequently, baboon spiders cannot dig new burrows if they are forcibly removed from their existing ones.

As ambush hunters, they wait inside their burrow entrances for an opportunity to catch prey at night. The spider becomes aware of approaching prey when the rim of web surrounding the lip of the burrow entrance is disturbed. Food comprises invertebrates, especially insects but also other spiders, solifugids, scorpions, millipedes, reptiles and amphibians. When approaching female spiders' burrows, males must be careful not to become prey themselves. They therefore tap out vibrations on the web at the burrow entrances to identify themselves.

ME

Baboon spiders belong to the more primitive group of spiders, the Mygalomorphs, whose jaws strike forwards and downwards. They are slow-moving and respond to threats by raising their forelegs intimidatingly. Predators may be startled by the black underparts and bright red hairs on the chelicerae. They have large fangs on their chelicerae and are able to administer a painful bite. Their venom is only mildly toxic, except the small baboon spider from the southwestern Cape that has relatively potent neurotoxic venom. Baboon spiders that lose a limb, replace it with a thinner version at the following moult.

255

Orb-web spiders

All spiders have silk glands that produce the silk protein and spinnerets for spinning it. Different glands produce different kinds of silk for different functions, most notably web-building. Orb-web spiders are renowned for their masterpiece webs, which they stretch out between gaps in vegetation. The construction starts with a bridge line, which is floated from one side of the gap between vegetation to the other and then reinforced with additional material as she crosses it back and forth. Then the foundation lines are constructed below the bridge, connecting various points to the vegetation to make up the frame or perimeter in which she will build the main web. Starting with a Y-shaped stand inside the frame, she gradually adds radial threads and then proceeds to build the hub in the centre of the web where the radial threads converge, using a mesh pattern. The catch web is spun concentrically around the hub. Some of the silk is not sticky, to allow the spider to move around without becoming ensnared in her own web. A trap line may be added to alert a spider sheltering to the side of the web that something has become ensnared and to quickly access her main web.

Garden orb-web spider

)) *Argiope* species

The garden orb-web spider measures about 3 cm with a leg span of 8 cm. Females are silver and yellow with black markings, the ribbed abdomen bearing serrated sides and the legs are long and banded. Males are between 2 mm and 1 cm in size and plain. While similar-looking to the golden orb-web spider, the two species are not closely related. There are 12 African species of garden orb-web spider.

ME

Garden orb-web spiders usually occur in built-up areas, in grass or in low vegetation. They are diurnal and sedentary, remaining on their webs and hanging head down with the two sets of forelegs and the two hind sets held together. They capture insect prey by wrapping it up in silk before administering a bite to kill it. If the spider is not hungry, the bundled prey will be left until later to be consumed. Males mate with females while they are feeding to avoid becoming prey. While harmless to humans, they can bite painfully.

The garden orb-web spider makes a huge, wheel-like web that may measure 75 cm across. The silk is colourless but an obvious white stabilimentum zigzags in a vertical stripe from the middle of the web. Specialised silk is used to construct the stabilimentum, which acts as a stabiliser and strengthener to the web. It is also obvious to avert large creatures from passing through it and damaging the web.

Golden orb-web spiders

)) *Nephila* species

The golden orb-web spider is a large spider with females measuring up to 4 cm long with a leg span of 8 cm. She has a cylindrical abdomen and long legs covered in tufts of hair. The abdomen is typically black, white and yellow and the carapace is covered in silvery hairs. Males are a mere 6 mm and plainer, dwelling on the edges of the females' webs. Golden orb-web spiders are diurnal and sedentary on their webs and they occur in forests, bushveld or wherever there is suitable vegetation. In Africa, 11 species occur.

The web of the golden orb-web spider is enormous, sometimes measuring 1 m across. The silk has a yellow colour and the reinforced bridge line is especially reinforced and obviously golden. The main web is strewn with debris that forms a makeshift stabilimentum to add to the support of the web. She waits in the centre of her web hanging head-down but if disturbed will dart off the web into the attaching vegetation. Spider silk is incredibly strong, equivalent to steel at the same thickness, and even small birds may get caught the web.

The bright golden colour of the orb-web is believed to advertise its location to large animals and flying birds so that they do not damage it. Replacing a broken web is energy-expensive to the spider and best avoided. The debris in the middle also offers an obvious marker of the web's presence as well as supporting the web and providing camouflage for the spider. It is thought that the UV properties of the silk may attract insects in the same way that floral UV pathways do.

The male spider waits for his mate to be distracted with feeding before darting in to deposit sperm from his pedipalps into her oviducts and then withdrawing again quickly. Females have the ability to store sperm and they produce four egg sacs in a single season. Spiderlings disperse after hatching by extending a piece of silk and allowing the wind to lift and blow them away in a process called ballooning. They grow by ecdysis, shedding their exoskeletons to accommodate for a larger body size.

All spiders have venom glands but few are dangerous to humans, the golden orb being a good example of a harmless spider despite its fearsome appearance. Furthermore, they are more prone to running away than attacking in defence. Glands are situated on the cephalothorax with sac-like sections where the venom is stored. A duct terminates at the end of fang and venom is injected into prey via muscle contractions.

Other common spiders

There are 63 families of spiders in southern Africa and of the 30 000 known species, as few as 30 per cent of all the species on earth are thought to have been discovered. People's fear of these 8-legged creatures seems misdirected since few can cause harm. Rather, they should be more accurately viewed as the highly adaptable creatures they are, being found across a multitude of habitats and performing the essential role of controlling pest insects. Spiders occur in one of two main groups: Araneomorphs and Mygalomorphs. Araneomorphs are mostly web-bound spiders with sideways striking jaws and they have just one pair of book lungs. Mygalomorphs are typically more primitive and are ground-dwelling with downward-stroking chelicerae and two pairs of book lungs.

Wall spiders

))) *Anyphops* species

Sometimes called 'flatties', these spiders have flat bodies with crab-like legs and are mottled grey, brown and black. They may be 5 mm to 2 cm in size. Usually found on rocks or under bark where they camouflage well, they do visit homes where they pursue moths, fishmoths and cockroaches but here they stand out on the plain walls. They do not spin webs but take refuge in crevices. They are agile spiders and move rapidly.

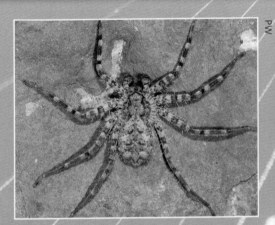

Garbage-line spiders

))) *Cyclosa* species

This mottled grey, 1 cm-long spider with a lumpy abdomen uses its appearance to camouflage itself amongst debris suspended on a stretched stabilimentum. The garbage line comprises the remains of its prey or old egg cases and moulted skin. It hides from predators and ambushes its prey in this manner.

Dew-drop spiders

Argyrodes species)))

Measuring just a few millimetres, dew-drop spiders make their living stealing food from the webs of other spiders on which they reside. Sometimes they even eat their hosts! These kleptoparasites have swollen, conical abdomens coloured metallic-silver and resemble drops of mercury, or as their name suggests, dew. They have long, thin, tapering legs. Dew-drop spiders belong to the same family (Theridiidae) as the venomous black button spider but are themselves harmless.

Trapdoor spiders
Family Ctenizidae))

Measuring up to 4 cm, these dark brown spiders with relatively short, spiny legs burrow into soils across southern Africa, making silk-lined living quarters up to 20 cm into the ground. A cryptically camouflaged lid is constructed like a trapdoor over the burrow. Prey is captured by ambush at night and from the cover of the half-open trapdoor that can also be shut to keep out blowing sand of enemies. The carapace of this spider is shiny while the legs and abdomen are haired. They have a specialised rastellum on the jaws for digging.

Tropical tent spiders
Cyrtophora species

Creamy grey or black and white, these spiders measure about 1 cm long and have pairs of pimple-like bulges on the abdomen. Sedentary and web bound, the tropical tent spider typically lives in colonies identifiable from their unique webs. Each spider builds a finely meshed orb-web on a horizontal plane, surrounded by trip lines. The middle of the orb is pinched upwards and resembles a pitched tent. The spider hangs upside down in the centre of the web well camouflaged amongst debris and egg cases. When insects get entangled in web, the spider bites it through the horizontal web layer. These spiders occupy low vegetation and are common in gardens.

Kite spiders
Gasteracantha species))

The kite spider is brightly adorned with red, yellow, orange, black and white on its flat, hard, shiny abdomen complete with spiny projections. It has short legs and measures about 1 cm in size. It builds a fine-stranded orb web in vegetation and the females typically rest in the centre, wrapping prey in silk and biting it to dispatch it. This is a diurnal spider, which is easily spotted dangling like a kite in its fine web.

Bark spiders
Caerostris species

Coloured like a piece of bark or lichen and adorned with warty protrusions, the bark spider is a superb mimic, hiding in plain sight on a tree branch by day, legs tucked in at its sides. They are about 2 cm in size. These spiders are nocturnal and reconstruct their enormous orb-webs nightly, hanging head down in the centre to catch prey. Webs may span 1.5 m between trees. Each morning, the web is abandoned or dismantled except for the bridge line and the silk reabsorbed. Venom is harmless to humans.

Rain spiders

Palystes species))

A free-running spider that has no web and often resides in human habitations. At 3 cm large with a leg span of 11 cm, they look fearsome but are harmless. They are useful to remove household pests, in particular crickets. The body is dark brown with darker patterns on the abdomen with strong, banded legs. The female spiders construct balls of leaves and white silk for the egg sac, which she protects even once the spiderlings have hatched.

Daddy longlegs

Pholcus species))

A small spider but with very long, slender legs. The greyish body measures just a few millimetres but the leg span reaches 3 cm. These spiders often make their loose, untidy webs in the corners of homes although in the wild they do this between rocks or in leaf litter. If it is disturbed, daddy longlegs spiders shake their webs by vibrating briskly. The female carries her egg sac in her mouth until hatching time.

Buckspoor spiders

Seothyra species))

Named for their habit of creating a lair that resembles an antelope track, this small spider has a robust appearance with robust legs. The abdomen is oval-shaped and yellow-brown with velvet hair. Sometimes they resemble the dangerous velvet ant (see page 238) with redder cephalothoraxes and spotted abdomens. They live in dry savannah or semi-desert in soft sand, creating a mat of densely woven silk at the entrance to their silk-lined subterranean burrows. They typically eat ants but other insects are taken as well.

Grass funnel-web spiders

Olorunia species))

These spiders are sooty grey with pale spots on a hairy abdomen and thin, banded legs. Long spinnerets protrude from the rear of the abdomen. While both nocturnal and diurnal, they are seldom seen due to a shy nature. They hide away in an open-ended tubular funnel exiting onto the ground or vegetation should escape be necessary. The funnel opens above onto a horizontal silk mat about 50 cm across. This is used to ensnare prey at which time the spider storms out to retrieve it. She feeds in the cover of her retreat. Webs are used lifelong, the size modified as required.

Jumping spiders
Family Salticidae)))

Small to medium-sized hairy spiders with blunt faces and obvious eyes. Males are most colourful and jumping spiders exhibit blacks, whites, greys and browns. They are habitat generalists and free-living. They hunt prey by stalking and leaping upon it, using the large eyes to locate prey in the first place. Jumps are effected by means of hydraulic pressure and not leg muscles. Some species imitate ants to deter their own predators. While jumping spiders do not construct webs, they still use silk in their daily lives, releasing a line when they attack prey to use to draw back and at night they hide in crevices sealing themselves into a silky, sac-like vessel. Males fight or attract females by raising the front legs and circumnavigating branches as they display.

Fishing spiders
Thalassius species)))

Sturdy spiders about 3 cm long with elongated and tapered abdomens patterned in browns with a white band down either side, extending from the carapace. These spiders are free-living and inhabit areas alongside streams and ponds where they wait to spot prey and then dive on it. Fishing spiders can stand on the water surface by spreading their legs out in all directions. The leg span is about 7 cm. Their fish-dispatching venom has no effect on humans and their diet is more diverse than other spiders, including insects, shrimps, tadpoles and frogs as well as fish. The female carries and protects her egg sac, guarding the hatchlings in a leafy nursery.

Crab spiders
Family Thomisidae)))

These attractive spiders are expert ambushers, matching their colour to the flowers they sit on, hiding in wait for insects to pass. Colours vary from white to pink or yellow and green. They attack insects much bigger than themselves and have potent venom, which enables them to kill bees, its commonest prey. Harmless to humans, these spiders are often found in gardens. They are diurnal and free-roaming so they have developed the ability to move forwards, backwards and sideways. There are 356 African species in this family. The male is much smaller and rides piggy-back on an immature female until she moults, which is when he mates with her. Some species tie up their mates with silk before mating.

White ladies
)) *Leucorchestris* species

These are desert-dwelling spiders that are free-living on dunes and in loose sand where they build trapdoor tunnels. They hunt in a frantic manner, pouncing on insects like desert crickets, spiders or geckos. Their style of hunting has resulted in them being referred to as 'dancing' white ladies. They are pale-coloured with hair and the long legs, spanning 9 cm, are armed with spines.

Community nest spiders
Stegodyphus species))

Community nest spiders are pale grey spiders covered in velvety hairs and bearing large abdomens. Spiders measure 2 mm to 2 cm. They nest communally in vegetation, their complex webs resembling untidy birds' nests. The nest is made from woolly silk combed and teased into that texture by a sieve-like spinning organ called the cribellum in front of the anterior spinnerets. A multi-angled catch web encompasses the main nest and traps insect prey. Numerous spiders inhabit a single web, retreating into separate tunnels or chambers but a group works cooperatively to overcome prey, taking it back to be shared by all in the nest.

DANGEROUSLY VENOMOUS SPIDERS

There are just six dangerously venomous spiders in South Africa and all bites are treatable with few, if any, resulting in death. These are the black and brown button spiders and the small baboon spider that have neurotoxic venom, and the violin, sac and six-eyed crab spiders that have cytotoxic venom. Neurotoxins result in a painful bite and affect heart and respiratory function causing headaches, chest pain, body temperature fluctuations and anxiety. Cytotoxins cause localised ulcerations and secondary necrosis of the tissue, accompanied with fever and resulting in scarring. The six-eyed crab spider is most dangerous with potent cytotoxic venom. Damage to the tissue is not localised around the bite site like with other spiders but spreads, causing tissue damage throughout the body and, potentially, death.

Black button spider

Six-eyed crab spider

Scorpions

Scorpions inhabit a diversity of habitats, can tolerate severe temperature extremes and are exceptionally effective predators. By using microhabitats like burrows, rock crevices or bark hideaways, they evade desiccation and freezing. They ambush prey often much larger than themselves, including insects, spiders, other scorpions, small vertebrates, snails, reptiles, mammals and amphibians. By spending most of their time totally inactive, they are able to lower their metabolism and avoid the need to feed frequently.

Scorpions are modified for their lifestyles, most notably with enlarged pedipalps that terminate in pincers. These are used to hunt, defend themselves or in courtship. The legs are equipped with stiff spines for grip while burrowing or curved claws enable it to navigate upside-down. Scorpions orientate themselves by using wind direction, scent trails, landmarks, visual items and possibly even the stars. Their eyes see poorly but register light and depth.

Scorpions can produce sound by stridulation. This involves rubbing various body parts against one another. Special rough surfaces on the tail may be brushed with the sting to make clicks that apparently startle predators. Bristles on the mouthparts also produce noises when rubbed over body ridges.

ME

ME

Scorpions have unique sensory capabilities. They have a well-developed sense of touch and can pick up vibrations through organs on their feet or discern something touching them with microscopic slit organs on the legs. Hairs on the body detect physical and chemical stimuli. A set of comb-like pectines on the ventral surface helps them to interpret their environment, including information about temperature, humidity, substrate or pheromone trails left by females.

While scorpions are excellent predators, they often form prey to larger animals. Hornbills, owls, frogs, snakes, bats, large lizards, centipedes, solifugids, spiders, baboons, honey badgers and mongoose all eat scorpions. Many species have developed ways to avoid or remove the sting in order to consume them. Centipedes use their toxic venom to kill them.

A male locates a mate by following her pheromone trail and tapping out vibrations to identify himself as a mate, not food. The pair joins pincers and move dance-like over a large area, sometimes for as long as 30 minutes. Once the male finds an appropriate surface on which to deposit his spermatophore (hooked sperm capsules), he directs the female over it until her genital opening aligns with the spermatophore and can hook them. He may lift and drop her to employ her body weight in triggering the release of the sperm. She remains still for a while, at which point the male releases her and makes a hasty retreat, often not without some ensuing commotion.

Gravidity lasts 2–18 months and 8–30 babies are born alive. In some species, eggs simply hatch inside the female and then emerge. Some species have a form of placental development usually reserved for mammals. The female gathers her babies one at a time as they appear, sometimes taking up to an hour. She raises her body and arches her tail, forming a basket with her legs. The pale, under-formed babies clamber upon her back and stay there for protection until their first moult about 2 weeks later. Like other invertebrates, scorpions grow by shedding their hard exoskeleton. After ecdysis they lack the fluorescence they otherwise have under UV light. Scorpions live for about 10 years although 30-year lifespans have been recorded.

The idea of a scorpion immediately conjures up images of coal-hot venom, and rightly so since scorpion venom is the most potent venom known. The venom is neurotoxic and scorpions sting prey to subdue it or enemies in defence. They may also use venom to relax their mates during courtship. Scorpion venom is manufactured in venom glands and injected into its target via the sting or telson at the tip of the tail and they can regulate just how much they inject.

The size of a scorpion's tail indicates how important venom is to its lifestyle and also the potency. Members of the **Buthidae family** all have relatively small pincers and enlarged stings because they rely more on their venom to catch prey than on their pincers. A Buthid's sting is excruciating and stings of the *Parabuthus* species require medical attention. Members of the **Scorpionidae family** have very large pincers yet small stings because they mechanically catch prey in their formidable forceps and the sting is of secondary importance. These scorpions have milder venoms.

Bark scorpions
Uroplectes species))

Small scorpions measuring about 5 cm that are variable in colour, from yellow or orange, sometimes with striping, to black, brown or dull green. Pincers are small and the tail enlarged with a very sharp stinger. While the venom is not lethal, it does require medical attention and is exceptionally sore. This scorpion is common and causes most scorpion stings in southern Africa. It typically resides under the bark of trees or in leaf layers but also frequents human habitations. It hunts cockroaches and crickets.

Thick-tailed scorpions
Parabuthus species))

Olive, brown, yellow or black and measuring between 4 and 14 cm, this group has slender pincers and a thick tail and telson. These scorpions are dangerously venomous and stings require medical care and can be lethal. They can also squirt their neurotoxic venom at the eyes. They hunt insects, geckos and even mice and shelter under stones or around homesteads, usually in arid habitats. To make intimidating sounds, the thick-tailed scorpions rub the stinger on ridges on the first two tail segments.

Burrowing scorpions
Opistophthalmus species))

Olive, brown or yellow scorpion measuring up to 10 cm and bearing a long, thin tail and large pincers. They burrow in soil or underneath rocks and prefer arid areas. They hunt beetles, grasshoppers, cockroaches and spiders under the cover of darkness, using the sting only to subdue larger prey. Venom is neuro- and cytotoxic but while a sting is painful, it is not lethal. Hisses if alarmed.

Rock scorpions
Hadogenes species))

Flat black scorpions with medium-sized pincers and a thin tail. They measure about 10 cm long. These scorpions take refuge in rock crevices by day and hunt geckos and insects at night. The sting is harmless and relatively painless.

Solifuges

)) Order Solifugae

Also known as a red roman or sun spider, solifuges are arachnids but not true spiders as they lack venom glands and spinnerets. They occur in hot, dry areas and are active and voracious predators, moving extremely swiftly as they wander in search of prey in the form of insects, small reptiles and birds, spiders and scorpions. One-third of the solifuge is head and jaws and they are able to inflict a painful bite. The modified jaws secure and shred prey scissor-like until it is liquidised enough to ingest. Since no venom is used, digestion is internal. Leg-like pedipalps are large and sensitive to tactile stimuli. These are held off the ground to navigate, have adhesive pads to assist with climbing, are used to grab prey, cupped to drink water or employed to determine how to attack enemies. Taste, smell and hearing organs are present on the feet and mouthparts and the body is covered with sensory hairs. Females are equally

WMC/BD

aggressive to males and the latter must induce a trance in order to mate. He may stroke her gently or stun her with an all-out charge. Sperm is deposited on the ground and transferred to her genital orifice with his pedipalps after opening it with his jaws. Solifuges take refuge in shallow scrapes under rocks and logs.

Millipedes

Locally referred to as a *shongololo*, the millipede is a common and obvious detritivore feeding on rotten vegetation or fungi. The cylindrical body is reinforced with a calcareous shell for pushing through humus and soil, projected forward by wave-like movements of the legs, of which there are two pairs per segment. These work in pulses, some legs pushing, some legs readying for the next stroke. Food and mates are located with tapping movements of the antennae in front of itself and millipedes respond to danger by coiling up tightly with the softer legs on the inside. Millipedes contain and secrete cyanide and other chemicals, to deter predators.

Centipedes

Centipedes are voracious carnivores and are brightly coloured to warn of their ability to flick toxins in defence. The body is flat with a single pair of legs per segment and achieves a quick serpentine movement. Centipedes use their venomous claws to capture and dispatch prey, including earthworms, snails, frogs, snakes, mice and birds. The terminal pair of legs is enlarged to perform sensory functions but can also nip in defence.

ME

African giant land snail

Achatina achatina

The largest snail in southern Africa, reaching about 20 cm, this is a scavenger that scrapes up food with a radula – a conveyor-like ribbon membrane with backwards facing teeth for rasping. They have colourful shells and a large, muscular foot with lubricating mucous for locomotion. Living in moist habitats, they move at night to avoid drying out and hide in damp vegetation when it is hot. It is preyed on by reptiles, birds and mammals, even by people who eat or export the escargot. The giant land snail is a hermaphrodite, but two individuals do still exchange sperm bundles to cross-fertilise one other. Eggs hatch as miniatures of the adults.

ME

Red velvet mite

Dinothrombium tinctorium

These little arachnids are tomato red and covered in soft, velvety hairs as the name suggests. The carapace looks somewhat folded and undulating. They measure about 0.5 cm long. Red velvet mites live in sandy areas and appear after good rains. They are predatory and consume other invertebrates. The larvae parasitise various insects and arachnids, before entering the free-living adult stage.

Ticks

Subclass *Acari*

These blood-sucking arachnids are ectoparasites that come in a variety of forms and colours. The cephalothorax and abdomen are fused and the body is soft to allow it to expand with a blood meal. Larger, bloated ticks are blood-engorged females, males are smaller. Adults are 4-legged while larvae are 6-legged. The larvae are miniscule and known as pepper ticks, as once a nest has been breached with a passing body, the tiny parasites spread out over the person or host animal resembling grains of pepper. Ticks have 1-, 2- or 3-host life cycles, depending on the number of times they fall off and recolonise hosts before maturing, ecdysis taking place in between hosts. Ticks are prevalent during the rainy season and carry diseases like tick-bite fever. Different species include, amongst others, cattle and dog ticks, which are red-brown, flat and have a hard shield; bont ticks which have brightly coloured brown, yellow and red patterns on their shields, and mouthparts measuring a third of the body length; and bont-legged ticks which have red legs with white bands.

ME

PO

Plants of many varying descriptions provide the bigger canvas upon which the rest of ecology is painted. Plants provide food and/or shelter (in addition to life-giving oxygen) to every creature on the planet. But being useful to animals is not their sole purpose and every species exhibits designs and functionalities of their own, not to mention delivers useful medicinal, cultural and ecological qualities. Although perhaps harder to perceive than with animals, they also all have unique identifying traits that set them apart one from another. Trees are one of the harder aspects of the environment to identify for amateurs but not as prohibitively so as many people believe. In this section, common trees and shrubs of the sub-region are introduced in a simple manner by way of easily accessible descriptions and close-up representative images. A section on smaller plants and wild flowers aims to showcase a handful of these striking plants too.

TREES

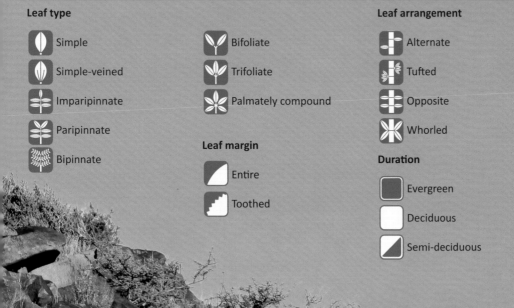

Leaf type

- Simple
- Simple-veined
- Imparipinnate
- Paripinnate
- Bipinnate
- Bifoliate
- Trifoliate
- Palmately compound

Leaf margin

- Entire
- Toothed

Leaf arrangement

- Alternate
- Tufted
- Opposite
- Whorled

Duration

- Evergreen
- Deciduous
- Semi-deciduous

Baobab

🔊 *Adansonia digitata*

Adansonia = named after the French surgeon Michel Adanson (1727–1806), and *digitata* = hand-shaped, referring to the shape of the leaf.

Height: 25 m

An enormous tree with bulging trunk and branches and a mushroom-like, dark green canopy. Oldest specimens may have a circumference of 30 m. Old baobabs may exceed 4 000 years of age. Because they expand and shrink to some degree, aging a tree is difficult. A 5 m wide tree is probably about 1 000 years old, an 8 m wide tree may be over 3 000 years old. Baobabs grow in hot, dry woodland at low altitudes.

Smooth, shiny, fibrous **bark** covers the enormous, swollen trunk and is dimpled with old wounds. Sections stripped by elephants reveal fibrous strips.

Palmately compound **leaves** are bright green when new, darkening with age. Leaflets are tear-shaped and number between 3 and 9 with those nearest the stalk being smallest. New leaves are simple.

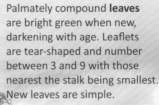

Large, creamy **flowers** with a pollen-rich, powder brush-like stamen bundle borne on a central column. Flowers hang downwards and open just before dark, lasting only 24 hours before falling off the tree. Flowers occur on the trees between October and November and have a strong carrion smell.

Velvety, mango-sized, hard-shelled **fruit** hang on long stalks from January to May. They are green or brown in colour and contain many large, dark seeds coated in white powdery pulp.

270

A tree of many uses

Much of the tree is edible: dried roots make porridge, leaves are eaten as spinach, the fruit is eaten fresh or mixed as a drink, seeds are sucked to relieve thirst or roasted and ground for coffee or soups. The pith and seeds contain tartaric acid. The seed is high in protein and the oils extracted are rich in vitamin D and fatty acids and thus used in body products to moisturise and heal the skin. The fibrous bark is employed in weaving sacks, fishing nets and clothes or as twine, instrument strings and snares. The heartwood is 40% water and used extensively by elephants. Humans and other animals also chew on the fibre for moisture. Animals browse accessible foliage, primates eat the fruit and herbivores eat fallen flowers. Straw-coloured fruit bats pollinate the flowers. Prone to natural cavities, the tree provides homes to myriad birds, reptiles, rodents and bats, reservoirs for rainwater and sites for beehives. Humans have used natural cavities in baobabs as granaries, kilns, hideouts, abodes, burial sites, prisons or bars.

Shepherd's tree

◗ *Boscia albitrunca*

Boscia = named after the French professor of agriculture, Louis A.G.Bosc (1777–1850), *albi* = white, and *trunca* = trunk.

Height: 7 m

Especially visible due to its crooked white trunk, the shepherd's tree has a compact, often flat-topped canopy. It grows in hot, dry woodland and bushveld in sandy and rocky areas where it is frequently used by herdsmen for shade and from whom it gets its name. It is an immensely useful tree. Branches are cut off the tree to provide high-protein browse to stock, although local culture forbids its total destruction and badly damaged trees recover slowly. Wild animals also browse heavily. Natural cavities collect water, an essential resource to people living in arid areas. The roots are nutritious and are eaten raw, boiled, dried and ground into porridge, or taken as a drink or coffee substitute. Crushed roots act as preservatives and extend the life of milk or butter, and prevent mould on citrus, bread, tomatoes and potatoes. The flower buds offer a caper substitute and while on the tree attract insects. Birds eat the fruit. Medicinally, haemorrhoids and epilepsy are treated with the plant. There is a cultural superstition that if fruits wilt before a millet crop is ripe, the harvest is doomed.

Narrow, leathery, grey-green **leaves** with no obvious veins grow in spirals around the branches or cluster on side shoots. The leaves terminate before the ends of branchlets that subsequently appear spiky on the edges of the crown.

ME

WMC/MS

Small, green-yellow strong-smelling **flowers** occur profusely in spring, usually after the first substantial rain.

Small, round, green **berries** that ripen to yellow occur from November to April.

The **bark** is pale, almost white. The texture is rough and blocky with smoother panes of white superimposed upon this. The trunk is robust and kinked, often with cavities.

False olive

🔊 *Buddleja saligna*

Buddleja = named in honour of Rev. Adam Buddle (1660–1715), an amateur botanist, and *saligna* = willow, the leaves resemble those of a willow tree.

Height: 7 m

A densely branching, smallish tree with a grey-green drooping canopy that grows on rocky hillsides or in more wooded areas. As its name implies, the tree resembles a wild olive and makes an attractive garden ornamental. They are fast growing and hardy trees. The dark, hard, durable wood is used for assegai shafts and fencing posts or as fuel. Several medicinal applications include for coughs and colds or as a purgative or emetic.

Deeply, longitudinally furrowed, pale, creamy brown **bark** and four-angled twigs.

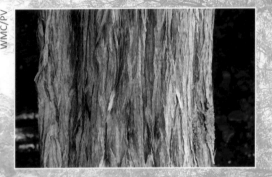

The **fruit** are pale green-yellow, ovoid capsules about 2 mm long. They occur between October and March in similar clusters to the flowers and turn brown with age.

Linear, shiny, dark grey-green **leaves** are hairy and white underneath with distinct, raised veins. The tips are tapered and the margins roll under.

Whitish, many-flowered sprays incorporate tiny **flowers** in fist-sized masses. The flowers have long anthers, a honey fragrance and occur between August and January.

Wild seringa

 Burkea africana

Burkea = named for the British botanist and plant collector Joseph Burke (1812–1873) who undertook several collecting expeditions with the noted South African botanist Carl L.P. Zeyher, and *africana* = from Africa.

Height: 8 m

The wild seringa has a relatively flat canopy and is crowned with red in autumn. There is a slight kink in its erect trunk and branches, which form a characteristic V-shaped fork. Wild seringas usually grow on deep, sandy soils or less often, on termite mounds. Elephants browse leaves and monkeys eat flowers and pods. The wood is hard and popular for uses such as railway sleepers, wagons, grain stampers, parquet flooring and mine props. Dried bark can be used as fish poison and to flavour beer and the roots produce a red dye used with the bark for tanning leather. Medicinal applications include cures for dysentery, septic sores, pneumonia and various pains.

BvW

The wild seringa has relatively small, flat, brown **pods** each containing a single seed. The pods are abundant and contribute to the autumn dress of the trees between February and July.

Plain, dark grey-brown **bark** that forms coarse blocks and shaves away leaving behind a red colour. New twigs have velvety, maroon-coloured tips.

Edible and harvestable caterpillars of the emperor moth, *Cirina forda*, subsist on **gum** from the tree.

ME

Strong-scented white **flower** spikes appear with the new leaves in spring and cluster together at the ends of the thickened twigs.

BvW

The **leaves** are large and double compound with visibly oval leaflets that look confetti-like against the sky. The leaves cluster on the ends of thick, pencil-like twigs. They are dark green above, paler below and the leaf stalks and main vein on each leaflet are yellow. Leaves become coppery-red in autumn.

White stinkwood

>)) *Celtis africana*

Celtis = the Greek name for the laurel tree, and *africana* = from Africa.

Height: 30 m

The white stinkwood is an enormous, regal tree with a strikingly pale, upright, buttressed trunk and pale branches and a dense and spreading canopy. It grows in a wide range of habitats but favours high-rainfall areas. It is often found on dolomite-derived soils. The tree's reputation stems from the obnoxious smell of newly cut wood, which is strong and used for furniture, carvings, household items and utensils, panelling and shelving and as a protective charm. The white stinkwood is a popular ornamental and shade tree used in gardens, parks and along streets. It grows 1–2 m per year, is drought resistant and frost tolerant. Birds and primates are attracted to the fruit and mammals and cattle browse the leaves, as do leaf beetles and butterfly larvae.

Very pale, smooth **bark** sometimes potholed in older sections. Young bark has a velvet texture and twigs have elevated dark rings. Ripples form where branches join the main stem.

White stinkwoods have tiny, round, yellow **fruits** that grow on long, slender stalks turning brown and then black when ripe. Fruits can be smooth or hairy and cover the tree profusely between October and February.

Small, green, **flowers** appear in spring (Aug–Oct). Flowers don't have petals and separate sexes occur in separate flowers but on the same tree.

The white stinkwood has dark green, simple, triangular **leaves** with a pointed tip, asymmetrical base and serrated margin. Three obvious veins arise from the base of the leaf and leaves hang from twigs but face upwards on a flat plane mostly. They change to yellow before falling and sometimes develop a yellow border from a disease. The leaves are soft or leathery and often hairy.

WMC/JMK

Mopane

◗ *Colophospermum mopane*

Colophospermum = from the Greek meaning oily or gum-producing seed, and *mopane* = derived from the local name for the tree.

Height: 30 m

Variable in growth form depending on growth conditions, fire and elephant activity, mopane may be a tall, erect tree with an untidy crown or a low branching shrub. It prefers low-lying clay soils but grows in a variety of habitats and outcompetes the undergrowth due to shallow roots. It tends to encroach and form monocultures, particularly attractive when leaves change colour. Hard, termite resistant stems are used for fencing, building cattle kraals or traditional Damara huts. Wood is also used to treat eye infections and inner bark for venereal diseases.

Rough, deeply fissured **bark**. Segments are not continuous, ending abruptly and often having a slight curve.

Bifoliate, butterfly-like **leaves** have fountain-like venation emanating from the point of stalk attachment (see opposite page). They start off bright green, darkening with time and turning yellow or red-brown

in autumn. Leaves are lost irregularly. Blades are joined together a small gland. Leaf surfaces pull together to reduce moisture loss when it's hot.

Pale, flat, kidney bean-shaped **pods** occur in winter en masse, each pod with a single, sticky seed. **Seeds** have many folds and oily resin glands and smell pleasant.

Many animals browse mopane, especially elephants, as the leaves are high in protein and retain much of this after they fall off too. The tree is rich in tannins as a defence against excessive herbivory. Tree squirrels nest in mopane cavities and eat the seeds. The resin of the seed is flammable and the genus *Colophospermum* means 'gum-producing seed'. Trees are also popular with hole-nesting birds and mopane bees.

Mopane worms, the larvae of the large *Gonimbrasia belina* moth occur in plague proportions on the tree at times and are rich in protein. They are harvested and eaten fresh, roasted or dried in rural areas in southern Africa. 'Mopane' means butterfly in Shona (Zimbabwe).

Red bushwillow

)) *Combretum apiculatum*

Combretum = a name used by Pliny for a climbing plant, and *apiculatum* = ending abruptly in a short point, referring to the leaf tip.

Height: 10 m

A relatively small, sparse tree with a shapeless canopy and one or several crooked trunks. Smaller branches tend to grow erect and at right angles to the main branches. The red bushwillow encroaches readily, preferring the sandy soils in dry, open woodland and rocky areas where they put on a colourful show before shedding. Famed for its hard wood – the densest and hardest in southern Africa, weighing 1 230 kg/m³. The timber is termite resistant, offering a good structural material. It is sometimes used for furniture that proves heavy. Coals are very long lasting. Game browses the leaves and brown hooded parrots enjoy the pods. People use the leaves and pods to brew tea but the seeds should be removed to prevent chronic hiccupping. Zulu people use the leaves for steam baths or as an enema for stomach ailments.

Bark is pale grey, brownish or charcoal coloured and smooth becoming rough with age and cracking to form a grid pattern. **Younger branches** have string-like bark fibres that peel away.

Fresh green, shiny **leaves** have hooked and twisted tips that contort the leaf blades somewhat. Leaves turn yellow in autumn and are sometimes sticky.

Four-winged **pods** are shiny green in the centre with blushing pink-red on the wings. They may be sticky to begin and become redder with age, drying brown. They are medium-sized at 2.5 cm and appear from March to August.

ME

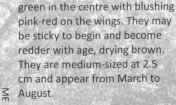

ME

ME

ME

Flowers are creamy-yellow spikes with long stamens, growing in the axils of the leaves. They resemble small bottlebrushes and are about 3.5 cm long.

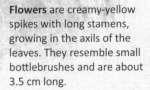

ME

ME

Russet bushwillow

 Combretum hereroense

Combretum = the name used by Pliny for a climbing plant, and *hereroense* = from Hereroland.

Height: 10 m

Impressively rusty-red when covered in pods, this small tree is usually multi-stemmed and has an irregular canopy with branches that may arch to the ground. Smaller branches grow erect off the larger ones. It is a bushveld tree preferring sandy soils or termite mounds. It is hard-wooded and earned its Afrikaans name 'kierieklapper' from its popularity for making walking sticks known as kieries. The termite resistant wood is also used for structural supports, kraal fences, furniture, pick-handles and wagon wheel-spokes. It burns for a long time because of its density. Lesser bushbabies eat gum that may ooze from wounds, and leaves are browsed or used with deseeded pods to brew tea. Tonsillitis, coughing, stomach problems, heart disease, heartburn or pain enemas are some of the medical conditions parts of the tree are believed to cure.

Rough, fissured **bark** is dark grey or grey-brown and cracked lengthways. **Young growth** is covered in brown hairs and younger stems may be green, reddish or grey with fine strings peeling off.

Relatively small, oval **leaves** are darker green above with brown hairs below. Leaves often grow on short side shoots and are decussate growing in pairs at right angles to the preceding pair. Veins are raised on the underside of the leaf with a russet-coloured overlay.

Flowers are greenish-yellow spikes with long stamens that resemble small bottlebrushes. They appear before the leaves and are about 3 cm long.

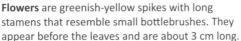

Four-winged **pods** are rusty-brown and small at just 2 cm. The seed in the middle is darkest. Clusters of pods remain on the tree from January to June, highlighting the russet bushwillow in the landscape as the entire tree takes on a russet colour when in pod.

Leadwood

🔊 *Combretum imberbe*

Combretum = a name that Pliny used for a creeping plant, and *imberbe* = beardless in Latin, referring to the lack of hairs on the plant.

Height: 15 m

A tall, stately tree which typically grows along rivers. Leadwoods are recognisable from high branches, an overall greyish appearance and dead 'sacrificial' branches. The tree ransoms these less vital lower limbs as a deposition site for toxins. Dead trees are iconic and stand for decades after they have died, offering excellent perching sites for vultures and other birds of prey. With very hard, dense wood (1.2 t/m^3), the tree is termite resistant and slow growing – some have been carbon-dated to over 1 000 years old. Leadwood is a difficult wood to work into furniture but ideal for maize mortars, hoes and for structural supports in mines or on railway tracks. The wood burns slowly and stumps smoulder for weeks after veld fires. The ash is abrasive, white and lime-rich, traditionally used as toothpaste or wall-whitewash if mixed with milk.

Leadwood **bark** is very pale grey and the light trunks of the trees stand out noticeably. The bark is very square and broken up into small scale-like tiles which look like a crocodile's skin.

The **leaves** are fairly variable in size, from smallish and narrow to medium-sized and broader. They have smooth but wavy margins. The upper leaf surface is greener than the lower one and the mid-vein on the underside has a russet colour. Both leaf surfaces are covered with tiny grey, snowy speckles. Inhaling the smoke of burning leadwood leaves is said to relieve coughs and colds.

Leadwoods have small, yellow, 4-winged **pods**, which house a single seed in the centre. These are present on the tree from April to June and in their profusion can make the whole tree appear yellowish.

The **spines** on younger trees are arranged in pairs, each alternating set at right angles to the preceding one. The spiny branchlets help to protect the tree from excessive herbivory while it is young. Leadwoods grow slowly and can't afford to keep losing a large amount of leaves to herbivores.

The **flowers** occur as creamy-yellow spikes. The calyx is bell-shaped on each individual flower and the anthers are relatively long. The flowers can occur quite profusely on the tree.

ME

ME

Large-fruited bushwillow

Combretum zeyheri

Combretum = a name that Pliny used for a creeping plant, and *zeyheri* = named after Carl L.P. Zeyher (1799–1858), German naturalist and explorer who first collected this species on the Magaliesberg range

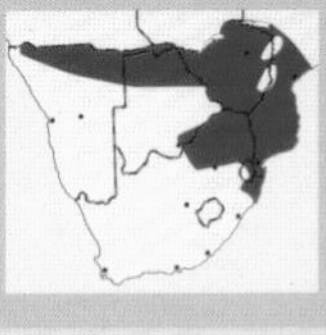

Height: 5-15 m

A shrubby tree with a short, curved trunk and sparse crown with sagging branches. The pods are conspicuous and once dry, rustle noisily amongst the yellow autumn foliage. It grows in varying soils in open woodland, on slopes, rocky terrain and along rivers. Elephants browse the leaves, baboons eat the seeds and the gum is edible for people. Medicinal applications range from antibiotic properties to eye lotions, a cure for gallstones and backache or nosebleed and haemorrhoid remedies. Fibrous roots are used to weave baskets and fish traps and the wood constitutes a relatively good general-purpose timber.

ME

Smooth, rather pale **bark** becoming coarser with darker patches that may flake off on older trees.

Fairly large, yellowish to dark green leathery **leaves** with raised veins on the paler underside and long leaf stalks. Young leaves are velvety.

Flowers are greenish-yellow spikes with long stamens that resemble small bottlebrushes. They appear before or simultaneously with the new leaves in spring and are about 70 mm long. Flowers grow in the axils of the leaves and are pleasantly scented.

Four-winged **pods** are large and green, ripening to brown. Profuse bunches hang from the branches, weightily remaining on the tree after the leaves have fallen off. They rustle noisily in the breeze.

ME

PJ

ME

Lavender fever-berry

 Croton gratissimus

Croton = Greek for a tick, referring to the shape of the fruit, and *gratissimus* = from the Latin meaning 'most pleasing'.

Height: 15 m

A small single or multi-stemmed tree that branches low and has a disorderly, V-shaped canopy with drooping leaves. There are orange speckles all over the plant – leaves, stalks, buds and stems – colouring the tree rusty brown overall. The silvery undersides of the leaves shimmer in the breeze. Aromatic oils give the leaves their lavender-like fragrance and San women crush the scented foliage and use it as perfume. The tree grows on rocky outcrops or hillsides and attracts bees to its flowers, and birds like crested guineafowl, terrestrial brownbuls and spurfowl to its fruit. Fever, coughs, bleeding gums, rheumatism, chest problems, indigestion, water retention, uterine disorders and insomnia are treated with this plant, despite it being poisonous.

ME

Coarse, cracked, brown **bark** with smooth and shiny young stems. Branches are covered with brown scales and have a silver or orange sheen.

The **fruits** are silver with orange speckles and comprise a row of hard, berry-like capsules on a long axis. They become yellow once mature bursting open into three sections, from December to June.

Rusty-coloured **flower buds** remain on the tree for a long time before the small, creamy flowers open to form a 10 cm long, unbranched raceme with several female flowers at the base and numerous male flowers above. These hang at the ends of the stems, from October to May.

Strap-like, drooping two-toned **leaves** that are dark green above and silvery underneath peppered with orange scales. The main vein on the underside protrudes. The long petioles are also covered in orange scales and new leaves are covered in russet hairs. There are usually totally orange leaves amongst the green ones and leaves are lavender-aromatic when crushed.

Highveld cabbage tree

🔊 *Cussonia paniculata*

Cussonia = named after Pierre Cusson (1727–1783), Professor of Botany, University of Montpellier, and *paniculata*, referring to the paniculate (branching) inflorescences.

Height: 12 m

This small, squat tree with a stout trunk and only a few thickset branches with a palm-like fountain of lacy, grey-blue-green foliage, grows in the bushveld on rocky outcrops and in mountainous areas. Cabbage trees attract birds and insects such as Charaxes butterflies, and flies pollinate them. The wood is pale-grey and soft, and was used historically for brake blocks. Trees are frost-resistant and popular garden ornamentals.

Thick, corky, grooved, grey-brown **bark**.

Small, round, purplish **fruits** cluster densely together in spikes on the tumbleweed-like flower structure. The individual 6 mm fruits are fleshy, each containing a seed inside a stone (May to June).

Enormous, palmately compound **leaves** with jagged, waisted leaflets fan around a long stalk and cluster at the ends of branches. The leaves are leathery and pale blue-green. Leaflet blades are not subdivided and do not cut back to the midrib as in the common cabbage tree (see next page).

Yellow-green **flowers** grow in tight spikes in summer (January to April) from a spoked stalk with each of the multiple arms radiating outwards to form a huge spiky dome.

ME

ME

Common cabbage tree

🔊 *Cussonia spicata*

A much-branched tree with twice-compound, shiny, dark green **leaves** and leaflets that are subdivided and cut all the way back to the midrib. The flowers produce 8–12 finger-like yellow-green spikes in a candelabra-like double umbel in spring or summer. Fruit are angular, fleshy and purple. The many medicinal uses include treatment of fever, malaria, nausea, uterine discomfort, sexual diseases, stomach ulcers, indigestion and mental illnesses. It was also used as feeding troughs in the past.

Sickle bush

 Dichrostachys cinerea

Dichrostachys = two-coloured spike, and *cinerea* = refers to the greyish hairs of the typical subspecies which is confined to India.

Height: 7 m

A small multi-stemmed, low-branching, scrubby tree with a sparse canopy and flattened crown that encroaches aggressively and may form dense thickets. It grows well in disturbed habitats but is otherwise a habitat generalist favouring fertile clay soils. The sickle bush is very nutritious and browsed by game. Wood is exceptionally hard and termite resistant, and used for tool handles, fence posts or as lasting firewood. The inner bark makes strong rope and the flexible branches good hunting bows. Various medicinal preparations remedy stomach and chest problems, internal pain, toothache, pneumonia, skin sores, dysentery, sexual diseases or eye conditions as well as acting as a de-wormer, local topical anaesthetic and relieving scorpion stings, insect and snake bites. People keep charms or plant the trees near their homes to keep evil spirits away or collect the pods for decorative use.

Pale grey or brown **bark** finely striated with thin, vertical grooves.

The sickle bush has extremely rigid, hard, sharp **spines** from which the leaves may sprout.

The **pods** occur as twisted bunches and are obvious on leafless trees. They start green, drying brown but do not burst open (May to September).

The soft, feathery double-compound **leaves** are bright green, fading to olive and are often borne directly off spines. Many pairs of leaflets, each comprising tiny pinnules, make up the leaf.

The attractive two-toned Chinese lantern-like **flowers** grow on the tree from September to January. Each spike hangs down and has two parts – yellow fertile flowers at the tip and pink to white sterile flowers at the base. The multi-spiked flowers result in contorted bunches of pods.

Jackal-berry

 *Diospyros mespiliformis*

Diospyros = 'divine pear', and *mesos* = half + *pilos* = bullet, referring to the shape of the fruit.

Height: 25 m

Jackal-berries are enormous trees with a big, thick trunk that branches high and has a dark green, dense, spreading canopy. They grow largest along watercourses and on termite mounds. North of South Africa the jackal-berry is often called the ebony tree, as it is part of a family of dark wood trees. Timber is prized and used to make furniture, flooring, mokoros, maize-stampers, cups and knife handles. The fruit are its crowning glory and eaten by myriad frugivorous creatures and humans, who also make brandy, beer and preserves from them, or meal from the pulp. When fields are cleared for cultivation, jackal-berries are often left standing. The tree is high in tannins, used for tanning leather, to treat dysentery and as an antibiotic.

Dark, blackish **bark** is roughly textured and grooved, with an overlying white wash. Bark flakes in small chunks.

Green, hard-skinned **fruits** become yellow and fleshy once ripe. Round and measuring 2.5 cm, berries ripen around September but can be found on the tree all year. Immature fruit are hairy.

White, sweetly scented **flowers** grow in clusters with sexes on different trees. They are relatively unremarkable appearing after the new leaves between October and December.

GN

Strap-like, glossy, dark green **leaves** are alternately arranged on a flat plane. Margins are slightly wavy. New leaves are deep red while older ones turn yellow.

Wild pear

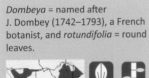 *Dombeya rotundifolia*

Dombeya = named after J. Dombey (1742–1793), a French botanist, and *rotundifolia* = round leaves.

Height: 10 m

A small tree with crooked trunk and irregular canopy through which one can usually see its multi-branched limbs and particularly conspicuous when in blossom. It grows in open woodland on hillsides, rocky areas or old termite mounds, and is fast growing and drought resistant. Flowers are used in love potions, the inner bark makes good rope and leaves are browsed by game. Wood is heavy and typically used for implement handles, bows, yokes and mine props. Medicinal applications include heart complaints, nausea, stomach ulcers and other stomach troubles, venereal diseases, rheumatism, menstrual issues, colic, fever and enemas.

Dark, grey-brown **bark** is rough and grooved lengthways, cracks making uneven blocks. Young bark is smooth.

Small, round, hairy **fruits** are enclosed by the dry flower petals (October to December). Seeds are hair covered.

Profuse white or pinkish **flowers** occur in spring (July to October). They are star-shaped, sweet smelling and cluster at the ends of branches. The wild pear is often the first tree to flower at the end of winter and flowers turn brown with age.

The **leaves** are round, sandpaper rough and rigid with 3–5 conspicuous veins from the base of the leaves that are raised below. The leaf stalks are also rough, the margins slightly toothed and the base of the leaf is often heart-shaped.

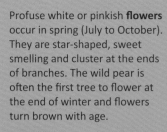

Stemfruit

)) *Englerophytum magalismontanum*

Engler = named after the botanist H.G.A. Engler (1844–1930) + *phytum* = plant, and *magalismontanum* = from the Magaliesberg mountain range.

Height: 10 m

This is a small, compact, evergreen tree with a thick, crooked trunk and a bluish-green canopy of branches that hang down. It grows between rocks in riverine forest or on rocky outcrops. The fruits of the stemfruit are its most unique feature with all manner of primate and bird relishing them. They are rich in vitamin C and used for making wine, brandy, syrup, jelly and jam. Fruits combined with the roots treat epilepsy and headaches, and powdered root alleviates rheumatism. Bushpigs dig up the roots. The tree makes an interesting and easily grown garden plant.

Bark is grey and smooth, yet scaly. New branches are covered in rusty hairs. Branches are scarred where fruits have fallen off.

The oval **leaves** are glossy, dark green and leathery with edges slightly turned under. Leaves are thick and cluster to form stiff rosettes at the ends of short twigs. **New leaves** are golden and look like flowers at the branch tips. They fold up along the main vein while young. The main vein is sunken above, raised below and numerous side veins run parallel near to one another. The underside is velvety red-brown or silver and leaves are often covered by a whitish **waxy layer** that rubs off. Leaf stalks are rigid, merge into the leaf bases and when plucked ooze milky latex.

The 3 cm **fruits** have a sharp tip and grow directly off the stems, crowding on older wood particularly (December to February). They have leathery skins which turn red when ripe, concealing a purple flesh with a milky juice and usually just one seed.

Smallish pink, purple-brown or white, star-shaped **flowers** grow in clusters off the knobbly stems between June and December.

Buds and stalks have a dense covering of red hairs and flowers have an unpleasant scent.

WMC/PV

WMC/JMK

ME

Magic guarri
 Euclea divinorum

Euclea = of good report or famous, perhaps referring to the fine quality of the wood, and *divinorum* = of the diviners.

Height: 8 m

Multi-stemmed, small tree or straggly shrub often growing in clusters in open, sodic areas, on riverbanks, hillsides or in thornveld. A useful bush that treats constipation, abdominal pain, infertility, headaches, convulsions, toothache and diarrhoea. Brown-black dye extracted from the roots is used on basket ware and the dark wood is used to make household utensils. Branches make handy toothbrushes, fire-beaters, pest-swats and brooms, and branches may be placed atop water-filled buckets to prevent spillage when carried on heads. The fruit produces alcohol or violet-coloured ink and is a purgative. A Zulu superstition suggests cutting a magic guarri down will result in the demolition of one's kraal and hunters carry pieces as good-luck charms.

Bark is pale grey and smooth becoming darker, rougher and more segmented on older branches.

Small, sweetly scented, white **flowers** cluster in the leaf axils with sexes on separate plants. The flower stalks have rusty spotting on them.

Bunches of purple-black **berries** occur between October and March. The berries measure 5 mm in size and have just a thin layer of flesh over the seed.

WMC/JMK

ME

Simple, leathery, dark green, shiny elongated **leaves** with wavy edges. The leaves are decussate, arranged opposite to each other with each pair at right angles to the previous pair. Leaf stalks are short and strong.

ME

Euphorbias
Euphorbia species

The genus Euphorbia is large and diverse, with more than 2 000 species of herbaceous, woody or succulent plants. They all produce milky, often toxic, latex which they exude when cut. The three species described here are succulent trees, which are often used as garden ornamentals because of their striking shape, and drought and heat tolerance.

Bushveld candelabra euphorbia

)) *Euphorbia cooperii*

Euphorbia = for Euphorbus, Greek physician of Juba II, King of Mauretania, and *cooperii* = for Thomas Cooper (1815–1913), English botanist.

Height: 7 m

This spiny, succulent tree has a cylindrical, dimpled **trunk** and upward curving branches forming a wineglass shape. Lower branches hang for a time before they die and fall off, revealing a new part of the trunk every year. It grows in the bushveld or wooded grassland preferring rocky areas. Its copious milky latex is one of the deadliest of all the *Euphorbias*, causing blistering and allergies or even blindness if inadvertently placed in the eye. The latex is used as fish poison. Baboons and doves eat the flowers and fruit without a problem and birds nest in the holes left behind by the severed branches.

ME

Each **branch** is notably constricted into heart-shaped sections and each segment bears 3–6 wings and has paired grey spines along the hard ridges.

A popular garden plant for its shape and attractive yellow **flowers** and red **fruit** that grow on the angles of the segments .

ME

ME

Common tree euphorbia

Euphorbia ingens

Euphorbia = for Euphorbus, Greek physician of Juba II, King of Mauretania, and *ingens* = unusually large.

Height: 15 m

A candelabra-shaped tree that, unlike the bushveld candelabra, does not shed its older branches. Consequently it has a massive, often almost V-shaped canopy on a short trunk. Branch segments have parallel sides and paired spines of only 2 mm on distinct cushions that are not aligned to form a ridge. The flowers and round fruits cluster on short stalks. Monkeys eat the fruit and porcupines gnaw the roots. The latex is used as a fish poison or to treat warts.

Rubber euphorbia

Euphorbia tirucalli

Euphorbia = for Euphorbus, Greek physician of Juba II, King of Mauretania, and *tirucalli* = derivation is obscure.

Height: 10 m

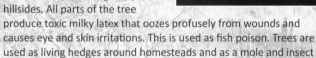

A sturdy, upright trunk bears a scrambled canopy of spaghetti-like, thin, green, spineless branches. The rubber euphorbia sometimes forms dense stands utilising numerous bushveld habitats but preferring rocky hillsides. All parts of the tree produce toxic milky latex that oozes profusely from wounds and causes eye and skin irritations. This is used as fish poison. Trees are used as living hedges around homesteads and as a mole and insect repellent. While there are risks of internal bleeding or death involved in ingesting the latex, it is used for medicinal purposes to relieve pain or sexual impotence and as a snakebite emetic. Black rhino eat the plant without ill effect. It was tested as a commercial substitute for rubber but rejected as a good substitute.

Ana tree
◈ *Faidherbia albida*

Faidherbia = for Louis Léon César Faidherbe (1818–1889), French general, colonial administrator and Governor of Senegal, and *albida* = somewhat whitish, referring to the colour of the stems.

Height: 30 m

An elegant, single-stemmed tree with a rounded or flat yet somewhat bare crown. It grows along rivers and in other alluvial areas, floodplains, pans, vleis or dry river courses with high water tables. Ana trees grow quickly, colonising and stabilising sandy banks and are protected in South Africa. The pods are very nutritious and the seeds are high in protein, providing food at the end of the dry season for wild animals, stock and people, who boil the seeds or pound the pods into flour. Elephants favour ana tree pods and disperse the seeds in the process of feeding on them, also providing food for guineafowl and baboons that pick through elephants' dung. Remedies using the bark relieve diarrhoea, eye inflammation, bleeding and induce vomiting.

Dark brown, rough **bark** occurs in older trees while younger ones have smoother greenish-grey bark. Twigs zigzag and may droop.

The **flowers** grow between March and September and are creamy, elongated spikes.

WMC/RC

The ana tree has paired, brownish-white, relatively short, straight **thorns**.

The **pods** are large, thick, flat and coiled like an apple peel. They are bright red-brown or orange and indehiscent. The tree yields copious pods, up to 1 000 kg in a year, and these provide essential food to myriad animals when the pods fall off, from November.

Leaves are twice compound. They vary considerably in size and in the number of pinnae and pinnules per leaf. A gland is present at the base of each leaflet pair. The canopy has an overall grey-green hue and often looks quite bare.

WMC/BD

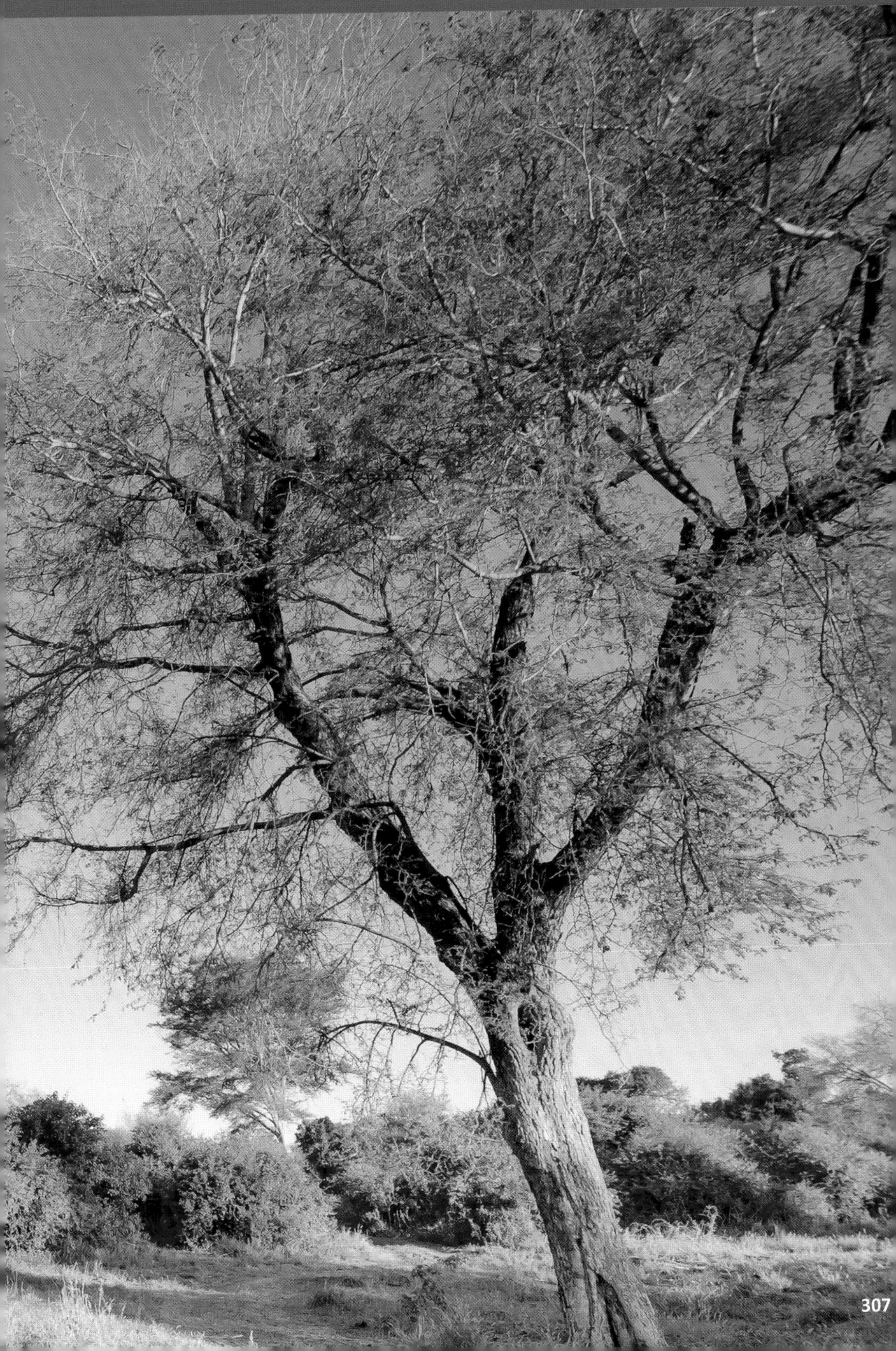

Large-leaved rock fig

)) *Ficus abutilifolia*

Ficus = name for the cultivated fig, and *abutilifolia* = with leaves resembling that of the genus *Abutilon*.

Height: 10 m

Obvious for its white bark, branches and roots, and for its habit of growing on rocks, even sheer rock faces, the large-leaved rock fig is an untidy tree with a crooked trunk and sparse crown. Fat roots grow like spider-legs over the rocks. They extract nutrients from the soil below the rocks and spaghetti-thin exploratory roots make their way down as soon as seeds germinate, expanding with time until they eventually crack the rocks, contributing to biological weathering. Frugivores – from fruit bats and bushpigs to turacos and green pigeons – relish the fruit. Leaves are used in traditional remedies and bark decoctions are drunk by men as a revitalising tonic.

Obvious, smooth, cream coloured or yellow-grey **bark** that may look mottled and develop flaky layers with age.

Very large, heart-shaped **leaves** with conspicuous yellow or pink veins, raised below, grow on long stalks and spiral around the branches. Plentiful milky latex oozes when a leaf is plucked.

The stalkless **figs** grow in the axils of the leaf between September and March measuring 1.5 cm in size. They are green and white-speckled, turning pink when ripe. The flowers grow inside the fig.

ME

ME

Sycamore fig

)) *Ficus sycomorus*

Ficus = the classical Latin name for the cultivated fig, and *sycomorus* = the Sycamore of the Bible.

Height: 30 m

The sycamore fig is a large and impressive tree obvious along river courses, sometimes in groves. The tree has a single, buttressed trunk that branches low and a vast, spreading, dark green canopy. It produces profuse sticky milky latex. Figs are in demand from all manner of fruit-eating creatures, from bats and birds to primates, swine, civets, porcupines and antelope. People eat figs fresh or dry them, make fig-soup or brew alcoholic gin. The leaves can be cooked as a vegetable. The latex is used as birdlime or to treat ringworm. Other medicinal applications include throat, chest and gland complaints. The wood is soft and used to make drums, mokoros or the base plates for fire drills. The inner bark makes a strong rope.

Powdery pale yellow-orange **bark** particularly obvious in golden light. It is smooth with irregular cracks and patches of bark may peel away from the trunk to reveal pink or green underneath. Trunks are often impressively buttressed.

Fairly large, roundish **leaves** that have a rough texture and slightly wavy margins. Leaves are thin but rigid with three obvious yellow veins from the base and those on the underside stand out. Some leaves grow off twigs around the base of the tree. Milky latex oozes from plucked leafstalks.

Round, pink, velvety figs grow directly off the trunk and branches in bunches. The **figs** are borne on broom-like stalks which, after being eaten by various animals, leave a woody stubble behind. Flowers are borne inside the fig, which is a thickened, hollow stem. These ripen into fruits once pollinated. The tree has ripening fruit on it all year.

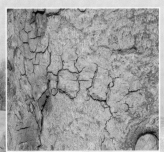

ME

Fig wasps from the Agaonidae family pollinate the fig's flowers, being the only insects small enough to fit through the tiny fig operculum. Every species of fig has just a few species of wasp that pollinate it. The females lay their eggs in the ovaries of the female flowers, depositing pollen they collected from the figs where they hatched. Wingless male wasps spend their entire lives inside the same fig, mating with females by boring into the galls before they hatch. The female fig wasp leaves through the small fig opening, collecting pollen from the male flowers in this region on the way out to deposit in a new fig.

WMC/JMK

Bushveld gardenia

» *Gardenia volkensii*

Gardenia = named after Alexander Garden, a medical doctor from South Carolina, and *volkensii* = named in honour of G. Volkens who collected plants on Mt Kilimanjaro during 1892–1894.

Height: 10 m

A relatively small, often multi-stemmed tree with rigid branches, a rounded crown and a generally tangled appearance. Pale branches bear stumpy twigs in whorls of three. The tree is most attractive when in flower. The gardenia grows in open woodland and tolerates a variety of soils, brackish or stony substrates. They are protected trees and believed to keep lightning and unwanted spirits away. The fine-grained wood is used for carving items, making sticks and fashioning spoons. Animals eat the fruit but it causes vomiting in humans.

Pale creamy to grey smooth **bark** peels in patches with yellow underneath.

Sweet-scented **flowers** occur between August and December. They are about 8 cm in diameter, trumpet-shaped with soft petals and open at night. They transform from white to creamy-yellow with time.

ME

The glossy green, spoon-shaped **leaves** are of variable size and whorled in threes at the tips of short twigs. The stalk is flanked to its base with tapering leaf blade and the margins are smooth, wavy and slightly scalloped near the tip.

ME

Egg-shaped bumpy green **fruit** grows on the tree between November and May. They have ribbing and raised white spots.

Sausage tree

🔊 *Kigelia africana*

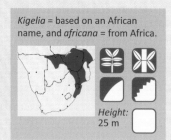

Kigelia = based on an African name, and *africana* = from Africa.

Height: 25 m

An enormous tree with a solid main stem and dense, leafy, domed canopy growing on alluvial soils along rivers or on floodplains. A variety of browsers consume the leaves and flowers and nectivorous birds and insects visit the flowers, which are pollinated by bats. Many animals may consume the fruits, including monkeys, baboons, giraffe, zebra, porcupines, bushpig, squirrels and hippos.

The sausage tree provides excellent shade and is used in picnic sites, as garden trees or for religious assemblies (beware falling fruit!). Medicinal applications include treatments for pneumonia, sore backs, wounds, toothache, epilepsy, syphilis, rheumatism, skin ulcerations, acne, stomach troubles in children, lactation problems and possibly genital enlargement rituals. Sausages are hung in homes to repel whirlwinds and the seeds can be roasted and eaten. Ripe fruit is used to brew beer and wood, which is resistant to cracking, used for planks, yokes and mokoros.

The pale brown or greyish **bark** is mostly smooth but peels in sections on older trees. The trunk can become gnarled and corrugated.

Deep red **flowers** with pretty yellow markings adorn the tree in spring. The large, cup-like flowers hang in multiples off long chandelier-like flower stalks. Flowers are unpleasantly scented and appear between July and October, generally before the leaves.

Large compound **leaves** have just a few pairs of leaflets with a solitary one at the tip. Leaves are thick and leathery but begin bright green and softer. The leaf margins are slightly wavy and sometimes a little serrated, and leaves cluster towards branch ends. The tree loses its leaves briefly at the end of winter.

ME

Huge sausage-shaped **fruits** hang on long stalks (sometimes more than one sausage per stalk) and can reach a metre long and a mass of 10 kg. Sausages remain on the tree for many months before ripening and falling off. Fruits are poisonous while green.

ME

Red milkwood

Mimusops zeyheri

Mimo = from the Greek meaning ape, and *ops* = resembling, and *zeyheri* = honouring C.L.P. Zeyher (1799–1858), a German botanist and plant collector.

Height: 15 m

A fig-like tree with a big, round, dense crown. The trunk may be tall and erect, or short and warped. It grows on dry, wooded hillsides, along riparian zones, in rocky locations, on old termite mounds and in hot, dry, open woodland. Fruits are edible and rich in vitamin C, and are eaten by people and myriad frugivorous animals and birds. The pinkish wood makes good all-purpose timber but causes sneezing if worked while green. The trees grow large and make great shade trees and especially large specimens are to be found at the Great Zimbabwe Ruins.

Dark grey, chunky, blocky **bark**. Younger branches have smoother bark but are somewhat knotted and coated with fine reddish hairs.

Shiny yellow-orange, plum-like, oval **berries** with prickle-tips and smooth, delicate skins. Fruits have 1–4 seeds and yellowish flesh. They occur between April and October.

Dark green, leathery **leaves** have thick, wavy margins and a raised yellowish, mid-vein below. The leaf shape is somewhat variable and their long stalks are often reddish. Young leaves are hairy with reddish hairs. The tree exudes milky latex.

Creamy, fragranced **flowers** form profuse clusters between October and March. Each star-shaped flower measures 1 cm and has red, hairy sepals and a long, thin stalk.

PJ

Wild olive

 Olea europaea subsp. *africana*

Olea = Latin for olive, *europaea* = from Europe, and *africana* = from Africa.

Height: 14 m

The wild olive is a small to medium-sized tree with a gnarled trunk, low branches and a smooth, dense canopy. Usually rounded in shape, trees can appear weather-beaten and stunted. The wild olive is a habitat-generalist but prefers rocky hillsides, streams, forest edges and old termite mounds. It is frost and drought tolerant. It is probably best known for its wood, which is hard, yellow-brown and attractive, and used extensively for furniture as well as ornaments, sticks, fence-poles and fuel. Younger leaves can be brewed into tea and fruit is edible albeit unappetising. Birds eat the fruit and ink can be extracted from it. Leaves are used to make medicinal eye lotions and bark to treat colic. Other conditions, including high blood pressure, headaches, fever, respiratory complaints and renal problems are also traditionally remedied using wild olive. A close relative to the cultivated olive species and popular garden ornamental.

The narrow, tapering, sharp-tipped **leaves** grow off slender stalks and droop slightly. They are shiny grey-green above, silvery grey below.

The leaf edges curl under and the midrib is sunken above and raised below. Leaves sometimes have tiny white scales on the green section or golden scaling below. Edges fray when pulled apart.

Wild olive **bark** is dark grey and coarse, flaking in irregular pieces. Younger branchlets are covered in pale lenticels, are ridged and have angled edges.

The small, white **flowers** grow in branched sprays from the axils of the leaves between October and February. They are fairly inconspicuous but have a sweet scent.

F&KS

The wild olive **fruits** are small (1 cm), round and purple-black when ripe. They are littered with fine white speckles and each fruit has a sharp tip. Fruits are only thinly fleshy and occur between March and July.

ME

Jacket plum

Pappea capensis

Pappea = named after Carl W.L. Pappe (1803–1862) who founded the SA Museum Herbarium and was the first professor of botany at the South African College (now UCT), and *capensis* = of the Cape.

Height: 10 m

The jacket plum is typically a single-stemmed tree with a rounded, tangled canopy, branches sometimes drooping fountain-like towards the ground (appearance can be variable). Jacket plums often grow on termite mounds but are adaptable habitat-generalists growing in various places except in dense forest. Humans, animals and birds seek out the fruit. People make a preserve, vinegar or alcohol from the fruit and the hard seed produces aromatic oil used for remediating baldness, treating ringworm or venereal diseases, purging the digestive system, making soap and greasing rifles. The wood can be used for making sticks, spoons, yokes and furniture and an infusion of the leaves is said to ease sore eyes. Jacket plum trees are also called 'Indaba Trees' for their popularity as a historical meeting place for Zulu chiefs.

ME

The jacket plum's **bark** looks like it has been sponged with different shades of grey paint. Younger trees have smooth bark. Older trees have the rougher sections where black blocks peel away from the main trunk and branches like roof tiles or like a brick wall where plaster has peeled. The bark is often lichen-coated.

Named for its distinctive **fruit**, the jacket plum produces clusters of hard, velvety green-coated fruits between December and July. These soften and burst open when ripe to reveal juicy, scarlet-red flesh inside the neatly ruptured skin. The berry appears to be wearing a green tuxedo with a red shirt.

WMC/DK

ME

ME

The elongated **leaves** have a rigid, leathery, oak leaf-like texture and an obvious yellow main vein. They vary in size and have both entire and serrated margins on same tree. Younger leaves have toothed, saw-like edges while more mature leaves have smooth margins. The leaves grow in rosette-like whorls.

There are greenish-yellow finger-like **flowers** on the tree between September and March. Inflorescences clump together in bunches at the ends of branches and have a sweet scent. The tree can become heavily laden with flowers, sometimes producing male and female flowers on separate trees.

African weeping-wattle

🔊 *Peltophorum africanum*

Peltophorum = shield-bearing, referring to the shape of the stigma, and *africanum* = from Africa.

Height: 14 m

A smallish, low-branching tree with bowing branches and an untidy canopy. The tree is spectacular in flower. It grows in well-drained soils in the bushveld and open woodland or along the edges of wetlands. The weeping-wattle got its name from its association with sap-sucking spittlebugs that tap moisture from its stems and excrete the fluid as quickly as they ingest it, which then drips off the tree. A popular garden ornamental for its flowers and the insects, and subsequently insectivorous birds, they attract. Black rhino eat the bark and cattle eat the pods. Bark is said to cure internal parasites, sore eyes and colic while the roots heal wounds, stomach troubles, sore throats and infertility. The pale wood with red heartwood is used for furniture, ornaments or tools like axe handles. Sometimes leaves are used as toilet paper.

The weeping-wattle has chunky, dark blackish **bark**. On older trees it is rough and cracked while younger bark is paler and smoother. Very new twigs have fine red or grey hairs.

The **leaves** are large, flat and twice compound with up to 9 pairs of leaflets per leaf and up to 22 small rectangular pinnules per leaflet. The stalks and main leaf veins are coated with soft, rusty-coloured hairs.

Thin, yellow-green to brown, tear-shaped **pods** reach about 9 cm long and grow in clumps from December to July. The fruit is winged with a single bulging seed in the middle.

The weeping-wattle's **flowers** are bright yellow with scrunched petals and a sweet smell (September to February). Long, thin stamens extend from each flower, bearing obvious pollen-bearing anthers. The erect sprays reach up to 15 cm long with bulbous, unopened flowers at the ends. Flower stalks and buds are covered in fine, rusty hairs.

ME

Apple-leaf

)) *Philenoptera violacea*

Philenos = Greek for tractable, *pteros* = wing, and *violacea* = violet-coloured.

Height: 20 m

The apple-leaf is a tall tree with a meandering trunk and few main branches. The rather shapeless crown has characteristically insect-chewed leaves. The apple-leaf grows largest along rivers but survives in many kinds of soil because it makes use of ground water. The tree is protected in South Africa and it is considered bad luck to cut one down. It gets its common name from the sound and smell of its crushed leaves and is also called the rain tree for its propensity to host moisture-dripping spittlebugs (see page 249). Apple-leaf wood is hard and heavy and is used for carving, building and making dug-out canoes, tool-handles or maize-stampers. The roots are used to treat snakebite or smoke from them is inhaled to relieve symptoms of the common cold. Poison in the roots and bark can be used as fish poison. Nectar-rich flowers attract bees and browsers eat the leaves, sometimes picking them off the ground. Many butterfly species use the tree as a larval-host and birds like rollers and barbets use the natural cavities for nests. Carrying a twig of the apple-leaf in one's pocket is said to encourage friendship.

The **bark** is pale, whitish-grey and smooth with rough patches in places or on older trees, where the bark peels off in small blocks showing a yellow colour underneath. It oozes reddish sap if it is damaged. Young bark is hairy.

The shiny green **leaves** are compound with large, leathery leaflets, which have a velvety feel when young. The terminal leaflet is largest with between 1–3 sets of lateral leaflets. The leaves have prominent midribs, thick stalks and are characteristically chewed and damaged by insects. Fresh leaves smell like apples when crushed.

The fragrant **flowers** are pale mauve and hang in grape-like bunched sprays, which can reach 30 cm long, at the ends of the branches. The tree flowers between October and December just pre-empting or coinciding with the new leaves. The tree sheds its flowers confetti-like, forming an attractive carpet under the tree.

The apple-leaf produces copious clumps of flat **pods** each bearing the bump of the seed in the middle. Pods are light green and velvety but dry to brown and remain on the tree for a long time (January to August). The pods can reach 15 cm long and 3 cm wide.

Common sugarbush

))) *Protea caffra*

Protea = named for the Greek sea-god Proteus, and *caffra* = from Kaffraria (Eastern Cape).

Height: 8 m

The most widespread protea in South Africa is a small, robust, evergreen tree or multi-stemmed shrub with a short, crooked trunk, low branches and a pale greyish canopy. It occurs in colonies on stony ridges and on south-facing slopes in grassland. Nectivorous insects and birds are drawn to the flowers. The sugarbush is burnt as firewood and bark tannins used for tanning leather. The bark is also used to treat diarrhoea and chest trouble. Other medical uses include cures for bleeding stomach ulcers or for dizziness. The flower head bases are used in treating psychological issues and sold for this purpose in muthi markets.

ME

Dark, almost black, **bark** with net-like texturing and coarse, corky blocks in mature trees. Young trees have smooth, pinkish bark. The bark is fire-resistant and trees often show signs of burning. Leaf scars are obvious on older branches.

The **leaves** are leathery, strap-like with a slight sickle-shape and stalkless, growing directly off and crowding at the ends of stubby branches. They are dull blue-grey with a pink or yellow midrib. New leaves form red rosettes at the tips of branches and turn bright green before greying.

Hairy nutlets develop at the base of each flower and these fruits are contained within a **cone**, which opens after fire (usually July–March). Cones remain on the tree for a long time sometimes only releasing the seeds to be dispersed by the wind a full year after flowering.

ME

Large, pink, nectar-rich, scented **flowers** grow singly or in small groups between October and March. A ring of brown woody bracts surrounds the flower head while the inner rings are pink or cream. Actual flowers are thread-like and velvety, housed within the bracts.

WMC/BD

Weeping boer-bean

)) *Schotia brachypetala*

Schotia = named after Richard van der Schot, head gardener of the Schönbrunn Gardens, and *brachypetala* = short petal.

Height: 25 m

A large impressive tree with an erect trunk and dense, bright green crown. They grow in relatively inaccessible places along drainage lines and rivers or conspicuously on termite mounds in warm, dry areas. A flowering tree is spectacular and scarlet-red flowers 'weep' nectar profusely, attracting insects and birds. The tree also hosts froth-forming spittlebugs that drip liquid out the tree. Monkeys, baboons, civet, warthogs and antelope eat the flowers and many species browse the leaves. Bark is eaten by black rhino. The bark is used by humans for leather tanning or dyeing fishing nets and medicinally is used with the roots in treatments for heartburn, hangovers, diarrhoea and nervous disorders. Smoke from burning leaves is supposed to help bleeding noses and ulcers are treated with powdered leaves. The tree provides good timber for furniture or floor boarding. Seeds are edible after roasting and traditionally used as a coffee substitute.

The **bark** is grey-brown and smooth with fine cracking, becoming blockier with age.

Shiny, dark green paripinnate compound **leaves** with a flattened, winged rachis and 4–8 pairs of stalkless, opposite leaflets that increase in size

towards the apex of the leaf (no terminal leaflet). The main vein on each leaflet is slightly off-centre and young leaves have a coppery colour.

ME

The boerbean **flowers** appear with or before the new leaves between August and October and are very showy. They are scarlet-red and form profuse clumps on older branches. The flowers have virtually no petals and the long stamens protrude out. The flowers produce copious nectar, which drips out of the tree.

ME

ME

The weeping boerbean has relatively large (17 cm), hard, woody, brown **pods** that persist on the tree for a long while before dropping. The pods are dehiscent and burst open to expose paler brown seeds with sticky yellow arils (fleshy covering). March–September.

Marula

◍ *Sclerocarya birrea* subsp. *caffra*

Sclerocarya = hard nut, *birrea* = 'birr', the common name for the tree in Senegal, and *caffra* = from Kaffraria (Eastern Cape).

Height: 18 m

A tall, upright, single-stemmed tree with just two or three main branches forking from the trunk high up and rounded, pencil-like twigs. The canopy is leafy in summer. They usually grow along rivers, on well-drained crests of the catena and in sweetveld areas. Elephants regularly strip the tree of its vascular tissue, uproot trees for their moist roots and relish the sweet, vitamin C-rich fruits. Their digestive systems scarify the hard kernel to assist with the germination of the seeds. Primates, antelope, squirrels and civets also relish the fruit. The fruit is used by people for jellies, jams, beer, port and Amarula Cream (a type of liqueur). The nut is also tasty and oil extracted from the seed is used as a preservative or in cosmetics. The inner bark has antihistamine properties, produces a pink dye used on basket-ware and is mixed with brandy to treat malaria. Marulas are used for marriage and fertility rites and typically left standing when other vegetation is cleared for cultivation.

The pale grey **bark** peels in oval discs to reveal a white colour underneath in a slight depression, giving the impression that a newly painted golf ball has struck the tree repeatedly. Elephant damage and scarring on the trunks is common.

Pink and white **flower** sprays appear with the new leaves. Sexes occur on separate trees.

Pale grey-green compound **leaves** usually have about seven pairs of leaflets with a single one at the tip. They cluster and hang down from the ends of rounded, pencil-like branchlets. Leaflets are long stalked (unlike the false marula which has no petiolules). New leaf stalks are pink.

Round, firm, golf-ball sized
fruit fall off the tree green and
ripen to yellow on the ground
between January and March. On
the tree, they are borne on rigid
stalks. Fruit are rich in vitamin C
(67.9 mg/100 g) and the thin
flesh is very tasty. A large, woody
kernel contains the walnut-
flavoured, protein-rich nuts
sealed in with 2–3 small caps.

ME

Karee

◀)) *Searsia lancea*

Searsia = named after Paul B. Sears (1891–1990), an American botanist, and *lancea* = referring to the lance-shaped leaflets.

Height: 9 m

The karee is a small, single-stemmed tree branching low with many thin branches and supporting a soft, drooping canopy. Karees often grow near water enjoy a wide variety of habitat, including calcareous soils and old termite mounds. Leaves are browsed during times of drought due to a high tannin content that makes the bark suitable for tanning leather. The flowers attract insects and ground birds and bulbuls consume the fruits, which people may brew into beer. The tough and long-lasting wood is reddish-brown with a spicy smell and was used for fence posts, implement handles, wagon parts, tobacco-pipe bowls and bushmen bows.

Rough, almost black **bark** on older trees; younger bark is reddish-brown.

The shiny, oval, pale green **fruits** bunch together, ripening yellow-brown when mature (September to January). Each fruit is about 5 mm, asymmetrically shaped and sometimes sticky.

The stiff, leathery **leaves** are trifoliate and look like a bird's foot. Three long, dark olive-green, finger-like leaflets originate from a long leaf stalk, each blade tapering to a point and sometimes slightly sickle-shaped. The central vein is raised on both sides with obvious

secondary venation. Leaves are hairless and may give off a shiny exudate. They have an aromatic scent when crushed.

The pale yellow, star-shaped **flowers** cluster on the tree between April and July.

Knob thorn

⟩⟩ *Senegalia nigrescens*

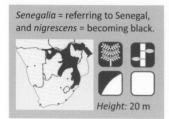

Senegalia = referring to Senegal, and *nigrescens* = becoming black.

Height: 20 m

A tall tree with an erect trunk branching high with a soft, confetti-like canopy of round leaflets. Knob thorns usually grow along rivers on clay soils and because of their affinity for clay, indicate sweet veld when growing away from rivers. The fertile soils in which the trees grow result in it being very nutritious and heavily browsed. Soils under the trees support swathes of nutritious grasses too. Woody knobs on the trunk and branches are distinctive and have numerous medicinal applications including cures for body pain and eye conditions, sexual arousal and breast enlargement. Elephants strip the bark in spite of the knobs and the tree may then become infested with woodborer. Knob thorns flower profusely at the end of winter and are frequented by droves of giraffe that are believed to facilitate pollination of these tall trees. As they feed, their heads and necks get dusted with pollen and this is transferred between trees as the giraffe moves around. Knob thorn wood is very hard and mainly employed as structural material. Erect trunks behave as lightning conductors and inner bark makes good rope.

ME

Dark, fissured **bark** on older trees, flaking yellow bark on younger trees. The trunks are covered with thorn-tipped **knobs**, which reduce in prevalence as the tree grows out of harm's way.

Long **bean pods** (up to 14 cm) occur in bunches and are indehiscent. They begin light green darkening to brown with maturity.

The double compound **leaves** with large paired leaflets resemble mini butterflies. The leaflets are assembled in pairs of two or three per leaf. The rachis is lined on the underside with small hooks.

In addition to the thorn-topped knobs on the stems of younger trees, branches are covered in very sharp pairs of hooked **thorns**.

Fluffy, yellow-cream, elongated **flower spikes** (August to September) are pollen-laden and have a sweet scent. Flowers develop from purplish buds.

335

Tamboti

 Spirostachys africana

Spirostachys = spirally arranged flower segments, and *africana* = from Africa.

Height: 18 m

These tall, erect trees with rounded crowns typically grow in groves along drainage lines and on clay soils. They have splendid red autumn foliage. The tamboti's toxicity is well known and it oozes milky latex when damaged, causing eye irritation, blisters and potentially death if swallowed. Inhaled smoke or meat cooked over burning wood upsets the stomach and brings on headaches. Latex is used as fish poison and to numb toothache. Animals eat the plant without ill effect – black rhino and porcupines eat the bark, elephant and antelope browse the leaves and ground birds eat the seeds. The red-brown wood has a sandalwood-like scent and is popular for furniture but it should be worked carefully for its irritant properties. Blocks of wood repel household insect pests. The knotthorn moth (Emporia melanobasis) breeds in the seeds of the tamboti, causing the beans to jump as the larvae wriggle in the sun.

Older trees have coarse, blocky, black **bark**. Younger branches and younger trees have smooth, white-grey bark. Young trees also have protective spines.

The small, yellow-brown, three-lobed **fruits** audibly pop open in summer (October to February).

ME

The **flowers** usually appear before the leaves. It has spikes with red-brown female flowers at the base and yellow male flowers at the end. The male flowers persist on the stalk while fruit develops from the female flowers.

The small, bright green, simple **leaves** have toothed edges.

Each leaf has a longish stalk, which oozes **milky latex** when plucked. Leaves turn bright red in autumn but there are usually a few red leaves amongst the canopy all year.

ME

ME

Black monkey-orange

🔊 *Strychnos madagascariensis*

Strychnos = from the Greek word for deadly, referring to the strychnine-containing seeds of an Indian species, and *madagascariensis* = from Madagascar.

Height: 6 m

A small, shrubby, untidy, plant with multiple stems that grow upright and bunch closely together. The canopy may be many-branched with scarred, knobbly side-shoots that are hard but not true spines and leaves hug the stems so the canopy is not dense. The tree grows in open woodland and rocky areas and is renowned for its fruits. These are relished by many animals and people who bury them until ripe and then dry and powder them, sometimes mixing in honey to improve the shelf life. The fruits are not especially tasty but this can apparently be improved by drying the fruit with fire. The fruit shells are used in traditional musical instruments. The green monkey-orange (Strychnos spinosa) is similar but has genuine, sharp spines.

Pale grey to brown-grey, smooth **bark** covers the younger trunks, peeling in messy sections on very old ones.

Leaves are 3-veined from the base, cluster on spiny-looking side shoots and hug the branches tightly. Younger leaves are bright green and hairy with hairy margins, becoming smoother and darker with age. The size varies quite a bit.

The orange-sized, greyish-green **fruits** look oversized on the shrubby trees (February to November). They are hard, woody, have thick rinds and ripen to yellow. Inside, many seeds are implanted in yellow pulp.

Small nondescript greenish **flowers** in clusters in spring.

Umdoni

◗) *Syzygium cordatum*

Syzygium = Greek word meaning coupled, alluding to the paired leaves and branches, and *cordatum* = heart-shaped.

Height: 20 m

Also known as waterberries, these elegant trees usually grow in groves in wooded areas or forests beside water. The tall, crooked trunk branches low with spreading boughs growing upwards bearing the dense, blue-green canopy. A favourite with frugivorous birds and animals, and people also eat the purple berries or make alcohol from them. The emperor moth (Microgone cana) uses the tree as a larval plant and the caterpillars are harvested and eaten by locals. The bark makes good fish poison and weaving material is typically dyed orange with dye extracted from the bark. The wood is red-brown to grey and durable, especially in water, and is used for canoe, boats and jetties, as well as beams and rafters, furniture and as fuel. Medicinal applications include diarrhoea, headaches, wounds, respiratory ailments, stomach troubles and as an emetic and purgative. A useful species for stabilising riverbanks.

Pale to darker grey, rough **bark** becomes cracked and corky with age. Younger branches have smooth, pale bark with white markings and are 4-angled.

Deep purple, fleshy, oval **berries** grow in clusters amidst the leaves (June to January). The calyx persists at the tip and inside the fruit is white and bears a single seed.

Almost round, shiny, leathery, dark green **leaves** with a yellow main vein are borne in pairs at right angles to one another and cluster at the branch tips like rosettes. Their bases clasp the stems and have virtually no stalk.

Pinkish-cream pincushions made up of well-developed stamens and much nectar constitute the **flowers**. They are sweet smelling and grow in branched heads at the ends of twigs (October to June).

Camphor bush

 *Tarchonanthus camphoratus*

Tarchos = the Greek word for funeral rites + *nanthus* = the Greek name 'anthos' meaning flower, and *camphoratus* = like the smell of camphor.

Height: 2-9 m

A small greyish-green tree or bush that grows across a wide range of habitats, from semi-desert to forest, preferring sandy soils and typically growing in clusters. It may be single or multi-stemmed and branches low. Taller trees grow where there is more rain and then tend to grow alone. The aromatic leaves are used as perfume or for massage and dried ones are smoked, proving slightly narcotic. The leaves and other parts of the plant are implicated in medicinal treatments for asthma, toothache, stomach pain, bronchitis, inflammation, venereal diseases, headaches, sinus and rheumatism. Animals browse the tree despite the aroma, but leaves are probably mostly used during drought times. The fruiting stems are used to stuff pillows. Hard, durable, grey-brown wood is used to craft ornaments, musical instruments or San bows.

The **bark** is pale with long fissures. Twigs are grey and ridged.

Branched sprays of small **nutlets** covered in woolly hairs endure through winter (June to September).

The strap-like dull green **leaves** have tiny dimples covering the upper surface and smell like camphor when they are crushed. Below, the leaf is white, velvety and has raised veins. Leaves feel leathery and vary in size.

Creamy yellow **flower** clusters occur between March and November. The branched sprays grow at the ends of branchlets and protrude past the canopy.

343

Green clusterleaf

Terminalia brachystemma

Terminalia = from the Latin word 'terminus', referring to leaves at the end of shoots, and *brachystemma* = from the Greek *brachys* for short, and *stelma* for crown or garland.

Height: 5-10 m

A shrub or small tree with a rounded, bushy but spreading crown. Branches form horizontal layers and branchlets tend to zigzag. It grows in bushveld on sandy soil (Kalahari Sands) or in areas where the water table is not too deep, often around vlei areas. It hybridises easily with the silver cluster-leaf (see page 347), which can make separating the two species difficult in some areas. The wood is hard and durable and is used for making axe handles and other useful items. The roots offer some medicinal value in remedying sore stomachs.

The **bark** is pale and grey. It is smooth but does become fissured and stringy. Branchlets have purplish bark that peels to show a paler under-colour.

The **fruit** is a pinkish pod of about 5 cm. The swollen seed in the middle is usually paler than the surrounding membranous wing that becomes cherry red when ripe and then reddish-brown on drying (January to June).

Flowers grow in small, creamy, spikes in the axils of the leaves and measure 6–11 cm long (October to February).

The **leaves** are simple and cluster at the ends of the branches; they and have a leathery texture, sometimes with hairs on the prominent midrib on the underside of each leaf. The leaves are green on the upper surface and bluer below and have virtually no leaf stalk as the base of the leaf overruns the stalk on either side.

BvW

Purple-pod clusterleaf

🔊 *Terminalia prunioides*

Terminalia = from the Latin word 'terminus', referring to leaves at the end of shoots, and *prunioides* = like a *Prunus*, referring to the bright plum-coloured fruits.

Height: 13 m

This is a small tree with fountain-like drooping branches. It is often multi-stemmed and untidy looking, growing in hot, dry bushveld and open woodland areas at low altitudes. It also occurs on rocky hillsides and deep alluvial soils. It has very hard, tough wood, which is used to build huts and kraal fences or for tool-handles and traditional clubs. It can be administered medicinally for sore throats, coughs and stomach pain. Stems are boiled to make a tea. Game browses the younger leaves, primates and parrots eat the green seeds and flies visit the flowers.

Dark brown to grey **bark** is deeply fissured.

Small, greenish-white, cylindrical **flowers** form slender spikes that grow from the ends of short branchlets. The flowers are smelly and occur from September to February.

Simple, small, thin, dull green, spoon-shaped **leaves** tapering on the end that attaches to the branch. They cluster on stubby side-shoots.

The **pods** are bright wine-red becoming brown when dry. A papery membranous wing surrounds a single, swollen seed. The long-lasting pods occur from January to September.

Silver clusterleaf

)) *Terminalia sericea*

Terminalia = from the Latin word 'terminus', referring to leaves at the end of shoots, and *sericea* = like silk, referring to the fine, silky hairs covering the leaves.

Height: 20 m

An erect tree with horizontal, layered branches and a silvery, blue-green canopy. The trees usually grow in bands along seeplines and on deep sandy soils. The wood is hard and termite-resistant and used to build huts and fences, make tool handles, furniture and other household items, or as fuel. The inner bark makes excellent twine. Leaves are not very nutritious but are browsed especially during drier times and the bark gum is edible.

Mature trees have dark grey, rough **bark** that is fissured lengthways. Younger bark is reddish and peels in strips. Very young twigs have silver hairs.

Clusters of pale to dark pink **pods** grow on the tree from January to June. They are two-winged with a swelling where the seed sits in the middle. The pods become brown when dry and persist on the tree for some time.

There are silver hairs on blue-green, leathery, elongated **leaves** and these cluster at the ends of branches. The new leaves are fresh green but grey with age.

Between September and January, clusters of cream-coloured, unpleasantly scented flowers grow in the angles of the leaves.

Bushveld Natal-mahogany

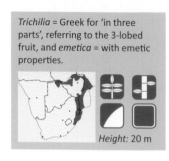

)) *Trichilia emetica*

Trichilia = Greek for 'in three parts', referring to the 3-lobed fruit, and *emetica* = with emetic properties.

Height: 20 m

An enormous mushroom-shaped tree with a stout trunk and dark green, domed canopy. Neither the branches nor the sky are clearly visible through the exceptionally dense foliage. The Bushveld Natal-mahogany usually grows along rivers or streams. Its species name emetica comes from its renowned medicinal property of being an emetic for stomach and intestinal problems. Seeds are poisonous but produce a milky broth when soaked that is eaten with spinach and the red seed-flesh is mixed with sweet potato. The seeds produce oil, which is used as a moisturiser, soap or in treatments for rheumatism and broken bones. A hot leaf-infusion relieves bruises. Pink dye is extracted from the bark and wood is used for carving, musical instruments, shelving, household implements, furniture or boats. The Bushveld Natal-mahogany is a popular shade tree and supports a variety of animals, from browsing antelope to fruit-loving primates. Nectivorous birds visit the flowers and hornbills relish the seeds.

The **bark** is dark, grey-brown in colour. It is mostly smooth with sections of cracked, coarse segments.

Small, silver-green **flowers** with velvety petals and a sweet scent make dense, round heads between August and October. They are trumpet-shaped as a result of the stamens fusing together in a short tube. Different sexes grow on different trees.

The tree has hard, 3-lobed, olive-green **fruit** capsules, each with a distinct neck, a sharp tip and a velvety texture. They grow together in bunches, turn brown when ripe and then burst into three sections to reveal six black **seeds** coated in fleshy, red jackets (November to April).

The large compound **leaves** are comprised of glossy, dark green, finger-like leaflets that are larger towards the tip of the leaf, overlap slightly and have smooth but rolled-under edges. Leaves cluster towards the ends of the branches off long, velvety leaf stalks. There are 4–5 pairs of leaflets and a single leaflet at the tip, and these have virtually no stalk attaching them to the central rachis. Leaflets have closely-spaced veins with brown hairs on the underside. New leaves are very shiny. They begin reddish, turning bright apple green before darkening.

ME

ME

Camel thorn

◗) *Vachellia erioloba*

Vachellia = named in honour of Rev. George Harvey Vachell (1798–1839), erio = woolly, referring to the covering of the fruit, and loba = lobe, referring to the fruit.

Height: 22 m

A large, attractive tree with crooked boughs and a vast, dense rounded or umbrella-like crown. The main stem splits low down into several stems. Adapted to dry conditions, it has extensive roots and grows in arid areas on deep sandy soils or along watercourses. It offers critical shade in arid environments and is often selected as a nesting site for sociable weavers. The pods are excellent and well-favoured fodder. The red-brown wood is tough and was used for mine-props and wagons in the past. The gum is edible and used by people and animals. Medicinally, it has applications for headaches and infected ears.

Brown-grey to black **bark** is rough with deep furrows and flakes in thick woody pieces. New shoots zigzag, beginning green and smooth then darkening to deep red with age.

The leaves grow in groups from the nodes. Bluish-green **leaves** have 2–5 pairs of sickle-shaped pinna with 6–18 relatively large pinnules. The short petiole and rachis are light green and the rachis is dotted with brown glands.

Pods grow singly on the tree for a protracted period extending from November to September. They are large (5 cm wide), thick, woody and ear-shaped, and do not burst open. They begin red dotted with purple glands, become grey-green and velvety and then dry light brown. The tip is rounded, the base is more tapered and the curved edge measures 6–15 cm long. Pods have up to 24 seeds in creamy pith.

Round **flower** heads have a deep golden colour and grow in groups of up to 10 at a node, all in different stages of maturity. Each flower measures about 1.5 cm and has long stalk (September to November).

Straight white or reddish **thorns** about 6 cm long with bases swollen and fused together forming 2 cm-wide ant galls, sometimes extending up the thorn. Normal and swollen thorns occur on trees at 90 degrees to the branch, or inclined slightly.

ME

Sweet thorn

🔊 *Vachellia karroo*

Vachellia = named in honour of Rev. George Harvey Vachell (1798–1839), and *karroo* = from the Karoo.

Height: 22 m

This is a single-stemmed tree branching at different levels with a round, spreading crown and dense, dark foliage. It has a wide distribution, growing in a variety of habitats and encroaching under disturbed conditions. It tolerates many different soils but thrives in fertile ones and is often used as an indicator of good grazing. The tree produces much gum where it is damaged, which is edible and is also used for glue. Monkeys, birds and insects make use of the flowers for food, browsers consume the leaves and no less than 13 butterfly species use the tree as a larval food plant. Seeds have been used as a substitute for coffee. The sweet thorn provides good shade, firewood and hard wood for building or for furniture. The bark produces effective string and tannins that dye leather red.

Rough, dark **bark** is cracked into squares, the fissures filled with red. Young branches are smooth and red-brown. New shoots are green or reddish with red glands, covered with a thin layer of bark that splits to reveal a green colour.

Straight, spine-like **thorns** are grey-white with a darker tip and tiny dark spots growing at right angles to the branches or raking forward. They are about 4 cm long and young thorns are longer than older ones with a yellow tip.

Between two and five bright yellow, round **flower** heads cluster at each node on new shoots with some buds unopened while others are in full bloom. Each bears an obvious ring of bracts and grows on a 2–3 cm long stalk. Flowers are spread out on the stalk and form a panicle.

Bipinnately compound, deep green **leaves** grow in groups from dark cushions at the nodes. There are up to 20 pinnules per pinna and 2–6 pinna per leaf, borne on a grooved petiole and rachis.

Flat, brown, linear **pods** measure up to 15 cm long and are smooth, brittle and sickle-shaped with raised edges, many veins and glands, and slight constrictions between the seeds. The pods bunch together and may tangle. They burst open to suspend their 12 seeds.

Umbrella thorn

 Vachellia tortilis subsp. *heteracantha*

Vachellia = named in honour of Rev. George Harvey Vachell (1798–1839), *tortilis* = twisted, referring to the shape of the pods, and *heteracantha* = different thorns (some straight and some hooked).

Height: 20 m

A flat-topped tree resembling an umbrella although sometimes also small, more rounded and shrubby. The umbrella thorn prefers clay soils, can grow in dry conditions and is an aggressive natural encroacher species. Leaves are nutritious and browsed by many herbivores while flowers are eaten by primates and the protein-rich pods devoured by giraffe, antelope, baboons and monkeys. Elephants strip the bark or uproot trees that often continue growing due to extensive root systems. Gum is edible to humans and forms a mainstay for lesser bushbabies when insects are sparse. Rope can be made from the inner bark and the hard wood makes good firewood or charcoal.

Dark brown, deeply grooved **bark** on adult specimens. Younger trees have redder bark with whitish markings.

Pairs of both hooked prickles and long, straight **thorns** reaching 8 cm occur on the tree.

Contorted, spiralled, hanging **pods** are green and found on the tree between May and June.

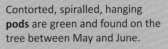

White, pom-pom, ball-like **flowers** are sweetly fragranced and dusted with yellow pollen (November to December).

ME

Bipinnately compound **leaves** are by far the smallest of the *Vachellia* leaves, measuring just 3 cm with 1–2 mm leaflets. They cluster at the nodes of the branches and hug closely to the branches.

Fever tree

Vachellia xanthophloea

Vachellia = named in honour of Rev. George Harvey Vachell (1798–1839), and *xanthophloea* = yellow bark.

Height: 15-30 m

The fever tree is a tall tree with an erect trunk and upward growing branches. The canopy is open and the crown is often flat-topped. Trees generally grow in stands, sometimes as forests, and are usually in the vicinity of water or in areas that flood seasonally. Malaria-causing mosquitoes occur in the same habitats as fever trees and are responsible for the tree's common name. Lower limbs may be sacrificed as toxin depots and turn black. Good luck charms are made from the bark, which is also used to treat stinging eyes and, ironically, fever. Roots may be finely ground as a malaria remedy or to relieve stomach pain. Browsers eat the leaves and pods, monkeys eat the pods and scented flowers, and bushbabies relish the gum. Red-billed buffalo weavers and other weaver species favour the tree as nesting site for its proximity to water and thorny protection from predators.

Powdery yellow-green **bark** punctuated with brown marks covers the trunk and branches with thin layers that peel off. Damaged bark turns brown-black.

The **pods** are yellow-brown, slender and papery with slight constrictions between the seeds. Pods grow in bunches and the points of attachment are narrow. Pods are indehiscent but sections do break off. The pods occur between January and April.

Small yellow **flower** 'balls' on slender stalks develop between the thorns from September to November.

Long, white, pairs of **thorns** of varying size (1–9 cm) grow from a common base and may bend slightly forwards.

The twice-compound **leaves** are fine and feathery with 4–7 leaflet pairs. The 10 cm long leaves grow out of cushions at the base of the thorn and the rachis of each leaf is rutted. Glands are present on the leaf stalk and at the base of the top pair of leaflets.

Nyala tree

 *Xanthocercis zambesiaca*

Xanthocercis = yellow rod, and *zambesiaca* = of the Zambezi region.

Height: 30 m

Nyala trees, called mashatu trees in Botswana, are enormous with fluted trunks and lovely dense, domed, shady canopies with drooping branches. Trunks branch low and may appear multi-stemmed. Nyala trees grow on termite mounds or along river courses, preferring fertile soil and access to water. Nyala eat the fruit off the ground and people make porridge from the dried fruits. Monitor lizards, genets, baboons and leopards may take shelter in the tree. Being leguminous, the nyala tree has rhizobium in the nodules of its roots to fix nitrogen into compounds that the roots can absorb. This increases soil fertility. The nyala tree has hard wood that irritates the nose and throat when worked.

Pale yellowish **bark** is rough and forms small squares with sections coming off the fluted trunk.

Date-like yellowish-brown **fruits** ripen between April and September and fall off the tree. This legume is the only one to produce berries rather than pea-like pods.

The small, unobtrusive **flowers** are sweetly scented.

FoZ/BW

Dark green compound **leaves** have small, oval, glossy leaflets (about 7 pairs) with the largest leaflet at the apex and those nearest the base, smallest. Some leaves grow directly and untidily from the branches and trunks.

FoZ/BW

Buffalo thorn

)) *Ziziphus mucronata*

Ziziphus = Latinised version of the Arabic vernacular name 'zizouf' for Z. jujuba, and *mucronata* = pointed, referring to the shape of the leaf tip.

Height: 18 m

The buffalo thorn is an untidy tree with drooping branches that have a distinct zigzag. It grows in a range of habitats, from semi-desert to forests, often along rivers or on termite mounds. Many cultural beliefs surround the tree. Zulu people call it the 'Tree of Life' with the straight and hooked thorns representing looking ahead and remembering the past respectively. Branches are also used to hook the spirits of people who have died away from home and bring them back, for which a journey is required and then body and branch are buried together. Buffalo thorns are often planted protectively on top of graves and they make useful hedges around homes. The San mix arrow poisons with juices from the tree. Buffalo thorn trees are short and renowned as shelters from lightning. Many animals browse the tree but especially giraffe. Blue waxbills nest amidst the thorny canopy and other birds are attracted to the fruit or to insects drawn by the nectar. Much of the plant is edible. Leaves can be eaten fresh or boiled as nutritious spinach. Fresh fruit is edible, but bitter – these are rather dried and ground into porridge meal or brewed as beer. The seed may be used as a coffee substitute. Buffalo thorns also offer an array of medicinal treatments for conditions including diarrhoea, dysentery, coughs, chest pains, fevers, eye diseases and abscesses.

Bark is grey and may be light or dark raked with thin, untidy fissures. Branchlets are distinctly zigzagged.

Tiny, yellow-green, star-like **flowers** grow in clusters in the axils of the leaf stalks. Flowers occur from November to February and are nectar-rich.

The dark green, glossy **leaves** have three evident main veins arising from the asymmetrical base of the leaf. Leaves are duller below and often a little hairy. The leaf terminates in a narrow point with a hair-like tip. Leaves grow on a flat plane.

Pairs of **thorns** grow at the nodes, one straight, the other hooked. Some specimens can be relatively spineless at maturity.

Shiny, round, red **fruits** are
about 1.5 cm and occur between
January and August. Sometimes
the berries are a more yellow-
brown colour and generally they
remain on the tree throughout
the winter.

361

FLOWERING PLANTS

SS

Fluted abutilon

)) *Abutilon angulatum*

Abutilon shrubs are common on riverbanks or alongside roads. The leaves are blue-grey and lighter below than above. The delicate flowers are yellow. The whole plant is velvety to touch, even the fruits.

Impala lily

)) *Adenium multiflorum*

Beautiful crimson-lined white flowers, about 5 cm in size, cover the succulent plant in winter while it is bare of its leaves. They grow in rocky areas and have robust underground stems. Waxy green leaves grow in summer, clustering at the branch tips. Fish and arrowhead poisons are prepared from the impala lily.

Leopard orchid

)) *Ansellia gigantea*

The largest orchid plant of the 500 species in southern Africa and the largest clusters may be up to 100 years old. Flowers are yellow with brown spots and have a gentle fragrance. The epiphytic plant looks like a pile of garden refuse caught in the fork of a large tree. It has aerial roots and composts its own material for nutrients. Vervet monkeys eat and disperse the seeds. The Zulu people use the leopard orchid as a love charm.

Ground lily

)) *Ammocharis coranica*

This bulbous plant grows to about 30 cm with strap-like fresh green leaves measuring about 45 cm long and 4 cm wide close to the ground. It produces a cluster of pink floral heads in a single rounded inflorescence numbering up to 20 and growing between November and January. These lilies prefer grassland regions and may be found in colonies.

ME

Pride-of-De-Kaap

🔊 *Bauhinia galpinii*

Attractive brick-orange flowers cover this
scrambling shrub in summer. It generally grows
along river courses or on rocky hillsides and is a
popular garden ornamental. The leaves are 2-lobed
and resemble butterfly wings.

WMC/JR

Wild foxglove

🔊 *Ceratotheca triloba*

This herb may reach 1.5 m in height and is a
pioneer species that colonises disturbed soils.
Attractive, trumpet-shaped, mauve flowers edged
with purple stripes open from the bottom of
the spike upwards. They are used in decorative
pressing. Leaves smell bad and are incorporated
in insect-repellent sprays but they are also cooked
and eaten as spinach, being rich in vitamins, iron
and calcium.

African wild violet

🔊 *Aptosimum lineare*

The small mauve flowers are similar to the
domestic violet, just smaller. The leaves are thin
and grass-like emerging from a central point like
a fountain. A delicate and beautiful specimen to
encounter in the bush.

Num-num

🔊 *Carissa* species

This is a small rigid multi-stemmed shrub with red-
tipped robust green thorns that are either single
(in *Carissa edulis*) or forked (in *Carissa bispinosa*).
White or pale pink star-shaped flowers grow in
clusters. Fleshy red fruit are edible. Fruit is used for
jam or to get rid of intestinal worms and the root is
implicated in traditional medicinal treatments.

Flame creeper

))) *Combretum microphyllum*

A robust climber, scrambling shrub or small tree that grows in bushveld, forest or along rivers and makes whatever it grows upon look as if it's on fire! Cherry-red flowers are striking growing from the ends of branches or in the angles of the leaves in panicles, before the leaves appear. Leaves are roundish and measure up to 12 cm long with 4–6 pairs of yellowish lateral veins. The leaf stalk base is thick and remains after the leaf falls as a blunt spine. Green-pink, 4-winged pods dry pale yellow-brown.

ME

WMC/HH

Knobbly creeper

))) *Combretum mossambicense*

Usually a climber but also a shrub or a small tree, this plant grows in low-altitude bushveld, mopane veld, on termite mounds or near rivers. The leaves are about 6 cm long and taper at both ends. The leaf stalk is up to 5 mm with the base thickest and these persist to form curved spines. Flowers are sweetly fragranced, white or tinged pink and grow in dense, showy spikes up to 6 cm long. These are held horizontally and occur before the new leaves in spring. Greenish-pink pods can be 4- or 5-winged and dry pale brown.

Wandering Jew

))) *Commelina erecta*

A small perennial herb that is low growing and produces delicate blue flowers measuring about 1.5 cm in summer. Flowers emerge from a folded spathe. Plants are widespread.

ME

ME

Crinum lily (Vlei lily)

))) *Crinum delagoense*

A spectacular lily with pink-striped trumpet-shaped flowers and contrasting broad green leaves than encircle the base of the plant, which grows in deep, sandy soils in early summer. Attractive burgundy-coloured fruits reach the size of a lemon when mature. A large, 20 cm bulb grows underground.

Devil's thorn

))) *Dicerocaryum eriocarpum*

The small oval green fruit is about a 1 cm across and has two sharp 'devils' thorns pointing up. The points adhere to animal hooves for dispersal. The plant is a creeper that grows on the ground and produces pink, trumpet-shaped flowers and blueish-green leaves. Leaves produce soapy foam when mixed with water and are used as an antiseptic or detergent.

White-berry bush

))) *Flueggea virosa*

The white-berry bush, a scrambling multi-stemmed shrub, produces fleshy, round white berries about 0.5 cm in size and 3-lobed. They grow profusely from December to March, leading to its other common name 'snowberry' tree. The flowers are small, creamy green-yellow and scented but otherwise inconspicuous. The bush is browsed readily and the fruits are popular with man and beast alike. The roots and fruits have medicinal properties. The supple wood is ideal for fish traps.

Papyrus

))) *Cyperus papyrus*

This is a grass-like plant that lacks nodes and has angular stems. It grows in moist areas in clusters and stays green all year. The Zulu and Tsonga people make sleeping mats out of papyrus. It can also be stuffed into trouser legs to make an emergency float during a flood.

Coral tree

))) *Erythrina lysistemon*

A smallish tree with a thick trunk and spreading crown – most notable in winter when covered in bright scarlet flowers before the leaves appear. The brilliant red flowers are slender, horizontal, stalked racemes measuring up to 10 cm long. The main petal is long and tube-like, enclosing the stamens. The constricted black pods bear the tree's most distinctive feature, its red 'lucky bean' seeds. The coral tree prefers north-facing, rocky ridges in bushveld and coastal areas. It is popular for its medicinal applications and a flowering tree supposedly signals the right time to begin planting crops.

Flame lily

)) *Gloriosa superba*

A spectacular flower with bright yellow or red flame-like petals that is lethally poisonous. The plant is usually a creeper growing over other vegetation. Porcupines relish the tuber and despite its toxicity, humans use the plant extensively in traditional medicine. It contains colchicines valued as an anti-inflammatory.

Ruby gnidia

)) *Gnidia rubescens*

A small perennial herb with a cluster of tiny red flowers with yellow highlights borne on a single stalk amongst the grass. Species of Gnidia are used to cure headaches, fevers and bad dreams.

Milkweed

)) *Gomphocarpus fruticosus*

This is a naturalised weed originally introduced from Australia. It may reach 2 m in height and bears bloated, green, heart-shaped fruit follicles covered in soft bristles. They dry blonde and burst open to expose dark seeds attached to silky hairs. The plant produces copious milky latex and is poisonous. Monarch butterfly caterpillars eat and assimilate these toxins as part of their defence strategy.

String-of-stars

)) *Heliotropium steudneri*

Heliotropium means 'to turn to the sun'. This is a perennial herb that grows in disturbed grassland areas. Tiny delicate white flowers appear in summer and grow in a tight row on a curved inflorescence. Sometimes two rows of flowers abut one another.

WMC/BD

Morning glory

))) *Ipomoea* species

This is a ground creeper that produces large, pink or white, trumpet-shaped flowers, the delicate petals joined by a seam that looks like a star from above. A large underground tuber can be dug up and used for moisture, scraping it clean and squeezing it into the mouth.

WMC

White button sedge

))) *Kyllinga alba*

A slender perennial sedge that occurs in dry woodland. It has a white, round button as an inflorescence.

Hibiscus

))) *Hibiscus* species

Wild hibiscus has large, bell-shaped flowers with scarlet throats. There are many different species, told apart by their leaves. The flowers are cooked as a vegetable and leaves host the larvae of certain types of hawk moths.

ME

Justicia

))) *Justicia* species

Small herbs that grow in disturbed places amongst the grass. Flowers may be white, yellow or blue. Leaf-like bracts enclose the delicate flowers and upright spikes are typical of the genus. They play a role in butterfly ecology and are named after James Justice, a famous Scottish horticulturalist.

ME

Hare's tail bush

)) *Kyphocarpa angustifolia*

This erect herb grows to about 60 cm tall in sandy soils. The inflorescence is 2 cm, elongated, creamy white and spiky, growing at the end of erect stems that bear a few thin leaves. The flower heads resemble the tail of a hare. Inflorescences appear between March and June.

Wild melon

)) *Lagenaria sphaerica*

A climbing herb obvious with its large round green fruit painted with paler patches. They climb over other riverine plants. *Lagenaria* means 'large flask fruit'. It produces white velvet flowers that attract insects like bees, flies and ants and the plant is used traditionally to cure swollen glands and sore stomachs. Many antelope relish the fruit.

Fever tea (Lemon bush)

)) *Lippia javanica*

Fever tea is a scrambling, messy shrub forming dark green banks in riverine vegetation. It is especially obvious when it is damp for its pungent lemon smell. Leaves are rough with scalloped margins and are often rather wrinkled. The flowers are small and white to creamy yellow. The spikes form a cylinder once they fruit and each fruit is small, hard and dry with two 1-seeded kernels. The plant is attributed with medicinal properties namely that the leaves can be brewed into a tea to relieve fevers.

Wild dagga

)) *Leonotis leonurus*

A plant with erect stems and ball-like orange flower structures. The hairy flower petals supposedly look like a lion's ear. Flowers are rich in nectar and attract butterflies and birds. While smoked by many tribes, this plant is not a narcotic and causes nausea when inhaled. When the leaves of *Cannabis* are very young they resemble those of the wild dagga plant.

Caterpillar bush

🔊 *Ormocarpum tricocarpum*

The 4 cm long fruit of this small bush or tree is coated in rigid hairs making it resemble a caterpillar. Fruits appear between October and March when butterflies and their larva are abundant. The plant has tiny compound leaves that cluster on short lateral branches. It grows against hillsides in hot, stony environments.

Common reed

🔊 *Phragmites australis*

A tall reed up to 4 m tall and adorned with fluffy, willowing inflorescences. It grows in dense stands near or in water channels. A hardy grass that performs numerous ecological functions, acting as a habitat for birds and as a natural purification system for the waterway. They also buffer areas from flooding. They are used to build fences, huts or as a substitute for thatching grass. This is the most widespread flowering plant in the world.

Blue water-lily

🔊 *Nymphae nouchali*

Obvious for its floating lily pad leaves and conspicuous floating flowers. The water-lily bud, like its developing leaves, begins under the water. It rises progressively to the surface and is mature by the time it emerges. The flower opens during the day and lasts just five days. As soon as it is pollinated, it is drawn below where the fruit develops. The fruits burst to release buoyant seeds that begin the life cycle anew. Its medicinal value is vast and many species of animal rely on it for survival.

Wild basil (Wild aniseed)

🔊 *Ocimum canum/*
Ocimum americanum

The flower heads of this small plant resemble commercial basil and the plant has an appealing scent after rain, when dew-drenched or when crushed. The wild variety can be used for cooking as well as herbal tea. It repels insects and rubbed on the body is a deodorant and muscle-relaxant. Leaves placed in ones shoes may alleviate soreness during long walks.

Potato bush

))) *Phyllanthus reticulatus*

A clambering shrub that grows in riverine vegetation. Leaves have thin red veins on the underside and look compound. Small, yellow flowers give off a potato smell on summer evenings. The leaves and fruit can be used to treat burns and other sores

Mistletoe

))) *Plicosepalus kalachariensis*

A hemi-parasite that grows on tree canopies inserting an absorbent organ into the tree's vascular tissue like a graft to extract nutrients. Once established, the plant photosynthesises its own food too. Bright pink-orange flowers grow in winter and attract birds and butterflies. Flowers burst open showering pollinators with pollen. Birds also disperse the seed through regurgitation and defecation. The fruit can be used as birdlime to catch birds.

Mother-in-law's tongue

))) *Sansevieria aethiopica*

Flat, tongue-shaped leaves grow up from the ground ending in a sharp point. They usually grow in clumps and have mottled markings. The leaves provide excellent fibre used by Bushmen for bowstrings or as fishing gut and to weave fishing nets and sleeping mats. Roots can be chewed for moisture. (Long, thin-leaved species = *Sansevieria pearsonii*)

Wild sesame

))) *Sesamum triphyllum*

Tall, upright stems bear pretty pink tubular flowers with dark throats. Leaves have 3 leaflets and smell strongly when crushed. They also give off a glutinous substance that can be used as a soap substitute. The fruits are cylindrical, 4-sided capsules that split when ripe. This plant grows in disturbed areas.

Flannel weed

◀ *Sida cordifolia*

A small grey-green shrub that grows in disturbed areas and produces delicate yellow flowers. Leaves have a soft velvety texture like flannel cloth. Plants repel pests, provide fibre for twine, contain saltpetre used as a food preservative or fertiliser and are used for treating children's illnesses.

Poison apple

◀ *Solanum panduriforme*

A small green shrub that has attractive purple flowers and small apple-like fruits that ripen yellow. The fruit is extremely poisonous, causing enlargement of the stomach and intestines, convulsions, coma and may ultimately prove fatal.

Purple pan weed

◀ *Sphaeranthus incisus*

This prostrate herb has sticky leaves and round, purple flower heads. It grows in pans with clay soils that retain moisture. It has aromatic oils and smells like sage and is sometimes used as potpourri (fragrant room-scenting dried flower mix).

Crane flower

◀ *Strelitzia regina*

A stunning, large shrub bearing 20 cm long crane-shaped orange and purple flower heads above the top of the leaves. Up to six flowers may be enclosed in the crane-like spathe. Plants grow up to 1.5 m tall and cluster together on rocky slopes near water and the coast.

Cape honeysuckle

🔊 *Tecoma capensis*

A showy creeper or shrub that grows under riverine forests and along drainage lines. Ruby-orange flowers attract birds and insects. Leaves are flimsy, shiny, dark green and compound. Margins are scalloped. Cape honeysuckle is broadly cultivated in gardens.

Dubbeltjie (Devil's thorn)

🔊 *Tribulus terrestris*

This is an annual, ground-creeping herb that forms a mat of attractive compound leaves and soft yellow flowers just less than 1 cm wide, in the rainy season. The seed husks are spiked with multi-pronged spokes and occur copiously. These easily penetrate the soles of bare feet and are the mechanism the plant employs to disperse its seeds as they adhere equally well to animal hooves. Tribulus grows in disturbed areas.

Lion's eye

🔊 *Tricliceras mossambicense*

A small, sparse herb found in grassy areas during summer especially early in the rainy season. Flowers are bright orange, borne on an upright albeit thin stalk and close at night. They are said to resemble lions' eyes, which are honey-orange coloured.

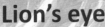

Cornflower (Vernonia)

🔊 *Vernonia glabra*

A common wild flower usually interspersed amongst grass and visible for the little purple heads that form dandelion-like seed heads once dry. They attract butterflies, especially brown-veined whites and the African monarchs. Local people use this herb medicinally.

ME

Black stick lily (Baboon's tail)

))) *Xerophyta retinervis*

Dark fibrous stems stand erect in the ground and look like monkey or baboon tails. Leaves are grass-like and fountain out of the top of the stem. Sprays of sweet-smelling white or mauve flowers appear at the end of spring. They grow in hot, dry, rocky places. Stems are used as pot scourers or to carry coals.

Red-star zinnia

))) *Zinnia peruviana*

This is an annual herb that was introduced from Peru but has become naturalised in South Africa where it grows in dry river valleys.

ME

Arum lily

))) *Zantedeschia aethiopica*

Well known as a garden plant, this is an evergreen species that grows in marshy areas, often in large colonies. The leaves are soft and large (30 cm) and borne on spongy stems. The flowers cluster on a central yellow spandex, which is enclosed by a broad, white spathe about 20 cm long. A shade-loving plant often frequented by arum lily frogs.

WMC

Bibliography

Alexander, G. and Marais, J. 2010. *A guide to the reptiles of southern Africa*. Struik Nature: Cape Town.

Apps, P. 1994. *Wild ways – Field guide to the behaviour of southern African mammals*. Southern Book Publishers: Halfway House.

Apps, P. and Du Toit, R. 2000. *Creatures of habit*. Struik: Cape Town.

Boon, R. 2010. *Pooley's trees of eastern South Africa* (2nd ed.). Flora and Fauna Publications Trust: Durban.

Branch, B. 1998. *Field guide to snakes and other reptiles of southern Africa*. Struik: Cape Town.

Branch, B. 2000. *Everyone's guide to snakes, other reptiles and amphibians of southern Africa*. Struik: Cape Town.

Butchart, D. 2001. *Wildlife of the Lowveld: Common animals and plants including Kruger National Park*. Struik: Cape Town.

Carnaby, T. 2005. *Beat about the bush – mammals and birds*. Jacana Media: Johannesburg.

Carruthers, V. 1997. *The wildlife of southern Africa: A field guide to the animals and plants of the region*. Southern Book Publishers: Johannesburg.

Carruthers, V. 2001. *Frogs and frogging in southern Africa*. Struik: Cape Town.

Chinery, M (Ed.). 2004. *Life in the Wild: Animal Survival*. Lorenz Books, London.

De Klerk, A. 2003. *The Waterberg Biosphere Reserve: A land use model for ecotourism*. Chapter 3. University of Pretoria: Pretoria.

De la Harpe, R. 1998. 'Cape Clawless Otter' *Africa Wildlife and Environment*. Vol 6: 4.

Dennis, N. Knight, M. and Joyce, P. 1997. *The Kalahari: Survival in a thirstland wilderness*. Struik: Cape Town.

Estes, R.D. 1991. *The behavior guide to African mammals*. Halfway House: Russel Friedman.

Estes, R.D. 1992. *The behavior guide to African mammals*. University of California Press: London.

Estes R.D.1995. *The behavior guide to African mammals*. Russel Friedman Books: Halfway House.

Emmett, M.C. and Pattrick, S.D. 2010. *Game ranger in your backpack: an all-in-one interpretative guide to the Lowveld*. Briza: Pretoria

Filmer, M.R. 1991. *Southern African spiders – an identification guide*. Struik: Cape Town.

Grant, R., Thomas, V. and Van Gogh, J. 2006. *Sappi tree spotting – Lowveld including Kruger National Park* (3rd ed.). Jacana Media: Johannesburg.

Grant, R., Thomas, V. and Van Gogh, J. 2004. *Sappi tree spotting – KwaZulu-Natal and Eastern Cape*. Jacana Media: Johannesburg.

Grant, R., Thomas, V. and Van Gogh, J. 2005. *Sappi tree spotting – Bushveld including Pilanesberg and Magaliesberg* (2nd ed.). Jacana Media: Johannesburg.

Glen, H. 2007. *Sappi tree spotting – What's in a name?* Jacana Media: Johannesburg.

Hall-Martin, A. 1993. *A day in the life of an African elephant*. Southern Book Publishers: Halfway House.

Hawthorne, T. 1998. *First field guide to spiders and scorpions of southern Africa*. Struik: Cape Town.

Hawthorne, T. 1998. *First field guide to snakes and other reptiles of southern Africa*. Struik: Cape Town.

Hine, G. 2004. *Bush knowledge and skills: study material for level I / II / III and trails guide*. The Interactive Wildlife Company: Johannesburg.

Hine, G. 2006. *FGASA Level 1 learner manual*. The Interactive Wildlife Company: Johannesburg.

Hine, G. 2006. *FGASA level 2 learner manual*. The Interactive Wildlife Company.

Hockey, P.A.R., Dean, W.R.J. and Ryan, P.G (Eds). 2005. *Roberts – birds of southern Africa*, VIIth ed. The trustees of the John Voelcker Bird Book Fund: Cape Town.

Kruger, W. Inside invertebrate information. Unpublished.

Lawson, B. and Lawson, D. *Specialist training manual for bird guides*. Lawson's Birding Academy.

Leeming, J. 2003. *Scorpions of southern Africa*. Struik: Cape Town.

Liebenberg, L. 2000. *A photographic guide to tracks and tracking in southern Africa*. Struik: Cape Town.

Liebenberg, L. 2005. *A field guide to the animal tracks of southern Africa*. David Phillips Publishers: Claremont.

Little, R., Crowe, T. and Barlow, S. 2000. *Gamebirds of southern Africa*. Struik: Cape Town.

Loon, R. and Loon, H. 2005. *Birds – the inside story*. Struik: Cape Town.

Marais, J. 2004. *A complete guide to the snakes of southern Africa*. Struik: Cape Town.

Maclean, G.L. 1993. *Roberts' birds of southern Africa*. John Voelcker Bird Book Fund: Cape Town

Mills, G. and Harvey, M. 2001. *African predators*. Struik: Cape Town.

Mills, G. and Hes, L. 1997. *The complete book of southern African mammals*. Struik Winchester: Cape Town.

Onderstall, J. 1996. *Sappi wild flower guide Mpumalanga and Northern Province*. DynamicAd: Nelspruit.

Palgrave, K.C. 1995. *Trees of southern Africa* (2nd ed.). Struik: Cape Town.

Picker, M., Griffiths, C. and Weaving, A. 2002. *Field guide to insects of South Africa*. Struik: Cape Town.

Pooley, E. 1998. *A field guide to the wild flowers of KwaZulu-Natal and the Eastern Region*. Natal Flora Publications Trust: Natal.

Roodt, V. 1998. *Common wild flowers of the Okavango delta – medicinal uses and nutritional value*. Shell Oil: Botswana.

Roodt, V. 1998. *Trees and shrubs of the Okavango delta – medicinal uses and nutritional value*. Shell Oil: Botswana.

Sinclair, I., Hockey, P. and Tarboton, W. 2002. *Sasol birds of southern Africa* (3rd ed.). Struik: Cape Town.

Skaife, S.H., Ledger, J. and Bannister, A. 1979. *African insect life*. Struik: Cape Town.

Skinner, J.D. and Smithers, R.H.N 1990. *The mammals of the southern African subregion*. University of Pretoria: Pretoria.

Smit, N. 1999. *Guide to the Acacias of South Africa*. Briza Publications: Pretoria.

Steyn, P. 1996. *Nesting birds*. Fernwood Press: Vlaeberg.

Tarboton, W. 2001. *Nests and eggs of southern African birds*. Struik: Cape Town.

Van Outshoorn, F. and van Wyk, E. 1999. *Guide to grasses of southern Africa*. Briza Publications: Pretoria.

Van Wyk, P. 1994. *Field guide to the trees of the Kruger National Park*. Struik: Cape Town.

Van Wyk, B. and Van Wyk, P. 1997. *Field guide to the trees of southern Africa*. Struik: Cape Town.

Van Wyk, B., van Wyk, P. and van Wyk, B-E. 2000. *Photographic guide to trees of southern Africa*. Briza Publications: Pretoria.

Venter, F. and Venter, J. 1996. *Making the most of indigenous trees*. Briza Publications: Pretoria.

Weaving, A. 2000. *Southern African insects and their world*. Struik: Cape Town.

Index

Page numbers in **bold** indicate main entries.